Innovations in
Rational-Emotive
Therapy

WINDY DRYDEN
LARRY K. HILL

SAGE Publications
International Educational and Professional Publisher
Newbury Park London New Delhi

For information address:

SAGE Publications, Inc.
2455 Teller Road
Newbury Park, California 91320

SAGE Publications Ltd.
6 Bonhill Street
London EC2A 4PU
United Kingdom

SAGE Publications India Pvt. Ltd.
M-32 Market
Greater Kailash I
New Delhi 110 048 India

Printed in the United States of America

Library of Congress Cataloging-in-Publication Data

Main entry under title:

Innovations in rational-emotive therapy / [edited by] Windy Dryden,
Larry K. Hill.
    p.   cm.
    Includes index.
    ISBN 0-8039-4300-8 (cl).—ISBN 0-8039-4301-6 (pb)
    1. Rational-emotive psychotherapy—Congresses. I. Dryden, Windy.
II. Hill, Larry K.
    [DNLM: 1. Psychotherapy, Rational-Emotive—congresses. WM 420
I583]
RC489.R3I55   1993
616.89é14—dc20   92-49498
DNLM/DLC

93 94 95 96 10 9 8 7 6 5 4 3 2 1

Sage Production Editor: Diane S. Foster

Contents

Preface

Rational-Emotive Therapy (RET) was founded in 1955 by Albert Ellis and thus became the first established approach within what has become known as the cognitive-behavioral approach to psychotherapy. RET has always been applied to a wide variety of clinical problems and client populations and numerous texts have outlined its broad therapeutic strategies and techniques.

In 1990 the American Mental Health Counselors Association (AMHCA), in association with the Institute for Rational-Emotive Therapy, hosted a World Congress on Mental Health Counseling at Keystone, Colorado, which had as its theme, "A 35th Anniversary Celebration of Rational-Emotive Therapy." This book contains 11 chapters (Chapters 2-12) that were first given as conference papers at that conference. The opening chapter was especially written for this volume by Albert Ellis and gives an up-to-date overview of the fundamentals of RET theory and practice.

The contributions to this book were chosen to illustrate innovations that have received insufficient coverage in the RET literature. As such, it demonstrates that 37 years after its inception RET is still vibrant and creative in its application to contemporary human problems.

—WINDY DRYDEN, *London, England*
—LARRY K. HILL, *Rock Springs, Wyoming*

Fundamentals of Rational-Emotive Therapy for the 1990s

ALBERT ELLIS

In some ways, rational-emotive therapy (RET) is remarkably similar in the 1990s to its fundamentals that I first began to delineate in 1955; but in other ways it is distinctly different. In this chapter, I shall describe its distinctive features today and shall try to concentrate on the most important aspects of its present day theory and practice.

The Basic Theory of RET

"Causes" of Emotional Disturbance

Emotional disturbance—and especially what is often called neurosis—has several important cognitive, emotive, and behavioral sources and does not only arise from but is heavily influenced by cognition or thinking. Humans are born easily disturbable, but they live in a social and physical environment, so that their "healthy" and "unhealthy" behaviors are "caused" by the interactions among their innate predispositions and their external milieu, particularly their social milieu. As I noted in my early writings (Ellis, 1958) people rarely, if ever, have "pure" thoughts, feelings, or behaviors. Instead:

> Thinking . . . is, and to some extent has to be, sensory, motor, and emotional behavior. . . . Emotion, like thinking and the sensory-motor processes, we may define as an exceptionally complex state of human reaction which is integrally related to all the other perception and response processes. It is not one thing, but the combination and holistic integration of several seemingly diverse, yet actually closely related, phenomena. . . . Thinking and emoting are so closely inter-related that they usually accompany each other, act in a circular cause and effect relationship, and in certain (though hardly all) respects are essentially the same thing, so that one's thinking be-comes one's emotion and emotion becomes one's thought (Ellis, 1958, pp. 35-36).

Following the views of several early philosophers, especially Buddha, Confucius, Epicurus, Seneca, Epictetus, and Marcus Aurelius, RET holds that people largely are responsible for their "emotional" disturbances and that they overtly and tacitly, con-sciously and unconsciously "choose" to disturb themselves. Con-sequently, they can consciously and actively, for the most part, choose to "undisturb" and to fulfill themselves (Ellis, 1962, 1991e; Ellis & Dryden, 1987, 1990, 1991). They mainly (not only) do this by taking their strong preferences for achievement, approval, comfort, and health and making them (yes, constructively and destructively changing them) into dogmatic, absolutist musts, shoulds, oughts, and demands.

The RET view of neurotic disturbance, following ancient and modern phenomenalism, posits an ABC model. People start with goals (Gs), usually to remain alive and reasonably happy, and then often encounter activating events or adversities (As) that block or thwart their desires for success, love, and comfort. They then tend to create or construct cognitive, emotive, and behavioral consequences (Cs) about these As—particularly, inappropriate or self-defeating feelings of anxiety, depression, and rage, as well as such dysfunc-tional behaviors as withdrawal, procrastination, and compulsions.

They construct these self-sabotaging Cs largely by their beliefs (Bs). These consist of, first, *rational beliefs* (rBs), which are prefer-ences and wishes and of, second, *irrational beliefs* (iBs), which are dogmatic musts and imperative demands. Thus, when *adversities* like failure and rejection occur (or people imagine or make occur) at point A, they choose rational beliefs (rBs) at point B—such as "I don't *like* failing and being rejected, but it's not the end of the world and I can still find some degree of happiness"—and they then feel appropriately (self-helpingly) sorry and disappointed, and try to change what is happening at point A. And they also choose irrational beliefs (iBs) at point B—such as, "*I absolutely must not* fail or be rejected. How *awful*. What an *incompetent and unlovable person* I am!"—and they then inappropriately (self-defeatingly) feel anxious, depressed, and self-hating.

People, then, largely (not completely) choose both rBs and iBs about the adverse As they experience; and RET theory says that if they *only* choose the former and never the latter, they would often create very strong *appropriate* feelings of sorrow, regret, frustration, and discomfort but would rarely create *in*appropriate feelings and neurotic behaviors. Moreover, RET theory states, when people do construct their own destructive feelings and acts, they frequently create *secondary* consequences (Cs) about their primary consequences. Thus, when they feel panicked, they create iBs like, "I *must* not be panicked! I'm no good for being panicked!" and thereby bring on panic *about* their panic. And when they behave neurotically—say, foolishly procrastinate—they tell themselves iBs like, "I *absolutely should not* procrastinate. I'm a no-good procrastinator!" and they thereby hate themselves *for* procrastinating (Ellis, 1979a, 1980a, 1986a; Ellis & Dryden, 1991).

The ABCs of rational-emotive therapy seem to be very simple and can easily be explained to disturbed people who want to help themselves, but they are exceptionally interactional and therefore in many ways complex (Ellis, 1985c, 1991d). This is because *activating events* (As) are perceived and thought about, and therefore have some beliefs (Bs) included in them and are also affected by past consequences (behaviors and feelings), and therefore have some Cs included in them. Similarly, beliefs (Bs) are affected by activating events (past and present) as well as by consequences (Cs), especially by feelings. Finally, consequences (Cs) are importantly influenced by activating events (As) and, especially by one's belief system (B). As noted above, people's cognitions, emotions, and behaviors importantly affect and include each other and are never really "pure," but the same goes for their ABCs, which again are interactional and far from pure (Ellis, 1991e).

To make things more complicated, when two or more people relate to each other, their As, Bs, and Cs often significantly affect each other's As, Bs, and Cs. For example, if Joe is married to Joann and he criticizes her, he creates an unpleasant activating event (A) for her. She may then tell herself—at B, her belief system—"He must not unfairly criticize me like that, that worm!" and at C, her consequence, largely makes herself furious at Joe. He then can experience her C, rage, and tell himself, "It looks like I criticized her too much, as I absolutely *should* not have done! How *awful* of me to act so badly!" and he may thereby make himself feel, at C, guilty and depressed. Then Joann may note his depression, think that she has gone too far with her rage, tell herself at B, "I was wrong in showing him so much rage. I *must not* be that wrong!" and she, while still feeling very angry at Joe, may cause herself to be quite guilty and depressed.

So Joe's rational beliefs (rBs) ("Joann acted badly and I wish she wouldn't!") may lead to his appropriate feelings of sorrow and disappointment and to his mildly criticizing her supposedly "poor" behavior; and his irrational beliefs (iBs) ("She *must* not act badly! I *can't stand* her acting this way!") may lead to his anger and his severe criticism of her. Joe's cognitions about Joann's consequence (C), rage, may lead him to have rational beliefs (rBs) ("I don't like Joann's rage, but I can live with it and still be happy"), and his cognitions about her rage may lead him to construct irrational beliefs (iBs) ("I criticized her too much, as I absolutely *should not* have done! How *awful* of me to act so badly!") and to thereby make himself depressed.

Similarly, Joann is affected or "pushed" by Joe's beliefs and emotional consequences to create both rational and irrational Bs and to bring about her own appropriate (self-helping) and inappropriate (self-defeating) consequences. When Joe and Joann have children, in-laws, friends, and business associates, you can see that the ABCs and the cognitions, emotions, and behaviors of all these individuals may importantly affect each other and may encourage each other to have (though not *absolutely make* each other have) self-helping and self-sabotaging (not to mention socially helpful and socially sabotaging) consequences.

RET, then, agrees with many systems-oriented thinkers that humans invariably live in some kind of (material and social) system; that the system importantly affects the people in it; that all the individuals in it affect each other and affect the system; and that to understand how people usually and abnormally behave, we had better understand (a) how people affect themselves (the ABCs of their thoughts, feelings, and behaviors); (b) how they affect each other; (c) how they affect the system; and (d) how the system affects them (Bateson, 1979; DiSalvo, 1989; Ellis, 1989a, 1991d; Huber & Baruth, 1989).

The difference between RET and most of the other personality and psychotherapy theories is that RET clearly distinguishes people's standards, goals, and values from their musts about these rules. RET agrees that, because they are innately teachable or gullible, most people most of the time significantly accept or learn the values and standards of their family, peers, teachers, and religious and political groups. Not always, of course, but often! They also partly, but only partly, learn or adopt musts or commands *about* these standards. Thus, when their parents say, "You must not be lazy!" they first learn that it is "wrong" or "undesirable" to be lazy—that in their social group they will probably be penalized for laziness and rewarded for effort.

Their learning the rules of their culture is generally good, because otherwise they would be severely penalized. They also invent their own personal rules—such as, "I will only try to succeed at tennis but not at golf." Or, "I only will try tennis for three months, and if I don't get pretty good at it, I will quit and try golf." Both their socially and personally acquired rules are okay as long as they are *preferences* and not *absolutist demands*.

People also take musts from their parents, teachers, peers, and cultures, but wrongly think that they are unconditional rather than conditional musts. Thus, your parents tell you, "You *must* do your homework," but really mean, "You *preferentially should* do your homework, or else you will fail at school and get bad results." If they literally meant, *"Under all conditions, at all times, you must do your homework,"* they would see you as a *thoroughly horrible person* when you didn't, and perhaps boycott you or give you away. Actually, they scold you for a short while and then go back to being nice to you—proving that they deplore your *behavior* but still accept and love *you* in spite of it.

You, however, frequently take their *preferential should* too seriously and turn it into an absolute, ever-to-be-obeyed *command*.

You then tell yourself, "If I don't do my homework, as I *must*, I am acting badly and *I* am a *bad person* for acting that way." Your parents (and others) rarely damn *you* for your poor behavior. But you easily damn *yourself*.

Similarly, you construct or invent absolutist musts *on your own*. You take your parents', your society's, and your personal preferences, even when they are expressed only and clearly as desires, and you change them into rigid musts. Thus, you take the view, "It is desirable to make a lot of money," and change it to, "I *have to* become a millionaire or see myself as a *total failure!*" You, like almost all people, are a born "musturbator" and will almost inevitably take parental, societal, and personal rules and foolishly make them into imperatives. So most—not all—of your profound musturbation is self-constructed, self-repeated, self-learned.

You often—not always—construct your dogmatic musts during your early childhood, when you tend to think badly, rigidly, and crookedly. Then you may carry them on, in spite of evidence that they are not valid and don't work, forever. But you also may easily construct many of them during adolescence and adulthood and, conversely, can also change or surrender them as you get older and wiser. The main thing RET emphasizes is that virtually all humans seem to be *active* acceptors of preferences and musts, *active* creators of demands *about* their desires, and *active* ongoing re-creators of self-disturbing and antisocial commands on themselves, on others, and on the world (Ellis, 1990f, 1991a, 1991e; Ellis & Dryden, 1987, 1991; Ellis, Young & Lockwood, 1987).

The Primacy of Absolutist Shoulds and Musts

When I first posited the ABCs of RET, I listed 10 major irrational beliefs (iBs) that people largely use to upset themselves, and that I empirically derived from asking my clients what they thought or told themselves when they were "emotionally" upset (Ellis, 1957a, 1957b, 1958, 1962). These have been put into 30 or more tests of irrational or dysfunctional beliefs and literally hundreds of studies have shown that disturbed people do acknowledge holding many of these beliefs (Baisden, 1980; Beck, 1991; DiGiuseppe, Miller, & Trexler, 1979; Ellis, 1979c; Smith, 1989).

When people change their irrational to more rational or functional beliefs, they significantly improve (Beck, 1991; DiGiuseppe,

Miller, & Trexler, 1979; Ellis, 1979c; Engels, & Diekstra, 1986; Jorm, 1987; Haaga & Davison, 1989; Lyons & Woods, 1991; McGovern & Silverman, 1984). After using RET for a few years, I was surprised to find that the original 10 iBs and my later additions to them (Ellis & Whiteley, 1979) could be put under three—yes, only three— main headings; and that each of these core iBs included an absolutist, rigid should or must. Thus: (1) *"I* (ego) absolutely *must* perform well and win significant others' approval or else *I* am an *inadequate, worthless person."* (2) *"You* (other people) *must* under all conditions and at all times be nice and fair to me or else *you* are a *rotten, horrible person!"* (3) *"Conditions* under which I live absolutely *must* be comfortable, safe, and advantageous or else the world is a rotten *place, I can't stand it,* and life is hardly worth living."

Other cognitive-behavior therapies—such as those of Beck (1976), Maultsby (1984), and Meichenbaum (1977)—also accept these shoulds and musts as irrational and disturbance-producing, but they do not, as RET does, see them as primary and do not see that the misleading inferences, attributes, and overgeneralizations that also are irrational largely stem from, or are tacitly derived from, disturbed people's musts, and would much less often exist without them. Thus, emotionally dysfunctional people, as RET has pointed out since the 1950s, catastrophize, awfulize, overgeneralize, personalize, jump to invalid conclusions, use emotional-reasoning, dichotomize, damn themselves and others, and make other major unrealistic, anti-empirical, often false inferences and attributions (Ellis, 1958, 1962, 1987c. 1987d).

If, for example, I reject your invitation to go to a movie, you may quickly infer: (a) You were wrong to ask me to go; (b) You selected a stupid movie; (c) I dislike you; (d) I hate movies; (e) You are a fool for inviting me, and so on. All these inferences are probably false, but you still create and believe them, and thereby may make yourself feel anxious, depressed, and self-hating.

Why does an intelligent person like you quickly manufacture such dubious, often ridiculous, attributions? The RET theory says, first, because you are naturally, innately, and by experiential training a slippery thinker who *easily* makes questionable or false inferences from observable (or imaginable) data. So you often, harmlessly or harmfully, see rightly and conclude wrongly. Many experimental and social psychologists agree with RET about this

(Ellis, 1987c, 1987d; Epstein, 1990; Kahneman, Slovic, & Tversky, 1985; Korzybski, 1933; Taylor, 1990).

RET adds another theory: that when you are "emotionally" disturbed by your erroneous inferences and attributions, these are usually (not always) derived from and secondary to your dogmatic, imperative musts. Thus, in the illustration given two paragraphs back, you *bring* to your inviting me to a movie the underlying, implicit, tacit, and preconscious powerful must: "Whenever I invite anyone I really like, such as Albert Ellis, to a movie, *he absolutely* must accept my invitation and clearly show he truly likes me or else." Because you devoutly, rigidly believe, and keep holding on to this *demand,* you *easily, semi-automatically, and rigidly* jump to the questionable conclusions, when I refuse your invitation (as I *must* not!), that you were wrong to ask me, selected a stupid movie, made me dislike you, discovered that I disliked movies, are a fool for inviting me, and so on.

RET assumes, in other words, that you are often a profound musturbator and that once you strongly construct absolutist *musts* and *must nots* you will very easily and often, when you, others, and the world contradict them, slide yourself into "logical" but misleading inferences that "confirm" and add to your disturbed reactions. Unlike cognitive-behavior therapy (CBT), therefore, RET's cardinal rule when people are thinking, feeling, and acting neurotically is "Cherchez le should! Cherchez le must! Look for the should! Look for the must!" RET assumes that people with disturbances overtly and/or tacitly have one, two, or three underlying musts, that these can usually be quickly found, and then actively and forcefully Disputed and changed back to preferences. However, to dislodge people's dysfunctional shoulds and musts thoroughly, RET also looks for and actively shows them how to Dispute their misleading inferences—especially their catastrophizing, awfulizing, I-can't-stand-it-itis, self- and other-damning, and overgeneralizing (Ellis, 1962, 1971, 1987d, 1991e; Ellis & Dryden, 1987; Ellis & Grieger, 1977, 1986; Ellis, Young, & Lockwood, 1987).

Disturbance About Disturbance

Soon after I started using the ABCs of RET, I realized that, once they disturb themselves (or accept the irrational beliefs of others), people largely construct secondary disturbances—or disturbances about their disturbances. Thus, they make themselves anxious about their anxiety, depressed about their depression, or self-hating about their anger at others (Dryden, 1990a; Ellis, 1962, 1971, 1973b, 1985c, 1988a, 1991a, 1991e; Ellis & Dryden, 1987, 1990, 1991). They also, as shown in the next section, often create ego disturbance about their low frustration tolerance or discomfort disturbance; and they create discomfort disturbance about their ego disturbance. RET, therefore, assumes that clients have primary and secondary emotional-behavioral problems, looks for both, and, if they exist, helps clients uproot both these important kinds of disturbances (Ellis, 1979a, 1980a).

RET and Discomfort Disturbance

When I first originated and practiced RET, I rightly emphasized ego disturbance—that is, people's damning themselves for not achieving success and winning others' approval. I soon saw, however, that although almost all my clients (and relatives and friends!) often tended to dysfunctionally denigrate their *self* or *being,* and not merely their poor *performances,* they also had *discomfort disturbance* or *low frustration tolerance* (LFT) in the course of which they destructively *demanded* that other people and external conditions *absolutely must* act and be exactly the way they preferred them to act and be. I therefore added to ego disturbance the central RET theory of discomfort disturbance or low frustration tolerance (Bard, 1980; Dryden, 1990; Ellis, 1963a, 1979c, 1980a, 1985c, 1988a; Ellis & Knaus, 1977; Grieger & Boyd, 1980; Walen, DiGiuseppe, & Dryden, 1992; Warren & Zgourides, 1991; Wessler & Wessler, 1980).

As I have noted in my writings and in many therapy sessions, ego and discomfort disturbance often coexist and significantly interact to cause severe neurotic problems. Thus, phobias may start with a client strongly convincing herself "It's *too* uncomfortable and dangerous driving across a bridge! I *can't* stand it!" and thereby creating LFT about bridges. Then she may put herself down (ego disturbance) by telling herself, "I *must not* be afraid of bridges! What a *weak person* I am for avoiding them!" and may thereby create a secondary disturbance. But she may also irrationally believe, "My life is *unbearable* when I avoid bridges and when I hate myself for having this phobia! How *horrible* for me to be this incapacitated!" and she may then have discomfort depression or

LFT *about* her phobia and *about* her self-downing. Her interactions among her discomfort disturbance and her ego disturbance may make her doubly or triply upset; and because of her LFT—"It's *too hard* for me to work on my emotional-behavioral problems! I *shouldn't* have to take so much time and energy to ameliorate them!"—she may refuse to give up her interactional disturbances. RET practitioners, therefore, assume that most clients have *both* LFT and self-damnation and try to help their clients discover and undo both kinds of disturbance.

RET and the Scientific Method

RET has always tried to be scientific in its theory and in checking its practice, but it first wrongly followed logical positivism (Ellis, 1962). Since 1976, it is close to Popper's (1962, 1985) critical realism (Ellis, 1985c, 1988a; Mahoney, 1991; Rorer, 1989), which focuses on critically assessing theories and trying to learn by falsifying them rather than on striving for their "truth" or "validity." As science recently has become more open-minded and probabilistic, RET in some respects tends to be synonymous with the scientific method.

How so? Well, modern science—and not, of course, dogmatic scientism—has three main facets. (1) It checks its theories with realism and empiricism to see whether they are falsifiable and anti-empirical. (2) It uses logic to see if theories are consistent with their own tenets and if they are contradicted by opposing, and presumably better, theories. (3) It is never dogmatic, doesn't claim that any theory is perfectly true under all conditions and at all times, and happily seeks for better, more workable, alternative theories (Bartley, 1962; DiGiuseppe, 1986; Popper, 1962, 1985).

I realized, after I had used RET for several years, that if people rigorously—not rigidly!—followed this kind of scientific outlook in their personal lives they would have a difficult time making themselves needlessly self-defeating or neurotic. They would presumably create few or no absolutist, dogmatic shoulds, oughts, and musts (because doing so is to be antiscientific) and if they did so, they would fairly easily and quickly challenge and dispute them empirically and logically—just as they are shown to do in RET!

RET, in other words, theorizes that much (not all) "emotional" disturbance is closely related to, and often essentially the same thing as, antiscientific, inflexible, absolutist thinking and that the main elements of "mental health" are flexibility, open minded-ness, and alternative-thinking. So RET's theory of neurotic distur-bance dovetails with contemporary scientific methods in several important ways.

The RET Theory of Force

I first thought, along with several ancient and modern philoso-phers, that people who had more irrational beliefs (iBs) were more "emotionally" disturbed then those with fewer such beliefs, and I still think that this concept has some evidential support. But then I changed RET so that it focuses mainly (not exclusively!) on the kinds of iBs that people hold—particularly on their absolutist shoulds, oughts, and musts.

A great deal of clinical evidence, however, led me to conclude, as Abelson (1963) had posited, that cognitions can be "cool" and "hot." I added to this theory that they could also be "warm." Thus, the cognition, "This is a deadly gun" is a "cool" cognition that merely describes an object. The cognition, "I dislike this deadly gun" is a "warm" cognition that evaluates the same object. The cognition, "I hate this deadly gun and I think that it has to be immediately destroyed, along with all other guns like it!" is a "hot" cognition that powerfully, forcefully evaluates this object, and constitutes a command, rather than a desire, about it.

RET now holds that when people have self-disturbing thoughts, these thoughts are often, perhaps usually, "hot" cognitions that they could hold mildly or lightly, on the one hand, or forcefully and heavily, on the other hand. People may easily, at one and the same time, have a "warm" or preferential cognition—"I like suc-cess but I can accept failure, learn from it, and still lead a happy life"—and also have a contradictory "hot," musturbatory cogni-tion"—I really *must* succeed, *must* not fail, and can only be quite miserable if I do!" RET theory says that if they hold the latter irrational belief (iB) more frequently and/or more strongly than the former rational belief (rB) they will tend to disturb themselves needlessly, while if they hold the rB more frequently and/or more strongly than the iB they will tend to make themselves less fre-quently and less strongly disturbed (Ellis, 1985c, 1988a).

Because RET asserts that people hold rBs and iBs weakly and strongly, it also theorizes that if people lightly and namby-pambily dispute their iBs and lightly or parrotingly change them into rBs, they often will still powerfully and tacitly hold onto their under-lying iBs and, therefore, will only temporarily and weakly surren-der their emotional-behavioral disturbances. Consequently, RET has invented and adapted a number of strong, dramatic-evocative, emotive therapy techniques, some of which are described below (Ellis, 1985c, 1988a; Ellis & Dryden, 1987, 1991). Preferential RET, unlike general RET and CBT, almost invariably employs vigor, force, and emotive, as well as cognitive and behavioral, methods of therapy (Ellis & Whiteley, 1979).

RET and the Concept of Efficiency

I started to do RET in 1955 largely because, as I jokingly and yet seriously often say in my talks and workshops, I have a gene for efficiency while poor Sigmund Freud—not to mention Carl Jung, Melanie Klein, and Wilhelm Reich—had a gene for inefficiency. Almost all methods of therapy work to some extent with some people—especially when they include the therapist's giving the client unconditional positive regard and encouraging some kind of in vivo desensitization. But psychoanalytic and many other therapies take much too long in many instances—while, alas, the clients are painfully and needlessly suffering.

RET, therefore, has always espoused efficiency-oriented meth-ods to supplement relationship, support, desensitization, and other conventional, widely used (and often effective) techniques. For the most part, it also minimizes or avoids, except in unusual cases, long-winded, inefficient methods like free association, dream analy-sis, detailed "explanations" of past history, and other methods that lead nowhere in the short, and often in the long, run. As noted below, on theoretical grounds it favors active-directive, questioning and challenging, distinctly didactic, homework-assigning, and other designed-to-be-efficient techniques (Ellis, 1962, 1971, 1973b, 1988a, 1990; Grieger & Boyd, 1980).

By *efficiency*, RET means a therapeutic theory and practice that is designed to get at clients' fundamental problems rapidly and show them, within a few sessions, how to start working to ame-liorate these problems. It also means a system that shows clients, as rapidly as feasible, how to achieve what RET calls an "elegant" or profound philosophical change, which is described below.

RET and the Self System

RET has been somewhat pioneering in being a "self" psychology, even more so than the psychoanalytic "self systems," such as those of Klein (Klein & Riviere, 1964), Hartman (1964), Guntrip (1971), Kohut (1977) and Kernberg (1975). This is because it gives more importance to people's self-constructions, even during their early childhood, than any of the psychoanalytic theories. As noted above, it sees humans as individuals who live in a social group (as also do the Adlerians and the object relations theorists). But it sees them as largely adopting social standards and values and then constructing or making them into rigid, absolutist musts and commands.

It is each person's unique "self" or "ego" that does most of this constructing and that is embedded in a social context, and even takes much of its "personality" from its sociality—as Adler (1964) and Sampson (1989) and others have shown. But one's "self" is both a taker and a creative constructor; and it largely runs human existence. RET objects strongly to *rating* or *measuring* one's "self" (as noted below), but it particularly favors self-development and self-actualization, as long as they are not taken to harmful extremes (Ellis, 1963c, 1973b, 1991a).

As for "object relations," RET agrees with the neo-Freudian analysts, especially Bowlby (1969, 1973), that people have a tendency to make their relationships with others of paramount importance and to believe strongly that they not only *preferably should have* but *absolutely need* the approval and love of their parents and early caretakers. They also believe that if they do not get "validated" by significant others they then have little *personal worth* and are *bad people.* Unlike psychoanalytic and many other therapies, however, RET holds that lack of early love and succoring does not *necessarily* seriously disturb all children, nor does it *make them* into "borderline personalities." Instead, most of the "borderlines" (as well as the psychotics) seem to have other, largely biological, deficits that contribute to their extreme neediness and severe disturbance. Because of the severity of their problems, they usually require more prolonged and intensive therapy than most "neurotics" (Ellis, 1989b).

RET especially tries to help borderline and psychotic individuals to fully accept themselves *with* their severe disturbances. It specializes in treating their neurosis *about* their psychosis and while it hardly cures the latter state, it appreciably helps many of them to achieve happier lives.

Humanistic and Existential Aspects of RET

RET has always been one of the humanistic-existential psychotherapies (Ellis, 1962, 1972b, 1983a, 1983b, 1985a, 1987b, 1987e, 1988a, 1990d, 1990f, 1991a). Although it has sometimes been accused of being sensationalistic and overly "rationalist" (Mahoney, 1991), RET is actually one of the most "constructivist" therapies. It holds that people do not merely *get*, or are "conditioned" to be, disturbed but that they largely create or construct their own grandiose musts and demands and that they actively, though often tacitly or "unconsciously," keep reconstructing them for the rest of their lives (Ellis, 1972b, 1985c, 1990f, 1991a, 1991e, 1991f).

As I noted in Dryden and DiGiuseppe (1990, pp. 79-93):

Unlike some of the other cognitive-behavior therapies, RET takes a definite humanistic-existential approach. It is not purely objective, scientific, or technique-centered in that it adheres to the following principles:

1. It deals with disturbed *human* evaluations, emotions, and behaviors. It sees humans as the basic creators or inventors of their own emotional problems and therefore as *humanly* capable of minimizing these problems.

2. It is highly rational and scientific but uses rationality and science in the service of humans in an attempt to enable them to live and be happy. It is hedonistic but espouses long-range instead of short-range hedonism so that people may achieve the pleasure of the moment and the future and arrive at maximum freedom and discipline.

3. It hypothesizes that nothing superhuman probably exists and that devout belief in superhuman agencies tends to foster dependency and increase emotional disturbance (Ellis, 1983a; Ellis & Tisdale, 1990; Ellis & Yeager, 1989).

4. It assumes that no humans, whatever their antisocial or obnoxious behavior, are damnable or subhuman. It respects and accepts all people just because they are alive and human.

5. It attempts to help people maximize their individuality, freedom, self-interest, and self-control rather than to submit to the control and direction of others (including their therapists). At the same time, it tries to help people live in an involved, committed, and selectively loving manner with other humans and to foster social as well as individual interest.
6. It particularly emphasizes the importance of will and choice in human affairs, even though it accepts the likelihood that some human behavior is partially determined by biological, social, and other forces.

Biological Bases of Human Irrationality and Disturbance

RET, more than most other psychotherapies, accepts the familial and societal influences on human irrationality and disturbance, but it *also* emphasizes their biological origins (Ellis, 1976a; Franklin, 1987). It does this for several reasons:

1. Practically all humans have a number of neurotic self-defeating tendencies, no matter where or in what culture or what ethnic group they were reared (Ellis, 1987c; Frazer, 1959; Freud, 1965; Hoffer, 1951; Levi-Strauss, 1962).
2. Although people tend to be more frequently and more severely disturbed when they are reared by dysfunctional, abusive, and incest-ridden families, they can also be highly neurotic when reared by highly functional, nonabusive, and nonincestuous families.
3. When people's disturbance is family-related, they often inherit a strong genetic factor from their close relatives. Several of the more serious mental-emotional disturbances—such as manic-depressive, severe depressive, schizophrenic, and obsessive-compulsive disorders—appear to have a distinct genetic component.
4. Even when seriously disturbed individuals—such as borderline personalities—significantly improve as a result of intensive therapy, they frequently fall back to disturbed ways of functioning.
5. Most therapists and their children display many unrealistic and self-defeating ideas and behaviors.
6. People commonly not only disturb themselves but needlessly depress and panic themselves about their disturbances. The "solutions" they choose for their problems often become part of or embrace the problem (Ellis, 1979a, 1980a, 1985a, 1985c, 1986a, 1987c, 1988a; Watzlawick, Weakland, & Fisch, 1974).

7. When people acknowledge their disturbances and their disadvantages, they still commonly resist working to change them (Ellis, 1985c; Wachtel, 1982). When they temporarily change themselves, they frequently fall back to self-defeating ways (Ellis, McInerney, DiMattia, DiGiuseppe, & Yeager, 1988).

8. Not only absolutist musts but erroneous attributions, inferences, and overgeneralizations seem to be ubiquitous among all humans (Beck, 1976; Burns, 1980; Ellis, 1957, 1962, 1985c, 1987d; Korzybski, 1933; Russell, 1965).

Because RET practitioners accept the biological as well as the social and interpersonal "causes" of human disturbance, they realize how difficult it is for people to make real and lasting changes, often show their clients that this is so, and encourage them to keep working and practicing to improve and to maintain their improvements (Ellis, 1985c, 1988a, 1991e).

Distinctive Practices of RET

RET was the original cognitive-behavior therapy (CBT) when I started using it in the beginning of 1955 and has always, in its general form, been synonymous with CBT (Ellis, 1969a, 1980b; Ellis & Whiteley, 1979; Lazarus, 1990). Like CBT, it uses a large number of cognitive, emotive, and behavioral methods, and it has many important integrative aspects, as it selectively adapts and employs a number of methods that are also used in existential, humanistic, eclectic, and other therapies. In its preferential form, however, it uniquely stresses a number of practices that most other modes of CBT and other therapies rarely espouse, such as the following techniques.

Active-Directive RET

RET practitioners assume that many, though hardly all, clients can actively and directively be taught the ABCDs of RET from the first session onward and can soon learn to use them effectively. I personally am highly active and directive with the great majority of my clients and find that at least a third of them can start improving within a few weeks. If they prove to be, as I experiment with rapid-fire RET, borderline or resistant, I usually slow down, repeat the main RET procedures and, avoiding my own possible low frustration tolerance, still keep pushing them to change for longer periods of time (and in a few cases for a number of years). I assume, however, that many neurotic, hardworking clients can benefit by an encouraging, active-directive approach, and that RET is one of the few intrinsically brief (or at least brief*er)* therapies for a good many less resistant clients (Ellis, 1992). I originated RET mainly because psychoanalysis and other therapies that I used up to 1955 were too inefficient and too prolonged. So I designed RET so that it can, but doesn't have to be, done in a relatively brief, highly directive manner (Bernard, 1991; Dryden, 1990; Ellis, 1962, 1973b, 1988a; Ellis & Abrahms, 1978; Ellis & Becker, 1982; Ellis & Dryden, 1987, 1991; Walen et al., 1980; Wessler & Wessler, 1980).

During the first few sessions, I outline the main principles of RET to my clients, especially show them how they largely disturb themselves; help them look for and dispute their musts and their other irrational beliefs; work out with them suitable cognitive, emotive, and behavioral homework assignments; and encourage them to unconditionally accept themselves and to improve their low frustration tolerance. Usually, one or two main symptoms—such as social anxiety, depression, and addiction—are repetitively tackled. But as my clients continue to improve, a more elegant, profound philosophic change is investigated and sought for (as is explained in the next section).

RET and the Concept of Elegant Change

Unlike some psychotherapies, such as pure behavior therapy and hypnosis, RET not only tries to help clients "cure" themselves of their presenting symptoms but also tries to help them achieve an "elegant" or profound philosophic change (Ellis, 1980b, 1985c, 1988a; Ellis & Whiteley, 1979; Ellis, Young, & Lockwood, 1987). This includes several possibilities:

1. Clients become less disturbed or even free of their presenting symptoms (e.g., of panic, depression, rage, or self-hatred).
2. They minimize their related and other disturbances (e.g., if they come to therapy about their sexual anxiety, they also make themselves

less anxious about work problems and overcome their neurotic procrastination).

3. They recognize and minimize their disturbances about their disturbance (e.g., their anxiety about their anxiety, depression about their depression, or self-downing about their rage).

4. They maintain their improvement for a long period of time, preferably permanently.

5. They rarely seriously disturb themselves about almost anything in the future.

6. When they feel disturbed again, they quickly use RET to reduce or eliminate the new disturbances.

7. By practicing RET over the years, they become less disturbable and prophylactically keep warding off potential needless upsets.

8. When even the worst things happen to them or their loved ones, they tend to disturb themselves minimally and mainly to feel *appropriately* sad, sorry, regretful, frustrated, and annoyed.

9. While steadily working at minimally disturbing themselves, they optimistically and energetically strive for greater happiness and self-fulfillment (Ellis & Dryden, 1991).

It is assumed in RET that people can make inelegant, though important, symptomatic changes through a number of different methods, including many of those used in RET. But when they make the kind of elegant change outlined above, they usually make a *profound philosophic change*. This can be achieved in several ways, especially by working hard and persistently to have strong preferences instead of grandiose demands. RET favors critical realistic acceptance, including:

Acceptance of self-change through hard work and practice.

Unwhining acceptance of what one cannot change.

Acceptance of human fallibility and imperfection.

Unconditional acceptance and nondamnation of oneself and others.

Acceptance of long-range rather than short-range hedonism.

Acceptance of probability and uncertainty.

Acceptance of the importance of one's self and one's social group.

Acceptance of one's own and others' mortality.

Acceptance of one's talents for greater happiness and self-actualization as one keeps working to minimize one's disturbance.

Clients are shown that though they can often make important personality and behavioral changes within a few months, their making an elegant change requires something of a lifelong dedication to acquiring, reconstructing, and steadily implementing an enthusiastic self-helping attitude. Therapy sessions are important but working in between sessions and after therapy has ended to be self-reliant and unconditionally self-accepting is even more crucial. RET sessions may be brief and infrequent, but self-determination and action to become consistently preferential and anti-musturbatory is endless (Ellis & Dryden, 1987, 1990, 1991; Ellis & Velten, 1992).

Therapeutic Relationship and Self-Help Materials

Theoretically, RET can be taught to people through books, pamphlets, audio-visual materials, lectures, courses, workshops, and intensives, with no personal relationship between a therapist and his or her clients. So can person-centered therapy, though Carl Rogers (1961) has denied this. Some of the most helped RETers I have known had little or no individual or group therapy; and a few mainly figured out its principles for themselves.

At the Institute for Rational-Emotive Therapy in New York, we use many self-help materials, especially some of my books and cassettes (Ellis, 1957a, 1972a, 1972d, 1973a, 1973c, 1974, 1975, 1976c, 1977a, 1977b, 1977d, 1978a, 1979b, 1980c, 1987f, 1988a, 1988b, 1990b; Ellis & Becker, 1982; Ellis & Harper, 1975; Ellis & Knaus, 1977) and those of Beck (1988), Burns (1980), Dryden and Gordon (1991), Hauck (1973, 1974, 1977), Knaus (1983), and Young (1974). We find that clients who use these materials tend to improve faster and more intensively than those who neglect them (Ellis, 1978b, 1990c, 1991c).

Like the writings and cassettes of Abraham Low (1952), RET is also well designed for self-help groups. In 1987, Jack Trimpey (1989) started Rational Recovery, which already has hundreds of self-help groups in the United States and several other countries that include alcohol, food, and other addicts who specifically use RET to help themselves with their emotional and behavioral problems (Ellis, 1991c; Trimpey & Trimpey, 1990). Many regular psychotherapy groups throughout the world—including eight weekly groups at the Institute for RET in New York—also use RET and CBT (Ellis, 1987a, 1990g; Ellis & Dryden, 1987; Ellis & Harper, 1961).

Ideally, however, people receive individual sessions of RET together with the use of RET self-help materials. Seriously neurotic and borderline individuals particularly benefit from this combination (Ellis, 1965/1989b). Realizing that perhaps the majority of therapy clients have a dire need for approval and love, including that of their therapist, RET practitioners usually avoid relating too closely to their clients and avoid having them maintain or increase their dependency tendencies. At the same time, rational-emotive therapists tend to be highly collaborative, encouraging, supportive, and mentoring (Ellis, 1990c, 1990d; Ellis & Dryden, 1991).

Most of all, RET practitioners, like person-centered therapists, unconditionally accept all their clients, *whether or not* these clients behave well in and out of therapy, and *whether or not* they are nice and lovable. Unlike Rogerians, moreover, they actively, forcefully teach their clients to *accept themselves* unconditionally. People can do this *practically*, RET teaches, by merely *deciding* that they are "good" or "worthy" just because they are alive and human. Or they can achieve unconditional self-acceptance more elegantly by deciding and actively practicing to rate *only* their deeds and performances and *not* to measure or evaluate their total *self* or *being* at all (Bard, 1987; Ellis, 1962, 1963c, 1972b, 1976b, 1988a, 1991e; Ellis & Becker, 1982; Ellis & Dryden, 1987, 1990, 1991; Ellis & Harper, 1975).

Emotive Techniques of RET

As noted above, RET hypothesizes that people often *forcefully* and *powerfully* create and hold on to their dysfunctional thoughts, feelings, and behaviors. Therefore, it has designed and adapted, and almost always employs, a number of vigorous evocative-emotive techniques. For example:

Shame Attacking. These exercises encourage clients to go out in public and deliberately do some act they consider "foolish" or "shameful" while working cognitively and emotively to feel *only* appropriately sorry and disappointed and *not* ashamed or sell-downing when they receive disapproval (Ellis, 1969b, 1973a, 1988a; Ellis & Abrahms, 1978; Ellis & Becker, 1982; Ellis & Harper, 1975).

Rational-Emotive Imagery. People imagine one of the worst things that could happen to them, implode their *in*appropriate feelings of horror, terror, depression, and rage, and then work to make themselves feel *appropriately* sorry, disappointed, or frustrated (Ellis, 1988a; Ellis & Harper, 1975; Ellis & Velten, 1992; Maultsby, 1971; Maultsby & Ellis, 1974).

Forceful Coping Statements. Clients are shown how to create realistic and philosophic rational self-statements and how to sink them *vigorously* into their heads and hearts until they *convincingly* believe them (Ellis, 1969b, 1988a; Ellis & Becker, 1982; Ellis & Dryden, 1987, 1991; Ellis & Harper, 1975).

Forceful Self-Dialogues. Clients make a tape describing their irrational beliefs (iBs), vehemently dispute them on the tape, listen to their own disputing, and have others listen to it to see if it is sufficiently powerful and convincing (Ellis, 1985c, 1988a, 1990b; Ellis & Velten, 1992).

Use of Humor. RET uses many forms of disputing a client's irrational beliefs, especially that of reducing them to absurdity. Disturbed people frequently lose their sense of humor, and it has been found that, if they interrupt their over-seriousness by laughing at some of their errors and inanities, they emotively as well as cognitively distract themselves from and tend to surrender some of their dysfunctional beliefs (Ellis, 1977c, 1987f; Fry & Salameh, 1987).

I began using a group of rational humorous songs, with my own lyrics set to popular tunes, in 1976. At the Institute for Rational-Emotive Therapy's psychological clinic in New York, we find that they are often effective when used with individual and group clients and in RET-oriented talks, workshops, and intensives (Ellis, 1977d, 1981, 1987f).

Use of Group Processes and Exercises. I began to apply RET to group processes in the late 1950s because I found that clients gained support from others who learned and used RET with them and that, when actively disputing others' irrational beliefs, they became more adept at and interested in disputing their own iBs. Consequently, RET uses several small and large-scale group processes, including regular group therapy, special women's and men's groups, workshops, and intensives. In the course of these groups—as well as in RET individual sessions—many experiential and emotive-evocative exercises are used (Dryden, 1990; Ellis, 1969b, 1973b, 1975, 1977a, 1979c, 1980c, 1985b, 1985c, 1987a, 1988a, 1990b, 1990c, 1990d, 1990g, 1990h, 1991a, 1991c, 1991f; Ellis, Sichel, Leaf, & Mass, 1989).

Interpersonal Relationships. From the start, RET has emphasized interpersonal and family relationships because most clients have problems in these areas and many would not come to therapy if they did not have them. RET actively deals with how people upset *themselves* about their relations with others, but it also shows them how to relate and cooperate better with others in the course of individual and group therapy and in workshops and intensives. It is consequently one of the main interpersonal relationship therapies (Crawford & Ellis, 1982; Ellis, 1957, 1962, 1969b, 1971, 1973b, 1975, 1976c, 1977a, 1977b, 1979b, 1980c, 1985a, 1985b, 1986b, 1988a, 1988b, 1990b, 1990d, in press; Ellis & Becker, 1982; Ellis & Bernard, 1985; Ellis & Dryden, 1985, 1987; Ellis & Harper, 1961; Ellis, Sichel, Yeager, DiMattia, & DiGiuseppe, 1989; Hauck, 1977).

RET Role Playing. Clients role play with a therapist, group member, or friend and stop when they display anxiety, rage, or depression to see what they are telling themselves to create their disturbed feelings (Ellis, 1988a; Ellis & Abrahms, 1978).

Reverse Role Playing. The rational-emotive therapist or a friend of the client plays the client's role and rigidly holds on to his or her irrational beliefs (iBs), until the client is able to talk the role player out of these dysfunctional ideas (Ellis, 1988a; Ellis, Sichel, DiMattia, DiGiuseppe, & Yeager, 1989).

Other Emotive Techniques. RET includes a number of other emotive-evocative methods, such as the therapist's using strong encouragement, forceful disputing, self-disclosure, stories, analogies, metaphors, and so on (Bernard, 1986; Bernard & Joyce, 1984; Ellis & Abrahms, 1978; Ellis & Dryden, 1987, 1991; Ellis & Yeager, 1989; Lazarus, 1990; Muran, 1991; Vernon, 1989).

Behavioral Techniques of RET

Because I got myself over my public speaking and social phobias at the age of 19 by forcing myself to *act against* them, RET has always heavily used a number of behavioral methods, and therefore pioneered in cognitive-behavior therapy (Ellis, 1962, 1969a, 1969b, 1971, 1972c, 1973b, 1988a, 1990e, 1991b; Ellis & Becker, 1982; Ellis & Dryden, 1987, 1990, 1991c; Ellis & Harper, 1975; Warga, 1989). Some of the most frequently employed behavioral methods of RET are discussed below.

In Vivo Desensitization. Rather than rely on Wolpe's (1982) imaginal systematic desensitization, RET favors in vivo desensitization and urges clients to do repetitively what they are afraid to do, such as speaking in public, encountering potential sex-love partners, and going for difficult job interviews (Ellis, 1962, 1971, 1988a; Ellis & Becker, 1982; Ellis & Dryden, 1987, 1990, 1991; Ellis & Harper, 1961, 1975).

Implosive Desensitization. In encouraging clients to do what they are afraid to do in order to overcome their dysfunctional fears, RET often favors implosive rather than gradual desensitization (Ellis, 1983b). Thus, people with elevator fears are encouraged to enter 20 elevators a day for about 30 days in a row while forcefully telling themselves, "I can handle this! I won't get stuck in this elevator and if I do, it's only a damned inconvenience, not a horror!" Not all clients agree to do their fear-attacking homework implosively, but when they do, they usually get better and quicker results than when they do so gradually—for they then experientially *see* that it is only uncomfortable, not harmful or "horrible" (Ellis, 1971, 1973a, 1985c, 1988a, 1991b).

Remaining in "Awful" Situations. RET often encourages clients to remain temporarily in "awful" situations—such as staying in a "rotten" marriage or with a "horrible" boss—until they work out their emotional problems and stop making themselves panicked, depressed, or enraged. *Then* they may be helped to leave the situation (Ellis, 1985c, 1988a; Ellis & Abrahms, 1978).

Response Prevention. With serious obsessive-compulsives, they are sometimes shown how to get a friend or relative to steadily monitor and restrain them, so that they are effectively prevented from indulging in their compulsive rituals (Ellis, 1985c; Ellis & Velten, 1991; Marks, 1978).

Penalization. RET not only uses a good deal of reinforcement when clients do their difficult agreed-upon homework assignments, but also recommends self-imposed penalties when they steadily refuse to do so. Thus, difficult customers (DCs) are urged to burn a hundred dollar bill or send it to an organization they violently disagree with when they fail to keep their promises to themselves to change their behavior. If necessary, they enlist a friend or relative to monitor their carrying out self-assigned penalties (Ellis, 1979c, 1985c, 1988a; Ellis & Abrahms, 1978; Ellis & Becker, 1982).

Medication. RET shows many clients how to live with little or no medication—such as large doses of Valium— but also often recommends experiments with antidepressants, lithium, and other suitable medication for clients afflicted with endogenous depression, manic-depressive illness, obsessive-compulsive disorder, and other serious emotional-behavioral problems. It specializes in helping clients to work on their low frustration tolerance and thereby be able to follow medical and psychopharmacological routines that they are dysfunctionally avoiding (Ellis, 1985c; Ellis & Abrahms, 1978).

Skill Training. RET, as I have noted on several occasions, is a "double-systems" therapy in that it usually first helps people function better in their present family, work, school, or social system and then, as therapy proceeds, helps them change the system so that they can lead happier, more fulfilling lives. Consequently, it often shows clients how to change the activating events (As) they encounter, how to solve practical problems, and how to acquire pleasure-enhancing skills. It has pioneered in teaching clients assertion training (Ellis, 1963a, 1975; Wolfe, 1974; Wolfe & Fodor, 1975), and it frequently emphasizes relationship, communication, sex, and social skills training (Ellis, 1957, 1962, 1963a, 1963b, 1971, 1973a, 1973b, 1975, 1976c, 1977a, 1979b, 1980c, 1985b, 1986b, 1988a, in press; Ellis & Becker, 1982; Ellis & Dryden, 1987, 1991; Ellis & Grieger, 1977, 1986; Hauck, 1977).

Avoidance of Inefficient Procedures

RET, as noted above, strives for efficient therapy and, therefore, largely (though not completely) avoids ineffective and potentially harmful therapy techniques. Thus, it is skeptical of and often avoids (a) Extensive free association; (b) Extensive dream analysis; (c) Too much therapist's warmth and enhancing of clients' dependency; (d) Compulsive exploration of clients' early life and endless narration of their present complaints and experiences; (e) Compulsive talking about clients' feelings; and (f) Overemphasis on positive thinking and on positive visualization rather than on Disputing of irrational beliefs (Bernard, 1986, 1991; Ellis, 1991f; Ellis & Dryden, 1985).

Emphasis on Self-Actualization

As mentioned previously, RET has two main aspects: helping people overcome their cognitive-emotive-behavioral disturbances and helping them actively to seek and arrange for a fuller, happier, and more self-actualizing existence. More specifically, as I point out in a recent paper (Ellis, 1991a, p. 15) and as I have collaboratively worked out with Ted Crawford (Crawford & Ellis, 1989), RET encourages clients to work at (a) actively choosing self-actualizing paths that they individually select; (b) preferring but not demanding that they solve self-actualizing problems; (c) unconditional acceptance of oneself and others; (d) overcoming procrastination and low frustration tolerance; (e) framing self-actualizing as a systemic problem to be designed and redesigned; (f) moving from either/ors toward and/alsos—by accepting ambiguity, paradox, inconsistency, and confusion and then pushing toward an integrated wholeness.

The RET approach to self-actualization, like its approach to treating cognitive-emotional disturbance, heavily emphasizes openness, skeptical questioning, and ceaseless experimentation. Critical realism is ever its watchword.

References

Abelson, R. P. (1963). Computer simulation of "hot" cognition. In S. S. Tompkins & S. Messick (Eds.), *Computer simulation of personality*. New York: John Wiley.
Adler, A. (1964). *Social interest: A challenge to mankind*. New York: Capricorn.

Baisden, H. E. (1980). *Irrational beliefs: A construct validation study.* Unpublished doctoral dissertation, University of Minnesota, Minneapolis.

Bard, J. (1980). *Rational-emotive therapy in practice.* Champaign, IL: Research Press.

Bard, J. (1987). *I don't like asparagus.* Cleveland, OH: Cleveland State University, Psychology Department.

Bartley, W. W. (1962). *The retreat to commitment.* New York: Knopf. (Rev. ed., Knopf, New York, 1985)

Bateson, G. (1979). *Mind and nature: A necessary unit.* New York: E. P. Dutton.

Beck, A. T. (1976). *Cognitive therapy and the emotional disorders.* New York: International Universities Press.

Beck, A. T. (1988). *Love is never enough.* New York: Harper & Row.

Beck, A. T. (1991). Cognitive therapy: A 30-year retrospective. *American Psychologist, 46,* 382-389.

Bernard, M. E. (1986). *Staying alive in an irrational world: Albert Ellis and rational-emotive therapy.* South Melbourne, Australia: Carlson/Macmillan.

Bernard, M. E. (Ed.). (1991). *Using rational-emotive therapy effectively: A practitioner's guide.* New York: Plenum.

Bernard, M. E., & Joyce, M. R. (1984). *Rational-emotive therapy with children and adolescents.* New York: John Wiley.

Bowlby, J. (1969). *Attachment and loss. I: Attachment.* New York: Basic Books.

Bowlby, J. (1973). *Attachment and loss. II: Separation.* New York: Basic Books.

Burns, D. D. (1980). *Feeling good: The new mood therapy.* New York: Morrow.

Crawford, T. (1990). [Letters to the author, May 7, May 11, & May 26.]

Crawford, T., & Ellis, A. (1982, October). *Communication and rational-emotive therapy.* Workshop presented in Los Angeles.

Crawford, T., & Ellis, A. (1989). A dictionary of rational-emotive feelings and behaviors. *Journal of Rational-Emotive and Cognitive-Behavior Therapy, 7*(1), 3-27.

DiGiuseppe, R. (1986). The implication of the philosophy of science for rational-emotive theory and therapy. *Psychotherapy, 23,* 634-639.

DiGiuseppe, R., Miller, J. J., & Trexler, L. D. (1979). A review of rational-emotive psychotherapy outcome studies. In A. Ellis & J. M. Whiteley (Eds.), *Theoretical and empirical foundations of rational-emotive therapy* (pp. 218-235). Monterey, CA: Brooks/Cole.

DiSalvo, J. (1989). *Beyond revolution: On becoming a cybernetic epistemologist.* New York: Vantage.

Dryden, W. (1990a). *Dealing with anger problems: Rational-emotive therapeutic interventions.* Sarasota, FL: Professional Resource Exchange.

Dryden, W. (1990b). *Rational-emotive counseling in action.* London: Sage.

Dryden, W., & DiGiuseppe, R. (1990). *A primer on rational-emotive therapy.* Champaign, IL: Research Press.

Dryden, W., & Gordon, J. (1991). *Think your way to happiness.* London: Sheldon Press.

Ellis, A. (1957a). *How to live with a neurotic: At home and at work.* New York: Crown. (Rev. ed., Wilshire, North Hollywood, CA, 1975)

Ellis, A. (1957b). Outcome of employing three techniques of psychotherapy. *Journal of Clinical Psychology, 13,* 344-350.

Ellis, A. (1958). *Rational psychotherapy.* New York: Institute for Rational-Emotive Therapy. (Reprinted from *Journal of General Psychology,* 1958, *59,* 35-49)

Ellis, A. (1962). *Reason and emotion in psychotherapy.* Secaucus, NJ: Citadel.

Ellis, A. (1963a). *The intelligent woman's guide to manhunting.* New York: Lyle Stuart and Dell. (Rev. ed., *The intelligent woman's guide to dating and mating,* Lyle Stuart, Secaucus, NJ, 1979)

Ellis, A. (1963b). *Sex and the single man.* Secaucus, NJ: Lyle Stuart.

Ellis, A. (1963c). Showing the patient that he is not a worthless individual. *Voices, 1*(2), 74-77. (Reprinted and revised as *Showing clients they are not worthless individuals,* Institute for Rational-Emotive Therapy, New York, 1985)

Ellis, A. (1969a). A cognitive approach to behavior therapy. *International Journal of Psychiatry, 8,* 896-900.

Ellis, A. (1969b). A weekend of rational encounter. *Rational Living, 4*(2), 1-8. (Reprinted in A. Ellis & W. Dryden, *The practice of rational-emotive therapy,* Springer, New York, 1987)

Ellis, A. (1971). *Growth through reason.* North Hollywood, CA: Wilshire.

Ellis, A. (Speaker). (1972a). *Conquering low frustration tolerance* [Cassette recording]. New York: Institute for Rational-Emotive Therapy.

Ellis, A. (1972b). *Psychotherapy and the value of a human being.* New York: Institute for Rational-Emotive Therapy. (Reprinted in A. Ellis & W. Dryden, *The essential Albert Ellis.* New York: Springer, 1990).

Ellis, A. (1972c). Psychotherapy without tears. In A. Burton (Ed.), *Twelve therapists* (pp. 103-126). San Francisco: Jossey-Bass.

Ellis, A. (Speaker). (1972d). *Solving emotional problems* [Cassette recording]. New York: Institute for Rational-Emotive Therapy.

Ellis, A. (Speaker). (1973a). *How to stubbornly refuse to be ashamed of anything* [Cassette recording]. New York: Institute for Rational-Emotive Therapy.

Ellis, A. (1973b). *Humanistic psychotherapy: The rational-emotive approach.* New York: McGraw-Hill.

Ellis, A. (Speaker). (1973c). *Twenty-one ways to stop worrying* [Cassette recording]. New York: Institute for Rational-Emotive Therapy.

Ellis, A. (Speaker). (1974). *Rational living in an irrational world* [Cassette recording]. New York: Institute for Rational-Emotive Therapy.

Ellis, A. (Speaker). (1975). *RET and assertiveness training* [Cassette recording]. New York: Institute for Rational-Emotive Therapy.

Ellis, A. (1976a). The biological basis of human irrationality. *Journal of Individual Psychology, 32,* 145-168. (Reprinted, Institute for Rational-Emotive Therapy, New York, 1976).

Ellis, A. (1976b). RET abolishes most of the human ego. New York: Institute for Rational-Emotive Therapy. (Reprinted from *Psychotherapy,* 1976, *13,* 343-348)

Ellis, A. (1976c). *Sex and the liberated man.* Secaucus, NJ: Lyle Stuart.

Ellis, A. (1977a). *Anger—How to live with and without it.* Secaucus, NJ: Citadel.

Ellis, A. (Speaker). (1977b). *Conquering the dire need for love* [Cassette recording]. New York: Institute for Rational-Emotive Therapy.

Ellis, A. (1977c). Fun as psychotherapy. *Rational Living, 12*(1), 2-6. (Also available as a cassette recording [1977] from Institute for Rational-Emotive Therapy, New York)

Ellis, A. (Speaker). (1977d). *A garland of rational humorous songs* (Cassette recording and songbook). New York: Institute for Rational-Emotive Therapy.

Ellis, A. (1978a). *I'd like to stop but . . . Dealing with addictions* [Cassette recording]. New York: Institute for Rational-Emotive Therapy.

Ellis, A. (1978b). Rational-emotive therapy and self-help therapy. *Rational Living*, *13*(1), 2-9.

Ellis, A. (1979a). Discomfort anxiety: A new cognitive behavioral construct. Part 1. *Rational Living, 14*(2), 3-8.

Ellis, A. (1979b). *The intelligent woman's guide to dating and mating* (rev. ed.). Secaucus, NJ: Lyle Stuart. (Original work published as *The intelligent woman's guide to manhunting*, Lyle Stuart and Dell, New York, 1963)

Ellis, A. (1979c). Rational-emotive therapy: Research data that support the clinical and personality hypotheses of RET and other modes of cognitive-behavior therapy. In A. Ellis & J. M. Whiteley (Eds.), *Theoretical and empirical foundations of rational-emotive therapy* (pp. 101-173). Monterey, CA: Brooks/Cole.

Ellis, A. (1980a). Discomfort anxiety: A new cognitive behavioral construct. Part 2. *Rational Living, 15*(1), 25-30.

Ellis, A. (1980b). Rational-emotive therapy and cognitive behavior therapy: Similarities and differences. *Cognitive Therapy and Research, 4*, 325-340.

Ellis, A. (Speaker). (1980c). *Twenty-two ways to brighten up your life* [Cassette recording]. New York: Institute for Rational-Emotive Therapy.

Ellis, A. (1981). The use of rational humorous songs in psychotherapy. *Voices, 16*(4), 29-36.

Ellis, A. (1983a). *The case against religiosity*. New York: Institute for Rational-Emotive Therapy.

Ellis, A. (1983b). The philosophic implications and dangers of some popular behavior therapy techniques. In M. Rosenbaum, C. M. Franks, & Y. Jaffe (Eds.), *Perspectives in behavior therapy in the eighties* (pp. 138-151). New York: Springer.

Ellis, A. (1985a). Intellectual fascism. *Journal of Rational-Emotive Therapy, 3*(1), 3-12.

Ellis, A. (1985b). Love and its problems. In A. Ellis & M. E. Bernard (Eds.) *Clinical applications of rational-emotive therapy* (pp. 32-54). New York: Plenum.

Ellis, A. (1985c). *Overcoming resistance: Rational-emotive therapy with difficult clients*. New York: Springer.

Ellis, A. (1986a). Anxiety about anxiety: The use of hypnosis with rational-emotive therapy. In E. T. Dowd & J. M. Healy (Eds.), *Case studies in hypnotherapy* (pp. 3-11). New York: Guilford. (Reprinted in A. Ellis & W. Dryden, *The practice of rational-emotive therapy*, Springer, New York, 1987)

Ellis, A. (1986b). Rational-emotive therapy applied to relationship therapy. *Journal of Rational-Emotive Therapy, 4*, 4-21.

Ellis, A. (1987a). Critical incidents in group therapy: Rational-emotive therapy. In J. Donigan & R. Malnati (Eds.), *Critical incidents in group therapy* (pp. 87-91, 105-109, 123-128, 141-146, 166-172, 189-192). Monterey, CA: Brooks/Cole.

Ellis, A. (Speaker). (1987b). *The enemies of humanism—What makes them tick?* (Cassette recording, No. 108). New York and Alexandria, VA: Audio Transcripts.

Ellis, A. (1987c). The impossibility of achieving consistently good mental health. *American Psychologist, 42*, 364-375.

Ellis, A. (1987d). A sadly neglected cognitive element in depression. *Cognitive Therapy and Research, 11*, 121-146.

Ellis, A. (1987e). Testament of a humanist. *Free Inquiry, 7*(2), 21.

Ellis, A. (1987f). The use of rational humorous songs in psychotherapy. In W. F. Fry, Jr., & W. A. Salameh (Eds.), *Handbook of humor and psychotherapy* (pp. 265-287). Sarasota, FL: Professional Resource Exchange.

Ellis, A. (1988a). *How to stubbornly refuse to make yourself miserable about anything—Yes, anything!* Secaucus, NJ: Lyle Stuart.

Ellis, A. (Speaker). (1988b). *Unconditionally accepting yourself and others* [Cassette recording]. New York: Institute for Rational-Emotive Therapy.

Ellis, A. (1989a). Foreword. In J. DiSalvo, *Beyond revolution . . . On becoming a cybernetic epistemologist* (pp. xi-xii). New York: Vantage.

Ellis, A. (1989b). *The treatment of psychotic and borderline individuals with RET.* New York: Institute for Rational-Emotive Therapy. (Original work published 1965).

Ellis, A. (1990a, August 17). *The advantages and disadvantages of self-help materials.* Paper presented at the 98th Annual Conference of the American Psychological Association, Boston.

Ellis, A. (Speaker). (1990b). *Albert Ellis live at the Learning Annex* [Cassette recording]. New York: Institute for Rational-Emotive Therapy.

Ellis, A. (1990c). How can psychological treatment aim to be briefer and better? The rational-emotive approach to brief therapy. In J. K. Zeig & S. G. Gilligan (Eds.), *Brief therapy: Myths, methods, and metaphors* (pp. 291-302). San Francisco: Jossey-Bass.

Ellis, A. (1990d). Is rational-emotive therapy (RET) "rationalist" or "constructivist"? In A. Ellis & W. Dryden, *The essential Albert Ellis* (pp. 114-141). New York: Springer.

Ellis, A. (1990e). My life in clinical psychology. In C. E. Walker (Ed.), *History of clinical psychology in autobiography* (pp. 1-37). Homewood, IL: Dorsey Press.

Ellis, A. (1990f, August). *A rational-emotive approach to peace.* Paper delivered at the 98th Annual Convention of the American Psychological Association, Boston.

Ellis, A. (1990g). Rational-emotive therapy. In I. L. Kutash & A. Wolf (Eds.), *The group psychotherapist's handbook* (pp. 298-315). New York: Columbia University Press.

Ellis, A. (1990h). Special features of rational-emotive therapy. In W. Dryden & R. DiGiuseppe, *A primer on rational-emotive therapy* (pp. 79-93). Champaign, IL: Research Press.

Ellis, A. (1991a). Achieving self-actualization. In A. Jones and R. Crandall (Eds.), *Handbook of self-actualization.* Corte Madera, CA: Select Press.

Ellis, A. (1991b). Foreword. In P. Hauck, *Hold your head up high* (pp. 1-4). London: Sheldon.

Ellis, A. (1991c, August 17). *The future of cognitive-behavioral therapies.* Paper presented at the 99th Annual Convention of the American Psychological Association, San Francisco.

Ellis, A. (1991d, August 16). *Rational recovery systems: Alternatives to AA and other 12-step programs.* Paper presented at the 99th Annual Convention of the American Psychological Association, San Francisco.

Ellis, A. (1991e). The revised ABCs of rational-emotive therapy. In J. Zeig (Ed.), *Evolution of psychotherapy: II.* New York: Brunner/Mazel. (Expanded version in *Journal of Rational-Emotive and Cognitive-Behavior Therapy*, 1991, 9(3), 139-172).

Ellis, A. (1991f). *Using RET effectively: Reflections and interview.* In M. E. Bernard (Ed.), *Using rational-emotive therapy effectively* (pp. 1 -33). New York: Plenum.

Ellis, A. (1992). Brief therapy: The rational-emotive method. In S. Budman, J. Hoyt, & S. Friedman (Eds.), *First sessions of brief psychotherapy.* New York: Guilford.

Ellis, A. (in press). Rational-emotive approaches to peace. *Journal of Cognitive Psychotherapy.*

Ellis, A., & Abrahms, E. (1978). *Brief psychotherapy in medical and health practice.* New York: Springer.

Ellis, A., & Becker, I. (1982). *A guide to personal happiness.* North Hollywood, CA: Wilshire.

Ellis, A., & Bernard, M. E. (Eds.). (1985). *Clinical applications of rational-emotive therapy.* New York: Plenum.

Ellis, A., & Dryden, W. (1985). Dilemmas in giving warmth or love to clients: An interview with Windy Dryden. In W. Dryden, *Therapists' dilemmas* (pp. 5-16). London: Harper & Row.

Ellis, A., & Dryden, W. (1987). *The practice of rational-emotive therapy.* New York: Springer.

Ellis, A., & Dryden, W. (1990). *The essential Albert Ellis.* New York: Springer.

Ellis, A., & Dryden, W. (1991). *A dialogue with Albert Ellis: Against dogma.* Stony Stratford, Milton Keynes, England: Open University Press.

Ellis, A., & Grieger, R. (Eds.). (1977). *Handbook of rational-emotive therapy* (Vol. 1). New York: Springer.

Ellis, A., & Grieger, R. (Eds.). (1986). *Handbook of rational-emotive therapy* (Vol. 2). New York: Springer.

Ellis, A., & Harper, R. A. (1961). *A guide to successful marriage.* North Hollywood, CA: Wilshire.

Ellis, A., & Harper, R. A. (1975). *A new guide to rational living.* North Hollywood, CA: Wilshire.

Ellis, A., & Knaus, W. J. (1977). *Overcoming procrastination.* New York: New American Library.

Ellis, A., McInerney, J. F., DiGiuseppe, R., & Yeager, R. J. (1988). *Rational-emotive therapy with alcoholics and substance abusers.* Elmsford, NY: Pergamon.

Ellis, A., Sichel, J., Leaf, R. C., & Mass, R. (1989). Countering perfectionism in research on clinical practice. I: Surveying rationality changes after a single intensive RET intervention. *Journal of Rational-Emotive and Cognitive-Behavior Therapy, 7,* 197-218.

Ellis, A., Sichel, J., Yeager, R., DiMattia, D., & DiGiuseppe, R. (1989). *Rational-emotive couples therapy.* Elmsford, NY: Pergamon.

Ellis, A., & Tisdale, J. R. (1990, January). The Ellis-Tisdale debate. *Newsletter of the Transpersonal Psychology Interest Group of the American Psychological Association, 9,* 3-11.

Ellis, A., & Velten, E. (1992). *When AA doesn't work for you: Rational steps to quitting alcohol.* New York: Barricade Books.

Ellis, A., & Whiteley, J. M. (1979). *Theoretical and empirical foundations of rational-emotive therapy.* Monterey, CA: Brooks/Cole.

Ellis, A., & Yeager, R. (1989). *Why some therapies don't work: The dangers of transpersonal psychology.* Buffalo, NY: Prometheus Books.

Ellis, A., Young, J., & Lockwood, G. (1987). Cognitive therapy and rational-emotive therapy: A dialogue. *Journal of Cognitive Psychotherapy, 1*(4), 137-187.

Engels, G. I., & Diekstra, R. F. W. (1986). Meta-analysis of rational emotive therapy outcome studies. In P. Eelen & O. Fontaine (Eds.), *Behavior therapy: Beyond the conditioning framework* (pp. 121-140). Hillsdale, NJ: Lawrence Erlbaum.

Epstein, S. (1990). Cognitive experiential theory. In L. Pervin (Ed.), *Handbook of personality theory and research.* New York: Guilford.

Franklin, J. (1987). *Molecules of the mind.* New York: Delta.

Frazer, J. G. (1959). *The golden bough.* New York: Macmillan.

Freud, S. (1965). *Standard edition of the complete psychological works of Sigmund Freud.* New York: Basic Books.

Fry, W. F., Jr., & Salameh, W. A. (Eds.). (1987). *Handbook of humor and psychotherapy.* Sarasota, FL: Professional Research Exchange.

Grieger, R., & Boyd, J. (1980). *Rational-emotive therapy: A skills-based approach.* New York: Van Nostrand Reinhold.

Guntrip, H. (1971). *Psychoanalytic theory, therapy and the self.* New York: Basic Books.

Haaga, D. A., & Davison, G. C. (1989). Outcome studies of rational-emotive therapy. In M. E. Bernard & R. DiGiuseppe (Eds.), *Inside rational-emotive therapy* (pp. 155-197). San Diego, CA: Academic Press.

Hartman, H. (1964). *Ego psychology and the problem of adaptation.* New York: International Universities Press.

Hauck, P. A. (1973). *Overcoming depression.* Philadelphia: Westminster.

Hauck, P. A. (1974). *Overcoming frustration and anger.* Philadelphia: Westminster.

Hauck, P. A. (1977). *Marriage is a loving business.* Philadelphia: Westminster.

Hoffer, E. (1951). *The true believer.* New York: Harper & Row.

Huber, C. H., & Baruth, L. G. (1989). *Rational-emotive systems family therapy.* New York: Springer.

Jorm, A. P. (1987). *Modifiability of a personal trait which is a risk factor for neurosis.* Paper presented at World Psychiatric Association, Symposium on Epidemiology and the Prevention of Mental Disorder, Reykjavik.

Kahneman, D., Slovic, P., & Tversky, A. (Eds.). (1982). *Judgement under uncertainty: Heuristics and biases.* New York: Cambridge University Press.

Kernberg, O. (1975). *Borderline conditions and pathological narcissism.* New York: Jason Aronson.

Klein, M., & Riviere, J. (1964). *Love, hate, and reparation.* London: Hogarth.

Knaus, W. J. (1983). *How to conquer your frustrations.* Hillsdale, NJ: Lawrence Erlbaum.

Kohut, H. (1977). *The restoration of the self.* New York: International Universities Press.

Korzybski, A. (1933). *Science and sanity.* San Francisco: International Society of General Semantics.

Lazarus, A. A. (1990). *The practice of multimodal therapy.* Baltimore, MD: Johns Hopkins University Press.

Levi-Strauss, C. (1962). *The savage mind.* Chicago: University of Chicago Press.

Low, A. A. (1952). *Mental health through will training.* Boston: Christopher.

Lyons, L. C., & Woods, P. J. (1991). The efficacy of rational-emotive therapy: A quantitative review of the outcome research. *Clinical Psychology Review, 11,* 357-369.

Mahoney, M. J. (1991). *Human change processes.* New York: Basic Books.

Marks, D. F. (1978). *Living with fear.* New York: McGraw-Hill.

Maultsby, M. C., Jr. (1971). Rational emotive imagery. *Rational Living, 6*(1), 24-27.

Maultsby, M. C., Jr. (1984). *Rational behavior therapy.* Englewood Cliffs, NJ: Prentice-Hall.

Maultsby, M. C., & Ellis, A. (1974). *Technique of using rational-emotive imagery.* New York: Institute for Rational-Emotive Therapy.

McGovern, T. E., & Silverman, M. S. (1984). A review of outcome studies of rational-emotive therapy from 1977 to 1982. *Journal of Rational-Emotive Therapy,* 2(1), 7-18.

Meichenbaum, D. (1977). *Cognitive-behavior modification.* New York: Plenum.

Muran, J. C. (1991). A reformulation of the ABC model in cognitive psychotherapies: Implications for assessment and treatment. *Clinical Psychology Review, 11,* 399-418.

Popper, K. R. (1962). *Objective knowledge.* London: Oxford University Press.

Popper, K. R. (1985). *Popper selections* (David Miller, Ed.). Princeton, NJ: Princeton University Press.

Rogers, C. R. (1961). *On becoming a person.* Boston: Houghton Mifflin.

Rorer, L. G. (1989). Rational-emotive theory: I. An integrated psychological and philosophical basis. *Cognitive Therapy and Research, 13,* 475-492.

Russell, B. (1965). *The basic writings of Bertrand Russell.* New York: Simon & Schuster.

Sampson, E. E. (1989). The challenge of social change in psychotherapy. *American Psychologist, 44,* 914-921.

Smith, T. W. (1989). Assessment in rational-emotive therapy. In M. E. Bernard & R. DiGiuseppe (Eds.), *Inside rational-emotive therapy* (pp. 135-153). San Diego, CA: Academic Press.

Taylor, S. E. (1990). *Positive illusions: Creative self-deception and the healthy mind.* New York: Basic Books.

Trimpey, J. (1989). *Rational recovery from alcoholism: The small book.* New York: Delacorte.

Trimpey, L., & Trimpey, J. (1990). *Rational recovery from fatness.* Lotus, CA: Lotus Press.

Vernon, A. (1989). *Thinking, feeling, behaving: An emotional education curriculum for children.* Champaign, IL: Research Press.

Wachtel, P. (1982). *Resistance.* New York: Plenum.

Walen, S. R., DiGiuseppe, R., & Dryden, W. (1992). *A practitioner's guide to rational-emotive therapy.* New York: Oxford University Press.

Warga, C. (1989). *Profile of psychologist Albert Ellis.* New York: Institute for Rational Emotive Therapy. (Original version published in *Psychology Today,* September, 1988).

Warren, R., & Zgourides, G. D. (1991). *Anxiety disorders: A rational-emotive perspective.* Elmsford, NY: Pergamon.

Watzlawick, P., Weakland, J., & Fisch, R. (1974). *Change.* New York: Norton.

Wessler, R. A., & Wessler, R. L. (1980). *The principles and practice of rational-emotive therapy.* San Francisco, CA: Jossey-Bass.

Wolfe, J. L. (1974). *Rational-emotive therapy and women's assertiveness training* [Cassette recording]. New York: Institute for Rational-Emotive Therapy.

Wolfe, J. L., & Fodor, I. G. (1975). A cognitive-behavioral approach to modifying assertive behavior in women. *Counseling Psychologist, 5*(4), 45-52.

Wolpe, J. (1982). *The practice of behavior therapy* (3rd ed.). Elmsford, NY: Pergamon.

Young, H. S. (1974). *A rational counseling primer.* New York: Institute for Rational-Emotive Therapy.

Treating Adult Children of Alcoholics

RAYMOND J. YEAGER
CAROLYN M. YEAGER
JENNIFER-ANN SHILLINGFORD

The psychology and self-help sections of most neighborhood book-stores have become increasingly stocked with texts describing what has become one of the more popular "syndromes" to hit the nineties, the adult child of an alcoholic (ACOA) syndrome (Black, 1981; Brown, 1988; Cermak, 1984, 1985). In fact, professional jour-nals in psychology, psychiatry, counseling, and social work are publishing more empirically and practically based articles de-scribing this population (Cermak & Brown, 1982; Hibbard, 1989; Jones, 1981; Parker & Harford, 1988; Reich, Earls, & Powell, 1988; Werner, 1986). Cable television shows, self-help groups, and na-tional alliances and foundations have all developed programs that address this newly identified group. The adult child of an alco-holic is a client who is being more widely and systematically investigated and treated (Hibbard, 1987).

The impact of one's childhood/family environment on the de-velopment of a healthy personality has received much attention

AUTHORS' NOTE: Address correspondence regarding this material to: Raymond J. Yeager, Ph.D., Institute for Cognitive Development, 2171 Jericho Tpke., Suite 235, Commack, NY 11725.

(Billings & Moos, 1982; Moos & Billings, 1982). Specifically, considerable attention has been paid to the effects of growing up in a family environment where parental alcoholism is prevalent. Although contemporary treatment approaches, in general, have tended to shift away from a focus on the etiology of one's current day problems (Brickman et al., 1982), few would disagree that significant, stressful, and often traumatic life events have a meaningful impact on one's adjustment (Holmes & Rahe, 1967) and development. We may acknowledge the role that past life events have in shaping personal schemata (Beck, Rush, Shaw, & Emery, 1979), while maintaining a focus on helping clients overcome and compensate for their troubled pasts.

It is estimated that there are currently 25 million children growing up with at least one alcoholic parent (Ackerman, 1983). These individuals have been identified as being at high risk for developing emotional and behavioral difficulties. Yet, only approximately 5% of these children ever receive treatment for their problems. Nevertheless, with the increasing attention and accessibility of services, children living in alcoholic environments and ACOAs are becoming increasingly identified and their problems are being better understood.

Adult Children of Alcoholics: An RET/CBT Conceptualization

The research with respect to the ACOA syndrome has thus far been equivocal (Fulton & Yates, 1990). Some studies illustrate distinct differences between ACOAs and their non-ACOA cohorts, while others fail to illustrate meaningful differences. Similarly, no one personality profile emerges from the empirical psychology literature. However, while definitive support is currently lacking for a specific diagnostic classification with distinct and differentiating characteristics, the detrimental effects an individual experiences growing up in a severely dysfunctional environment and the subsequent emotional and behavioral disturbances and dysfunctions are undeniable.

It is important to note that not all ACOAs are dysfunctional in every aspect of their lives (Goodman, 1987; Plescia-Pikus, Long-Sutter, & Wilson, 1988). In fact, many have developed the skills necessary to compensate for and overcome the influences of their disruptive alcoholic family backgrounds. It is no wonder, therefore, that the research literature has failed to identify one type of ACOA. Rather, like their specific experiences, ACOAs' behavioral, emotional, and interpersonal problems may be quite varied. What connects them is their shared experience and their tendency to develop similar weltanschauung (worldviews) consequential to these experiences. That is, they are similar in the manner in which they were conditioned to view themselves, their worlds, and their futures and pasts, (the cognitive triad, Beck, 1975, 1976).

Rational-emotive therapy and the allied cognitive-behavior therapies emphasize the primacy of cognition in the etiology and maintenance of emotional disturbance and behavioral dysfunction. Children raised in an environment marked by a severely disturbed and irrational philosophy and by inadequate and destructive problem-solving skills may never learn appropriate coping strategies or develop rational views of themselves and the world. Of importance is not what happened to a person in his or her past nor even what is currently happening. Rather, emphasis is placed on (a) the way individuals currently think about their pasts, and (b) how they think about themselves, their worlds, and their futures, as a possible function of past conditioning. Treatment, therefore, focuses on helping clients recondition and restructure their present-day thinking.

Before proceeding with a cognitive, emotional, and behavioral analysis of the ACOA, it is important to address the issues of "labeling." Individuals seeking treatment for ACOA-related concerns are typically globally labeled as "ACOAs." Such a label may stimulate self-fulfilling prophesies where clients so labeled may act in an "ACOA manner" to satisfy the requirements of the label and may similarly justify and excuse themselves of the responsibility for making personal changes because they have this particular "syndrome" or "disease." Any such label can lead clients to (a) maintain a past focus, (b) believe that they are helpless victims who are irrevocably programmed by their pasts, and (c) seek iatrogenic therapies that assert cathartic methods to relieve their "inner child's" suffering. As will be discussed later in this text, specific efforts can be made to prevent clients from such tendencies.

A distinct advantage of identifying and isolating the ACOA group is that it shows these clients that they are a valid population with special therapeutic needs. Similarly, the public interest in this group makes therapy less threatening and more readily approachable and available. In addition, the potential shame and embarrassment that may have prevented them from seeking help may be ameliorated.

Regardless of the potentially negative effects of assigning the "ACOA" label and the equivocal data regarding a discrete diagnostic categorization, millions of individuals and thousands of counselors and therapists espouse such a classification and actively seek to preserve it. Consider the disease model of alcoholism. Despite repeated scientific failures to show evidence for this model (Fingarette, 1988) and despite numerous studies that directly contradict it (Caudill & Marlatt, 1975; Higgins & Marlatt, 1973, 1975; Lang, Goeckner, Adesso, & Marlatt, 1975; Lied & Marlatt, 1979; Marlatt, Demming, & Reid, 1973; Marlatt & Rohsenow, 1980; Marlatt & Rose, 1980), the public (and many professionals) tends to maintain that alcoholism is a disease for all alcoholics. We as therapists and counselors must, therefore, be prepared to work with this group labeled "ACOA."

Rational-emotive therapy and cognitive-behavioral therapy provide a systematic and structured format within which we can parsimoniously conceptualize client disorders of various typologies. Addressed is a client's functioning among emotional and behavioral modalities and the specific and global cognitions that mediate these areas of functioning.

The following is a description of many of the issues that ACOAs present when entering counseling or psychotherapy. This chapter will illustrate some of the iatrogenic features of the alcoholic family environment and its effects on its children. The corresponding conditioning and development of an individual's belief system as well as the consequential emotional and behavioral patterns will also be discussed. Treatment strategies based on the principles of RET/CBT will be presented as will a case study of an "ACOA" client.

The Alcoholic Family Environment

In conceptualizing the diverse and complex dynamics of the ACOA syndrome, a therapist may find it useful to understand the patterns of behavior and interaction that are typical to the alcoholic family environment. It may be important to understand the mechanisms through which the schemata of the ACOA were conditioned, particularly since these clients tend to cling to their early memories of childhood traumata, which, in turn, reinforces and serves to maintain their current-day irrationalities. It is often useful to understand the "original data" from which ACOA clients developed and reinforced their thinking patterns. The conclusions formulated based on this "evidence" can then be challenged as to their veracity and reasonableness (Yeager, Yeager, & Shillingford, 1990).

It is impossible to characterize all of the conditions under which children mature. Children are influenced by a multitude of factors in their development. The family environment is one such influence, albeit a major and primary one. Factors such as a family's socioeconomic status, number of children, marital status of the parents, cultural background, enrichment opportunities, peripheral support systems, and personal factors such as intelligence and personality are all contributors to a child's growth. The current descriptions do not intend to detail all of the ingredients that interactively affect children. Rather, typical family dynamics and patterns of interaction will be explored. This chapter will, similarly, discuss many of the cognitive, emotional, and behavioral difficulties that children raised in alcoholic family environments experience.

Just as there is no one type of alcoholic, there is no one type of alcoholic family. Alcoholic families vary in terms of many of their patterns and their respective degrees of dysfunction. As stated earlier, there is no one type of "child of an alcoholic (COA)" or "adult child of an alcoholic (ACOA)."

It is almost the rule rather than the exception that individuals living, or having been raised in alcoholic families, are troubled (Drake & Vaillant, 1988). The alcoholic family environment is hardly conducive to normal development. While the data are equivocal regarding a univariate ACOA or COA personality profile, the following is a description of some of the more typical "issues," complaints, and areas of difficulty presented by this population.

Unpredictability

The moods, attitudes, actions, and reactions of the members of alcoholic family systems are typically unpredictable. Children often learn to scan their environments vigilantly, as they fear that conflict may unexpectedly be lurking around any corner. They typically make deliberate efforts to detect and avoid potential conflicts. Children will not risk being spontaneous, for fear they will be left unprotected and vulnerable to rejection, confrontation, or aggression. Clients will frequently report instances where they were enjoying the company of their (alcoholic) parents one moment and were being criticized for some personal flaw and spanked and sent to bed without dinner in the next. They learn not to trust safety or calmness and are hesitant to relax. As clients, they will often report that they "don't know how to relax" and have "never been able to relax." Feeling secure and comfortable is a foreign feeling, one that has historically represented the "calm before the storm." They have concluded from their experiences that being relaxed only leaves them unguarded and vulnerable to attacks (verbal or physical) by their alcoholic parent. Tension and vigilance, therefore, are means to ensure preparedness for any confrontation. ACOAs often live their lives from one "crisis" to another. They are uncomfortable with calmness and often "feel more at home" with their "crisis-oriented lives."

Rigidity of Rules

Alcoholic families tend to be extremely rigid. There are rules of conduct that are absolute and inflexible and the punishment for infractions typically exceeds the crime. Similarly, punishment is often unpredictable and inconsistent, a very iatrogenic parenting practice. There is little tolerance for error as family guidelines must be met precisely. Clients will often report having a favorite toy thrown in the garbage because their (alcoholic) parent argued that they were "making too much noise," or that they would be slapped across the face if they would put their elbows on the table during dinner time. They may be punished for talking with their mouths full at breakfast, and the same behavior may be ignored or even joked about at dinner. Although the family's rules may be ambiguous or not evident, individuals raised by alcoholic parents will typically assert that they "were supposed to just know better and follow them anyway." ACOAs report working hard to anticipate their parents' annoyances.

Alcoholic families tend to have little or no tolerance for either independent thinking or a question or challenge to parental authority. "Children should be seen and not heard" is a common rule. Parental authority is absolute and right. Children learn to think that there are absolute rules of behavior to which all people must unfalteringly adhere. Similarly, they come to believe that one's worth as a person is a direct function of the extent to which these rules are anticipated and followed. ACOAs typically endorse very conditional ratings of their personal value or often feel empty and as if they "don't know who they are." The latter of these features is very common to clients presenting with borderline personality.

Shame

Alcoholic families tend to actively maintain secrets. The rule that "you must not air our family laundry" rings loudly in individuals raised by this doctrine. No "outsiders" must know family "business" as they hide their "skeletons" in fear that they will be "found out."

Like all children, the child in an alcoholic family will typically compare him- or herself to peers. Such social comparison with children from more functional families tends to leave them feeling inferior, as "less than" and embarrassed by their own families. As a result, their interactions with others become quite superficial. No one is allowed to get too close and friendships are discouraged. Although a "stranger" may be made to feel comfortable, the implicit message is not to trust. The alcoholic family protects itself by displaying a facade that everything is normal.

Children of alcoholic parents will also experience a great deal of discomfort whenever there is a possibility that their parents may embarrass them. Children are typically embarrassed by their parents' drinking and behaviors. They will often refuse to participate in activities such as Cub Scouts or Little League, or any situation where their parent may potentially "misbehave." Intoxicated parents often make sexual innuendos to their children's peers or confront their peers in ways to discourage them from associating with their children. As a result, children from alcoholic families will often prefer to have no friends than to risk losing them due to their parent's behavior.

Conflict Resolution

All families experience conflict and healthy families address it and work to resolve it. The expression and resolution of conflict tends to distinguish alcoholic families from those that are less dysfunctional. Alcoholic families typically deny the very existence of conflict among their members. Interpersonal problems are never discussed, unless the participants are drunk. Usually, the proverbial carpet under which all problems have been swept develops a hump that can no longer be circumvented because of all the problems that are brushed under it. In the case where an alcoholic family is distressed by the behavior of a particular member, the problem will pile up so high that the family then either divorces from that family member or the individuals get drunk and fight under the guise of problem resolution. Rarely, if ever, is a constructive face-to-face confrontation either encouraged or tolerated. Instead, individuals will act as if they have no problem with each other and will typically talk to other family members behind the other's back. The members of alcoholic families are so fearful of conflict and so devoid of the skills to resolve it that problems come to be seen as an irreversible part of life.

Blame

The codependent members of alcoholic families also take the blame for family problems. Similarly, they take the blame for the alcoholic's drinking, emotional distresses, and any other problems that may exist. And they tend to accept such responsibility. Parents will often blame their children for their marital problems, for the family's financial pressures, for their own difficulties concentrating, and often for their own drinking behavior. Consequently, children accept this blame and reproach themselves for their roles in causing and exacerbating family difficulties. In addition, ACOAs grow up believing that they are incapable of managing their own lives and that their emotions are reactive to external circumstances.

Security/Safety

Healthy family environments inculcate in their children a sense of safety and security. Although children at preoperational ages cannot understand permanence of objects (Piaget & Inhelder, 1958), they learn as they develop that many things are constant and stable. They learn that daddy or mommy will come home after they leave the house, so there is no reason to throw tantrums. They trust that they will not be *abandoned*. However, alcoholic families often behave in ways to prevent the development of such trust. Few family rituals such as cooking, eating, cleaning, shopping, bedtime, and the like are ever constant, stable, or pleasant. Alcoholic parents often threaten their children that they will be given away or that the parents will run away if they are not "good." Similarly, children in alcoholic families often overhear a parent praying that their alcoholic spouse will get killed on the way home from the bar. Such threats of abandonment are terrifying for children.

Children typically trust that their parents have their best intentions at heart and that if a parent is acting in any particular way, it must be appropriate and justified. Yet, in alcoholic families, children are often threatened with or actually experience physical abuse, humiliation, and deprivation that they are told is justified. The alcoholic family controls its members through coercive, aggressive, or passive-aggressive means, hanging threats over each other's heads routinely. Trust, therefore, does not fully develop and fears of abandonment permeate much of their experiences.

Practical Skills

Healthy families also provide the structure and means through which the practical needs of their children are met. For example, parents typically make special efforts to teach their children such things as how to maintain bank accounts, socialize, or catch a baseball. Alcoholic families, however, rarely take the time for such specialized treatment. The cases where they do are usually marked by such anxiety, tension, frustration, and discomfort that the children find the experience most unpleasant and frightening. Learning, therefore, comes to represent pain, conflict, and embarrassment. The children learn to function for themselves, especially in terms of many basic daily activities. Children in alcoholic families will often have to iron their own clothes, prepare their own meals, and go to school without lunch money, for example, leaving them with a sense of personal unimportance and feeling deprived relative to their age peers. It may also teach them to be manipulative, sneaky, and sociopathic in order to get their needs met.

Self-Efficacy

Children develop their sense of personal competence (Bandura, 1982) through the feedback they receive from significant others (Cole, 1991). They use their parents, teachers, and peers to assist in their personal determination of their own competence (Darley & Goethals, 1980; Latane, 1966; Stipek, 1987). Similarly, they tend to respond to the expectations placed on them by such significant others (Brophy & Good, 1974). Children from alcoholic families typically receive little positive feedback, as the feedback they most frequently receive is corrective, negative, and destructive. They are challenged to develop neither patience, respect, nor confidence when learning new tasks.

Anger

Anger is a common emotion in dysfunctional families, in general, and in alcoholic families, specifically. Alcoholic family members often have short fuses and low tolerances for frustration. The tension that exists between family members is often high and the communication patterns are often quite disturbed. Anger is a means of expression that is likely to help coerce others into getting one's own way. As a result, children reared in this type of environment come to believe that that is "just how members of my family talk to each other." Anger is modeled as a way to communicate and as a typical manner in which to respond to frustration.

There is another important manner in which anger plays a significant role in the life of the ACOA. Given the strict and rigid rules for behavior, children in alcoholic environments are often not allowed to express negative feelings toward their parents or, for that matter, toward anyone in the family. Rather, interpersonal conflicts are swept under the proverbial rug. Children never learn assertive options or how to communicate their feelings. Problems, as a result, go unresolved and interpersonal frustration builds. Similarly, it is typically unacceptable for the members of an alcoholic family to "air their dirty laundry." That is, it is unacceptable practice to discuss the family's "problems" with anyone outside of the family. The result is that ACOAs harbor many negative feelings toward their past, especially since they were never "allowed" to be angry and are unfamiliar with the feeling. Instead, their behavior reflects a "bad attitude" toward the world that they have difficulty acknowledging or accepting.

People Pleasing

Need for approval is a common irrational belief espoused by many ACOAs. They are typically terrified of conflict and will instead martyr themselves for the sake of short-term peace or comfort. However, they are rarely comfortable since they are diligent to ensure that the needs of others are always satisfied. For the ACOA, it would be dreadful to be rejected or criticized. They often adamantly deny the existence of personal problems, for acknowledgment would only detract from their personal value. ACOAs learn that people are worthwhile only insofar as they meet the expectations of significant others and do not "disappoint them."

Peacemaking

As stated above, alcoholic families are replete with conflict. Conflict may be overt in the form of yelling and/or physical confrontations, or it may be "below the surface" as in the case of passive-aggression, threats, guilt trips, and the like. Children are typically terrified by this conflict since the risk of conflict for a child may often be quite great. For example, children are vulnerable in terms of physical and sexual attacks, parental separation, promises of deprivation or embarrassment, and protecting their loved ones. They will also often magnify the likelihood that they will be abandoned by their parents or their families. Fear of abandonment, in turn, leads them to behave in ways to guarantee security. As a result, children will often behave in ways that serve to dampen the conflict. They may simply "fade into the woodwork" and play the role of the "lost child" or they may draw attention away from their parents' conflict by misbehaving or getting into trouble themselves. Other children may become the family counselor, the "clown" or the "entertainer" in an effort to make peace. As adults, these individuals, terrorized by interpersonal conflict, often behave in similar ways. In turn, they will often stifle the emotional development of their own children or will have poor communication in their relationships.

Roles

Children play different roles and serve different functions in different families. These roles are hypothesized to maintain the balance or homeostasis of the family system (Crawford & Phyfer, 1988; Haley, 1976, 1980; Minuchin & Fishman, 1981). Whether the family is highly functioning or quite disturbed, the members' behaviors arguably keep the system intact. We all had our roles. In alcoholic families, however, these roles are typically rigid and dysfunctional. Some children play the "hero," whose success and achievement bring value and validation to the family, while others become "enablers," whose role is to fix the practical and interactive problems that result from alcohol abuse. Others become "scapegoats," to whom responsibility for family problems is attributed, and some play the role of "parent" to their siblings. There are many other roles and there are variations on the ones presented. Of concern, however, is the fact that these children are placed in positions where the homeostatic needs of the family override the developmental needs of the child.

These are some of the patterns that exist in alcoholic families. Such experiences arguably shape the ways in which children formulate their views of themselves and the world. Although there is no one "type" of alcoholic experience, children who grow up in these environments do share one thing in common. They were all influenced in their development by an alcoholic parent. The thrust of this chapter is to illustrate how such experiences affect the development of an individual's thinking and to provide a conceptual model for understanding and treating people with such backgrounds. Although the approach of the RET/CBT model is clearly oriented toward changes in the here-and-now, an understanding of developmental factors may facilitate a therapist's understanding of and ability to empathize with their clients. Also, adult children of alcoholics are often biased or "therapized" by the popular literature to explore their pasts the better to understand their personal dynamics. The RET/CBT approach is concerned with change above insight. However, just as you may have to jump into the water to get a drowning man to the shore, you may have to enter the past to get a client to change in the present.

Assessment

In order to begin treatment of any particular client, it is important that the therapist have an understanding of *that particular client*. All too often, therapists and counselors commence treatment independently of performing individualized assessments. As a result, therapists treat the "syndrome" and the symptoms and "issues" they believe to be part and parcel of that given syndrome. This is unfortunately the case when a therapist simply assumes that a client fits neatly into the profile depicted by descriptions of specific diagnostic categories. For example, to assume that your depressed client is depressed due to anger turned inward (a popular psychodynamic interpretation that is not supported by the empirical literature), and to commence treatment based on this assumption, would likely result in ineffective treatment. Assessment strategies can prevent a therapist from making such assumptions. That is not to say that we should not formulate and test our hypotheses about our clients. Rational-emotive therapy and the allied cognitive-behavioral approaches do maintain hypodeductive postures. However, a therapist who operates from any particular theoretical orientation and who forms hypotheses about the irrationalities or dynamics that are appropriate to a given client had better test them to see if they are, in fact, appropriate for *that* client. To assume so without assessing their accuracy is bad practice.

There are often great differences between individuals who meet the same diagnostic criteria or who have similar life experiences. For example, not all individuals who are diagnosed as "borderline personality disorder" or "panic disorder with agoraphobia" are alike. Although there are similarities, there may be great differences between individuals sharing the same diagnostic label. A similar example is the Vietnam veteran. While this population shared common experiences and likely common effects, there are broad differences in the overall levels of functioning between individuals. In order to treat any client responsibly, the therapist had better assess client particulars and direct treatment strategies accordingly.

Individuals raised in alcoholic environments will likely experience negative emotional, behavioral, and interpersonal effects. Similarly, the manner in which they perceive themselves, their worlds, the future, and the past may also be quite irrational and distorted. However, while similar experiences typically engender similar effects, individual variability still occurs. The following are some of the cognitive, emotional, and behavioral problems presented by the ACOA client. It is the responsibility of the therapist to discern which problems exist for any given client.

Cognitive Characteristics

A cognitive assessment of the ACOA client involves discerning the individual's thoughts regarding (1) him- or herself, (2) the world (including relationships, family, love, etc.), and (3) the future and past. Specifically assessed are irrational beliefs and cognitive distortions and the extent to which the individual's perceptions, interpretations, and evaluations along these dimensions are rigid, absolute, and demanding.

ACOA clients typically have a distorted view of self. They tend to be extremely demanding of themselves and have expectations for themselves that can never be met. They may have learned to personalize their family's problems and may attribute the chaos with which they were raised to their own behavior or personality. When evaluating their personal worth or simply taking a view of themselves, ACOAs often use standards to judge themselves that are severely more harsh than any standards they would use to judge anyone else. They are typically terrified that others will "find them out," see their "true colors" and consequentially reject them. As a result of such biased self-evaluations, ACOAs experience a great deal of emotional distress and find interpersonal relationships difficult.

The alcoholic family environment contributes to the development of the ACOA's view of the world as a punishing, inconsistent, unpredictable place. They learn to believe that they cannot trust others and that relationships are inherently unpredictable and insecure. Always anticipating the "negative," the ACOA scans the environment looking for data to support the hypothesis that the world (like their home) is a cruel place. Consequently, they minimize positive events and assert that they are accidental or merely temporary.

Looking back at the past or ahead to the future can be very painful for the ACOA. It is important to assess those past events about which ACOA clients are disturbed and the manner in which they think about them. ACOAs typically endorse catastrophic notions about past occurrences and concomitantly believe that their futures are, therefore, hopeless. It is common for the ACOA client to believe that they are victims of their pasts and that its effects are unrelenting. It is important, therefore, to assess the extent to which the ACOA client espouses such perceived external loci of control.

Emotional Characteristics

ACOA clients tend to report a variety of "feelings" when entering treatment. Therapists can structure their assessment by addressing the emotional excesses, deficits, and anomalies that clients experience. Emotional excesses are the self-defeating emotions that they experience with disproportionate frequency, intensity, and duration. Anger, depression, guilt, and anxiety are often considered to be emotional excesses, with the most common of these being shame and anger. Emotional deficits, on the other hand, include those feelings that are not experienced enough. For example, ACOA clients may rarely experience joy or happiness. Similarly, they may never experience even moderate annoyances or concerns. Their emotional flatness or numbness is considered to be a deficit of affect. Lastly, anomalies constitute those emotions that are considered not appropriate for a given situation. For example, an emotional anomaly includes becoming rage-filled upon receipt of a gift or overly (and maybe dramatically) unfettered in response to a life stressor.

ACOA clients typically present with a variety of emotional excesses, deficits, and anomalies and the therapist is advised to assess those particular emotional dysfunctions that need to be addressed. It is important for the therapist to project genuine caring when addressing the emotional distresses of the ACOA, since this client may interpret the counselor as "invalidating their feelings."

Behavioral Characteristics

Similar to the assessment of particular emotional disturbances, an assessment of the behavioral characteristics of the ACOA client will address the behavioral excesses, deficits, and anomalies. That is, which behaviors occur too much? Which occur too little? And which are peculiar?

A typical behavioral excess evidenced by many ACOA clients is popularly known as *codependency.* Codependency is a tendency to focus on satisfying the needs and desires of others at the exclusion of satisfying one's own. Underlying this tendency is the client's belief that the approval of others is necessary and that he or she is only valid and worthwhile with such approval. Similarly, because ACOAs believe that their personal worth is conditionally determined, they are forever working to please others so as to assure their own validity.

Another typical behavioral excess among ACOAs is their addiction proneness (Blane, 1988; Claydon, 1987; Wallace, 1987). ACOAs typically learn to cope with their negative emotions, resolve interpersonal conflict, forget and escape problems, sleep, interact, celebrate, and mourn through the use of alcohol and other drugs. They learn this through both direct instruction and modeling of their parents. What is lacking are appropriate social, coping, and problem-solving skills.

Deficits are typically evident with respect to the ACOA's self-regulation systems. ACOA clients tend to have particular difficulties managing how they act and react. They tend to experience intense emotional lability, on the one hand, or flatness, on the other. The ACOA client can go from calmness to rage in a matter of seconds. However, the return to baseline (calmness) is slow. In other words, they are easily upset and slow to recover. That which is lacking is the ability to manage their emotional and behavioral sensitivities and responses.

The ACOA client tends to be similarly unaware of that which is considered an appropriate emotional or behavioral response to a given situation. They have often had poor role models as parents or were simply instructed as to how one is "supposed to" act. As a result, anomalies in behavior that are learned include using vile language during an argument with a loved one, locking oneself in the bedroom for hours to avoid others, screaming or panicking in reaction to a minor stressor, and the like. A thorough assessment of the typical ways in which the ACOA client responds to activating stimuli and the manner in which problems are addressed is advised.

Interventions

There are a number of strategies that can be employed when working with adult children of alcoholics. Many of the techniques that are used with a variety of clients are recommended; however, many have to be tailored to meet the expectations and preferences of this group. Special considerations are advised in terms of making the therapy "user friendly" for the ACOA client. That is, a therapy style is recommended that does not alienate the sensitive (or highly sensitized) ACOA client. Many therapists approach *too quickly* without considering the extent to which their clients are ready. It is important for therapists to prepare their clients for treatment in terms of both increasing their willingness to make personal changes and in terms of their willingness to employ the prescribed procedures to make such changes. Essentially, the therapist seeks commitments as to both the *goals* and *means* of treatment.

It is important to note that different ACOA clients enter therapy with different levels of awareness about their problems, which may influence the course of treatment. For example, a client who has attended 12-step programs or read much of the popular press regarding the ACOA syndrome may already be aware of the influence their family has had on their personal development. Similarly, they may be biased and have distorted expectations regarding the goals and means of therapy. The therapist should, therefore, ascertain the extent to which the client is "ACOA-aware" and proceed accordingly. As it is important for the therapist and client to share a common orientation regarding problem resolution, information regarding how the clients perceive their problems and the treatment process is valuable. The therapist should ensure a proper orientation to the therapy process.

General Therapeutic Issues

Operationalize Vague Complaints

ACOA clients often enter therapy with complaints that are vague and are presented as inexplicit constructs. The popular literature and media representations of the ACOA syndrome typically employ a language not common in everyday (or professional) usage. For example, clients might describe their "inner child" as being in pain, that they have the "disease" of "codepend-ency" or that they are not "in touch with their feelings." It is important for the therapist to understand what a specific client means by these terms. By operationalizing and behaviorally an-choring such nebulous constructions, the therapist will ensure that the client and therapist are talking about the same thing. The client and therapist may have different understandings of many of the "issues" presented and, if a shared definition is not achieved, they may find that they have been talking about different things. A second advantage of operationalizing client complaints, espe-cially with the ACOA client, is that in doing so, the therapist models a *way* of thinking. That is, clients will learn how to define their own problems more clearly so as to make them more ap-proachable and subsequently more manageable. It is more direct to address, for example, the belief that one needs other's approval than to confront a intangible concept like "codependency."

Many people who present for treatment for ACOA "issues" often believe that since they grew up in an alcoholic or dysfunc-tional family environment, then they must fit the criterion for the "syndrome" and must therefore work to "relieve themselves of the pain that they have been denying for all these years." Although particular clients may not have manifested any significant distress or dysfunction as a result of their early experiences, they may come to believe that their "true suffering" is embedded in their unconscious and is hidden by their "denial." Therapists are ad-vised to confront this overpathologizing notion and the corre-sponding belief that one must, therefore, employ cathartic meth-ods to get in touch with one's pain so as to become purged of it. This perspective is not only ludicrous and empirically unfounded but it also fosters client dependency on a lifetime of therapy (Ellis & Yeager, 1989). Therapists should orient their clients toward here-and-now explorations and change strategies.

Maintaining Session Focus and Structure

An important strategy for all therapists, and one that distinguishes rational-emotive therapy from its more traditional counterparts (e.g., psychoanalysis, psychodynamic psychotherapy, client cen-tered therapy, etc.), is its orientation toward maintaining session focus. RET is a solution-oriented and directive form of therapy.

However, this can often become a difficult task when treating clients who believe that they will solve their problems merely by talking about them. Clients who believe that free association will provide them with change-motivating insight or who believe that you, as the therapist, must understand ever iota of past information, need to be oriented to the rational-emotive approach. It is important that the client accept a here-and-now, structured, directive, and change-oriented therapy process.

In order to orient an ACOA client toward a "working," as opposed to a "passive," posture in therapy, therapists can employ various methods. Therapists had better be cautious not to "activate" their ACOA client's irrational beliefs, however. For example, ACOA clients might believe that their therapists "are supposed to" know every detail about their pasts or that a failure to know such information either indicates that the therapist "really does not care" or "will be ill-equipped to help." The therapist should anticipate such distorted interpretations and, in general, be sensitive to the irrationalities that might be activated in the course of the therapy process. It is important for the therapist to convey genuine concern while also conveying that he or she is there to help and not just understand. Clients are often looking for support, but similarly do not understand that which is truly helpful. You can support clients (figuratively) by putting your arms around them and rubbing their heads while saying "poor, poor you!" Or, you can support them by supporting their action toward change. This involves direction. You are supporting them by helping them change.

A concern may arise. ACOA clients will often assert that their therapists do not understand them. The therapist should consider this feedback and test its veracity since it is possible that as a fallible human being you may have misunderstood or misinterpreted something presented to you. However, when ACOA clients assert such a statement they are often equating a lack of agreement with a lack of understanding. The therapist should distinguish for the client that he or she may, in fact, understand the client quite well, just may not be in agreement. ACOA clients may endorse an irrational belief that the therapist must agree with everything they say and must never confront their "irrationalities."

An RET session with the ACOA client will be problem-oriented and focused toward change above insight. As stated earlier, however, you do not want to dismiss the influence of your client's past completely. This may engender resistance and the belief that you either do not care about them as individuals or that you have an agenda independent of their particular therapeutic needs. Rather, it may be important to assess past and present family and environmental influences as a means to ensure an adequate understanding of your client and to facilitate the establishment of rapport.

Understanding Cognitive/Personality Development

Our views of ourselves, the world, and our futures are shaped by our experiences (Beck, Rush, Shaw, & Emery, 1979). These views may be realistic and empirically based or may be distorted and fallacious. While the past may have contributed to a person's development, however, it is in the present that we have the tools for change. It is through cognitive restructuring that this change occurs. Very simply, *cognitive restructuring* is *any process* where a person's beliefs are challenged and restructured. Employed may be verbally confrontive means, behavioral challenges, emotional or evocative procedures, or any other means generated by the creative therapist.

One strategy to restructure irrational or distorted thinking is to show clients that the original formulation of the belief was based on an arbitrary decision and was not initially well founded. For example, clients who believe that they are worthless will support this claim by asserting that this is what they were always told as children. One strategy involves having them illustrate the evidence that they initially used to validate their worthlessness. That is, what evidence did they have as children to support such a claim? This technique will help them see that even as a child they were concluding something about themselves in the absence of evidence and that they continued to embrace such a notion throughout their lives. Every experience they had since the inception of this belief had then been colored by the belief. Showing clients that there was never any real evidence is often a useful way to help clients overcome current-day irrationalities.

Exploring the development of clients' irrationalities is often useful in helping them to empathize with themselves rather than berate themselves for endorsing irrational notions. ACOA clients often benefit from such validation. Help them see how it is understandable why they learned to think as they do, especially given their early family environments. For example, it is no wonder that a child who is beaten moments after being hugged by an alcoholic parent has come to see relationships as insecure. Also, it is understandable why children who lived through constant ridicule and put-downs have come to think that they are incompetent and that no one will ever find them attractive or useful. An understanding into the development of their thinking patterns can be most useful in helping clients go beyond such patterns.

Specific Strategies

As stated earlier, any strategy that a counselor or therapist employs that serves to challenge a client's irrational or distorted way of thinking is known as cognitive restructuring. Cognitive restructuring involves strategies designed to test the accuracy and soundness of a person's belief system and to develop a more reasonable way of thinking. Clients are challenged to support their beliefs with realistic and logical evidence. Beliefs that are supportable and empirically based are maintained while those found to be unsupported are reconsidered and new beliefs and reformulations are developed. It is important to note that cognitive restructuring does not seek to "brainwash" clients into new ways of thinking. Rather, it supports the establishment of reasonable and realistic thinking patterns. The resistance presented by an ACOA client can often be circumvented by the reassurance that your strategies are aimed at helping them "see" things differently and in a manner that will not only help them manage their current problems but that is also more reasonable. It is important for therapists to remind their ACOA clients that the purpose of any confrontation to their thinking is simply to help them relieve themselves of their personal suffering.

Accept the Past: Serenity Prayer

While it is important to reorient the ACOA client out of the past toward increasing the focus toward changing current-day problems, it is often important for clients to work at learning to accept their pasts for what they were. In traditional psychotherapy parlance, this is referred to as "working through past issues."

In order to help a client accept the past, the therapist will assess which past activating events are important and how the client currently interprets and evaluates those events. For example, the client may catastrophize specific past events or may catastrophize the more general fact of having had a difficult upbringing. Some ACOAs believe that a person needs loving and caring parents to be a valid and worthwhile human being. The therapist should assess which irrationalities are maintained about past events and restructure accordingly. Essentially, the therapist seeks to change the client's current philosophy in a manner more congruent with that which is known as the Serenity Prayer, which states: "God grant me the serenity to accept the things I cannot change, the ability to change the things I can, and the wisdom to know the difference." The past is not changeable. Only one's evaluation and reaction to it are.

Anti-Labeling/Self-Fulfilling Prophecy

A belief that typically needs reconstruction is ACOA clients' tendency to rate themselves globally as "ACOAs." Labeling themselves as such will often lead them to believe that they have some "disease" or "illness" due to past conditioning and must proceed through an indefinite recovery process. Similarly, such clients will often excuse themselves of responsibility for maintaining their current distress by attributing cause to past events. They thus argue that they are victimized by their pasts and are, therefore, "powerless" over their emotions and behaviors. This notion of powerlessness is antithetical to common sense and the fundamental principles of rational-emotive therapy.

Therapists are advised to work to help their ACOA clients to delabel themselves and, instead, to adopt a more behavioral view of their current problems. That is, if they accept that their current attitudes, emotions, and behavioral patterns are learned, then they could similarly come to accept that they can be unlearned and substituted with newly learned patterns. This simple premise of behavioral psychology challenges the hopeless and helpless implications of the "powerlessness" notion and is important in helping the ACOA become reoriented toward here-and-now change.

Changing Self Rather Than Others

Most clients, regardless of their presenting problems, are initially interested in modifying their life events rather than changing their responses to them. So, too, with the ACOA client. ACOA clients typically seek changes in the current family environment or in any other activating events that are important to them. Or, they believe that people can only change once external conditions have changed. This is quite unreasonable given that many of the activating events presented by ACOA clients are past-related. It is often useful to illustrate examples of how people do change in spite of their pasts not changing. For example, most people get over their grief or depression following the death of a loved one. They did not get over it by the person "undying." Rather, they gradually changed how they thought about the death. As people work through their respective grieving processes, they come to see that they can, in fact, go on with their lives and accept death as part of life. Using such examples can often help the ACOA client accept that it is current thinking that needs to be addressed. As with other clients, the therapist should orient the client toward changing emotional and behavioral consequences through changing beliefs, rather than focusing exclusively on changing external stimuli. A therapist could also illustrate how the probability of changing external events might increase once the client's reaction to them becomes moderated. Extreme negative emotions or dysfunctional response patterns are hardly useful in helping clients modify their life circumstances. Rather, approaching problems in a more rational and managed way might (without guarantee) help facilitate such change. Also, even if their external conditions are not rectifiable, at least the clients will be experiencing less distress than they would otherwise. Helping the ACOA client focus on changing him- or herself rather than spending the bulk of the session time focusing on how to make an alcoholic family member change, for example, would help the client function independently of whether the significant other ever changes.

Anti-Shame and the Need for Approval

As mentioned earlier, shame is typically a central feature of the alcoholic family. As a result, the lives of ACOA clients tend to be colored by it. Many anti-shame strategies can be effectively employed. The objectives of such procedures are to modify clients' irrationalities with respect to: (1) need for approval, (2) intolerance of discomfort, and (3) rating of personal worth.

1. Disinhibition Exercises. Disinhibition exercises serve to help clients overcome inhibitions by helping them realize that: (1) discomfort is tolerable, (2) what other people think is not so important, and (3) their personal worth is not a function of how they present themselves publicly. These exercises, commonly known as "shame attacks," proceed by having a client expose something about which they are ashamed while concomitantly employing rational self-statements. A client might, for example, leave the house without looking "perfect" if doing so would typically be associated with shame, embarrassment, or anxiety. They might also increasingly draw attention to themselves by engaging a checkout clerk in conversation or asking questions of a person at the deli counter. Essentially, you encourage them to do the things that they are typically inhibited in doing. It is important *not* simply to engage in the disinhibiting behaviors but to also restructure their thinking accordingly. Such exercises should be arranged hierarchically in terms of difficulty.

2. Secret Telling. People can overcome their shame by writing down the things about themselves or about their experiences that they consider shameful. This is a particularly good strategy to employ in groups. Once clients have written their secret(s) down, have them throw them into a pail and shake them up. Next, have different members of the group pick one out and read it aloud. Anonymity, however, is maintained. Then have the person who read the secret discuss how it must feel to hold such a secret. You can then facilitate a group discussion about how things that people think are shameful are not really that dreadful once they are exposed. Illustrate how the client's prediction that everyone would think that this "shameful" secret was "horrible" was not realistic. You may even encourage the group members to break their anonymity about some of their respective secrets once the exercise is completed. This facilitates group cohesion and reciprocal empathy.

3. Disputing. Disinhibiting exercises are a form of behavioral disputation. Verbal disputation simply involves assessing the specific internalized statements that clients employ that engender shame and challenging them with counterarguments that are more realistic and reasonable. For example, consider the belief that "People must not know my flaws. They would think that I am no good." Underlying this notion is that "other people determine my worth and I must not be disapproved of." You could confront this notion by employing the following: "Consider you were standing in front of a line of people. The first person, for some reason or another, thought very negatively about you. Does this *prove* that you are no good? The next person, however, again for some reason or another, finds you particularly attractive. Does this mean that your worth has now changed? Or is this second person really crazy? The third person could take you or leave you. Where does this leave you in terms of personal worth? Does someone's worth as a person actually fluctuate? How could someone's appraisal of you actually affect your real value? Is your value or worth really ratable?" Questioning, as such, is intended to highlight the illogic of a person's thinking and to steer the person toward developing more rational alternatives.

Anti-Blame

Shame and blame often coexist for the ACOA client. Whether they are caught in the cycle of self-reproachment or parental condemnation, ACOA clients feel both intense anger and intense guilt. Guilt exists when we blame ourselves, while anger exists when we blame others. It is important to note that there is a distinct difference between *blaming* someone for something and asserting that they were (or are) *responsible* for something. Blame involves condemnation. It is giving someone responsibility *and* believing that they should be punished for it. If we stop blaming or condemning ourselves, yet still take responsibility for our actions, we will feel regret rather than guilt. Similarly, if we stop blaming or condemning others, while still attributing causal responsibility to them, we will reduce our anger to more manageable and less intrusive levels. It is, therefore, important to show clients that although they may have made poor choices or their parents may have had severe problems (yes, give responsibility where it is due), blame or condemnation is neither appropriate nor helpful.

Empathy and Perspective Taking

ACOA clients, like any client who experiences significant anger or guilt, have difficulty empathizing with themselves and others. Empathy involves understanding (not agreeing with) how someone thinks, feels, and acts. It is a process where a person tries to put him- or herself in the shoes of the other person (or themselves for that matter) and understand that person's perspective. You need not agree with that perspective to be empathic. Rather, you want to understand it.

Once you can understand and empathize with another perspective, you can validate it. You do *not* validate it in terms of agreeing with it but rather in terms of accepting it. ACOA clients often benefit by understanding and empathizing with a troubled parent. Rather than blaming the parent, help the client at least try to understand that it was because of the parent's problems that he or she acted that way. Empathy can help to ameliorate blame.

Don't Believe Everything You Are Told (Dismissing Parental Statements)

ACOA clients typically give credibility to the irrational statements that their parents have made or continue to make about them. They are essentially giving credence to crap. They have been conditioned to believe that what your parents say is invariably true. First of all, alcoholics typically have distorted views of reality (Yeager, DiGiuseppe, Leaf, & Resweber, in press; Yeager & Muran, 1991; Yeager & Rothschild, 1990). Therefore, to believe what they say is not good practice. Yet people do believe what their parents tell them. It is important to have ACOA clients address and challenge the "truths" that their parents taught them and that they currently endorse. It is the objective of the therapy to help clients think more objectively.

Anger Management Strategies

Anger is a predominant emotion among ACOA clients, and its management can be accomplished through a combination of cognitive and behavioral strategies.

A particularly useful strategy in relieving anger related to past experiences is based on the work of Novaco (1975). This counter-conditioning procedure involves:

1. identifying anger-related activating events (past or present)
2. identifying mediating irrational beliefs and cognitive distortions
3. instruction in relaxation procedures
4. establishing rational coping and self-reinforcing self-statements
5. hierarchically ordering anger-related activating events
6. pairing relaxation and self-instruction with anger-related stimuli in imagino

Cognitive strategies involve a sequential process in which the therapist initially teaches the client the relationship between thoughts and feelings. Mediating irrational and distorted cognitions are then assessed. Assessed are not only those irrational beliefs that are (a) anger-producing, but also those beliefs that clients endorse regarding (b) the appropriateness or usefulness of their anger. Angry clients often believe that their anger will help them protect themselves or that it will be useful in managing external situations. Next, a collaborative effort is made to "test" the accuracy and utility of the clients' beliefs. This is known as disputing or cognitive restructuring. Challenging a client's belief regarding the "function" of the client's anger is known as *functional disputing* (Ellis, McInerney, DiGiuseppe, & Yeager, 1988; Yeager, DiGiuseppe, Olson, Lewis, & Alberti, 1988). Alternative and more reasonable beliefs are then developed and substituted for their more irrational predecessors.

Assertion Training

Assertion training serves several purposes for ACOA clients. It helps them (a) to express their thoughts and feelings appropriately with reduced anger and anxiety, and (b) to realize that they have the right to have certain preferences and to express them without feeling guilty. Assertive behavior is an effective alternative to anger, anxiety, and guilt. Additionally, behaving assertively involves having clients accept that they do, in fact, have the right to have their preferences satisfied and that they need not be victimized by others. ACOA clients typically feel guilty expressing a desire to have their personal preferences satisfied and consequently feel resentment that they are being victimized. This guilt-resentment pattern is often manifested in the form of passive-aggressive behavior. ACOA clients feel too guilty to confront significant others directly and tend to hold in or "stuff" their feelings. As a result, they become resentful, thinking that the other person "should just know" how they feel and should change without any requests. However, the ACOA is afraid to express any resentments and would feel guilty if he or she did so. The client will then feel resentful over having to feel guilty. As a result, ACOA clients will express themselves in a passive-aggressive manner, where there is no direct confrontation. Training these clients in appropriate assertive behavior is often quite useful in breaking this self-defeating pattern.

Assertion training involves cognitive restructuring and skill development. It involves (a) teaching clients the difference between passive, assertive, and aggressive behavior; (b) restructuring irrational beliefs regarding the right to express preferences and regarding the "need" to have preferences satisfied once articulated; (c) skill development procedures including role play, in vivo practice sessions, and the like; and (d) emotional management strategies (e.g., relaxation training, disputing, self-instruction, etc.) to ameliorate the interfering effects of extreme negative affect. For a more detailed program of assertion training, the reader is advised to see Lange and Jakubowski (1980) and Alberti and Emmons (1979).

Self-Acceptance

ACOA clients often endorse beliefs regarding conditional self-acceptance. Like most clients presenting for therapy, ACOA clients believe that their personal worth is determined by external factors. Their personal worth is a function of satisfying internalized parental values. If they meet the requirements set forth by their parents (or by significant others in the present), then they have value. But only for the moment. They believe that they must always work to satisfy these requirements.

ACOA clients will rarely feel "worthwhile" or "valuable." They may, at times, feel good about themselves, but rarely unconditionally. The pressure of having to satisfy certain requirements to be considered "valid" is quite burdensome. As a result, the ACOA client will often assert that "there is no use, I can never make my parents happy." Implied in such a statement is the belief that they "must" make their parents happy and that their personal worth is a function of such an accomplishment.

There are a number of strategies that can be employed to help clients modify the extent to which they endorse the belief that they are "unworthy" or "conditionally worthwhile." Some of these are discussed below.

1. Disputing. Challenge your clients to prove that they are worthless. Actually give them this assignment. Ask them to keep a log of all of the evidence that "validates" that they are "invalid." Have them prove this to you "beyond a shadow of a doubt." Be sure to explain that you will agree with them that they are, in fact, worthless, but that you want first to see the proof. Although you may present this as a paradoxical strategy, ask clients to approach this task seriously. Of interest is an assessment of the data they use to validate their irrational belief. When they return with their assignment, have them use the data to convince you that they are "worthless." Obviously, the data will not support their conclusions. The therapist helps them see the illogic of their conclusions of personal worthlessness.

2. Lists. Another strategy to help clients to increase self-acceptance is to have them generate a list of their attributes and a list of their liabilities. Have them attend to their assets. They probably already attend disproportionately to their limitations. This problem is typical not only in individual and family problems, but in the corporate environment as well (Yeager & Miller, 1991). You do not want them to dismiss their faults, but rather to approach them more constructively. Similarly, have them generate strategies to (a) add more items to the asset list and (b) reduce the limitation list. It is important to note that you want to help clients see that everyone has both lists (i.e., we all have limitations). The simple acknowledgement of one's assets disputes that one is "worthless" or "asset-less." Also, illustrate that more assets does not equate with more worth. Emphasize the difference between rating one's assets versus rating one's "being."

3. *Affirmations.* ACOA clients will often respond well to employing self-instructional comments (Meichenbaum, 1977; Meichenbaum & Cameron, 1974) aimed at confronting thoughts of personal worthlessness or ineffectiveness. Statements such as, "I am not ruled by my past," or "I am a lovable person," are just two examples of affirmations. Once clients can understand (although not yet accept or believe) that certain thoughts are irrational, they can then generate rational alternatives that are (a) more accurate representations of reality and (b) more helpful to them in minimizing distress and increasing their abilities to function. These rational statements should be used in an instructional manner, as reminders or as cognitive distractions. Such an approach will be particularly useful with clients who are not yet skilled at assessing or disputing irrational thoughts or who may need strategies to help them through "crisis" situations.

4. *Writing.* Writing can be used as a therapeutic technique in several ways. Letters that will never be delivered can express anger, resentment, or any other emotion that the ACOA finds difficult to express. Stories, poetry, and autobiographies can all be used as vehicles to help clients realize (a) how current cognitions, emotions, and behaviors developed and (b) the irrationality and dysfunction associated with particular patterns of behavior. Such writings can be very revealing for ACOA clients inasmuch as they can begin to understand their past; have empathy for themselves; and, eventually begin to put the past in perspective so that they can move on.

5. *Confrontation.* Speaking out about the "ACOA experience" can serve several functions. When speaking to other family members about shared traumas, ACOA clients can begin to realize (a) that they were not to blame for the family's problems and (b) that they were not alone. Together siblings, cousins, and close relations can validate for each other that something really was wrong and that it was a shared experience. Of course, any two members of the same family could have experienced the same events very differently. When an individual believes that he or she can never change until the alcoholic parent has been confronted, then confrontation may be indicated. Through assertion training (see above), the therapist can teach the ACOA how to confront the alcoholic and end the cycle of victimization that occurred in the past. Many clients, however, never need to confront their family members

directly. Rather, they can do so in role plays with the therapist or in letters that are never mailed.

Conclusions

There are an indefinite number of strategies one may employ in working with the ACOA client. Included herein were a variety of strategies designed to introduce the reader to the treatment of this emerging client population. However, the particular strategy one employs is less important than the theory from which one operates. Very simply, it is recommended that one conceptualize the ACOA client as an individual who has experienced the effects of being raised in a dysfunctional childhood environment. What is important is not the particulars of these experiences but rather the effects in terms of how these clients currently think, feel, and behave. It is the therapist's responsibility to assess these cognitive, emotional, and behavioral particulars and to arrange for restructuring strategies accordingly. The therapist should also be sensitive to clients' expectations regarding treatment and to reorient them as appropriate. Care should be taken *not* to activate client resistance by being insensitive to their preexisting conceptualizations of their problems or of the therapy process. The ACOA client may have read some of the popular literature about the "syndrome" or may have attended lectures or workshops describing ACOA "recovery needs." Therefore, the informed therapist should carefully establish a collaborative and open-minded relationship with the ACOA client even when presented with suggestions that are ostensibly ludicrous. For example, try to be sensitive to the client who asserts that his or her "inner child" has been "traumatized" or that "psychic release" is needed. It is not the fault of the clients that the popular press has filled them with such inane conceptualizations. Be patient and understanding and systematically steer them toward a more realistic, humanistic, and pragmatic means to solve their current-day problems.

Case Example

Mary was a 27-year-old single woman with a graduate degree in Business Administration. She had been employed by her current company for 6 years and was a well-respected employee. Although her employer considered her to have great potential, Mary balked at advancement opportunities and seemed to stagnate in her job.

Mary characterized her family background as "alcoholic" and herself as an "adult child." She described her father as a chronic and active alcoholic and her mother as a codependent who reportedly "just kept the peace." Mary is the oldest of three children. Her younger siblings have histories of cocaine and alcohol abuse.

Mary was raised in a home environment where expression of either positive or negative feelings was discouraged. No family member, save the father, was "allowed" to voice an opinion. Conflict between family members was ignored or "forgotten about without resolution." Similarly, the children were not allowed to discuss problems they were having outside of the home. Rather, they were told to "work them out by yourself."

Mary also reported that it was her job to care for her younger siblings. She complained that she never felt appreciated and asserted that similar household responsibilities prevented her from partaking in typical teenage activities. As a result, she found herself isolated from her peers. Mary indicated that she never felt like she "belonged" anywhere.

Mary indicated that family life was always "eventful" and unpredictable. She similarly reported getting into a great deal of trouble with her parents, and having never been able to figure out what would have made them happy. Mary experienced a great deal of both guilt and resentment because of this.

Mary indicated that she was always ashamed of her family, which is another thing about which she felt guilty. She never wanted friends to meet her parents and often made excuses for their behaviors. Mary never felt safe at home, especially when her father would be drinking or when they had company (which was rare). She reported that her father would embarrass her in front of others and make her feel "worthless."

Mary struggled to please her parents, especially by getting good grades in school. She reported that her parents never made much of a fuss when she would do well but made a "big fuss" when she would get less than "A"s. Her parents provided little support or encouragement.

Mary entered therapy stating that she "felt like something is not right." Initially, she was unable to provide concrete or specific examples of her complaints, save that she was "just generally dissatisfied with her life." Mary denied suicidal interest, intention, or plan. She reported having no prior treatment but stated that she attended 12-step self-help meetings. In response to questions assessing her expectations regarding therapy, Mary asserted that she needed to heal the "child within."

The early stages of therapy helped Mary identify problem areas and treatment objectives in measurable and concrete terms. Of primary concern were her thoughts about (a) herself, (b) the world, and (c) the future and past, as well as any consequential emotional and behavioral disturbances. Similarly, specific efforts were made to orient Mary toward a here-and-now perspective in terms of making changes. A didactic and supportive dialogue highlighted the importance of focusing on current conditions. Mary was assured that the past may be important in terms of understanding the development of her problems, but that it is in the present that we help her to compensate for her conditioning history. An empathic therapeutic posture was maintained throughout this redirecting process so as to help Mary understand that the therapist not only wanted to *understand* but also to *help.*

At this point, the dangers of labeling were discussed. The "adult child" label served to maximize Mary's sense of hopelessness, helplessness, and powerlessness. This point directly contradicted information Mary was previously given at her "meetings." Although she was quick to realize that the label of "ACOA" could potentially, and subconsciously, interfere with the treatment process, many clients can benefit from therapy while still cradling such a label. It is often not worth the resistance it creates to strip a client of such a label that they ardently embrace (Miller, 1989).

Mary presented with depressed mood and feelings of guilt, anger, and resentment. In addition to her emotional pain and distress, she found herself not realizing her vocational potential and without meaningful or lasting relationships. Primary in Mary's emotional distress and behavior dysfunction were several irrational beliefs and distortions. Assessed was her tendency to denigrate her personal worth and, similarly, believe that she was only worthwhile if validated by others (particularly her father). She also evidenced a biased tendency to attribute failures to personal traits and successes to chance conditions. Mary also espoused an extremely unforgiving and perfectionistic standard for her own (but not others') behavior. She saw herself as an "ineffective person" who was "less than" others. Mary had never learned to appreciate her attributes. Rather, she minimized them in favor of focusing on her limitations and liabilities. She similarly believed that she was doomed to a life of unrelenting unhappiness, particularly since she believed that the experience of a "horrible" past leaves "irreversible scars."

Mary viewed the world as an unfair place where relationships are inevitably conflict-laden and "more harm than good." She would argue that she would "lose a part of herself" if rejected by someone about whom she cared. Mary trusted no one and believed that people are "just out to use you." As a result, she made no efforts to establish intimate relationships and saw herself as "unrelatable."

Mary had poor and strained relations with her family. She experienced a great deal of anger regarding them and would quickly berate herself and feel guilty for having such "unacceptable" feelings. Anger was an unacceptable emotion for it represented conflict, pain, and danger. She similarly believed that children are never supposed to be angry toward their parents. In general, Mary was afraid of her feelings and subsequently turned them off. She feared losing control.

Therapy proceeded by empathizing with Mary's situation and enlisting her as a collaborator in the therapy process. Although she initially asserted that she needed to lean on rather than collaborate with a therapist, she soon accepted her position on the "therapy team." It was important for Mary to recognize that the therapy would provide both support *and* strategies for change. This helped her feel optimistic about her therapy.

It was important for Mary to understand the role her belief system played in the etiology and maintenance of her current emotional and behavioral difficulties. Particular caution was employed to ensure that she did not misread the therapist as blaming her for feeling like she was feeling. Rather, she was presented with an optimistic and hopeful model within which she learned how to take charge of her life. Although she initially felt helpless, she soon realized that she had the capacity to change. She learned that neither the past nor her family need change in order for her to be happy in life.

Therapy proceeded by challenging Mary to confront her beliefs in terms of their (a) accuracy and (b) function. It was relatively straightforward in showing her that her thoughts about herself, the world, and the future and past only contributed to helping her *maintain* her current distress and behavior problems. Mary soon agreed that she would benefit by reconditioning these beliefs. This led to cognitive restructuring procedures that served to help Mary develop a more rational and empirically based philosophy. Addressed were her self-downing cognitions, distorted views of relationships, her catastrophizing views of her past, and her sense of hopelessness about the future. Similarly addressed was her failure to empathize with herself and allow herself to have negative (although less extreme) feelings regarding her family. She also learned that she will not "lose control" or "go crazy" if she allows herself to feel her feelings. Mary learned to "play new tapes" other than the ones she had been playing since childhood. She consequently learned to act and react in a more assertive, confident, and less disturbed and self-defeating manner.

Skills development procedures were also employed. Mary learned anger management and assertion skills so as to improve her ability to relate to her family. Similarly, she learned to live her life independently of them and with reduced guilt. This was a big step for Mary, since she historically believed that children (even adult children) are always "supposed to" do what their parents want. Overcoming guilt and concurrently managing her anger left her with an appropriate and "adult" manner in which to deal with her parents' influence. Mary chose to decrease contact with them and to set limits on the extent to which they "controlled" her. Mary reported that she felt like she was finally "free" to live her life the way *she* wants.

Mary increasingly learned to trust people. First, however, she was challenged to define trust as a continuous, rather than as a dichotomous, variable. Mary initially believed that you either trust people or you do not. She learned that there are degrees of trust and that you do not have to "give your entire being" to someone when you do trust them. Varying degrees of trust were operationalized and Mary was encouraged to systematically and incrementally trust people. First, she was asked to disclose mildly revealing personal information with a friend and gradually and increasingly "open up." Concurrently, Mary's belief that it would be "awful" if she was betrayed and that she must have a guarantee that the person is trustworthy were disputed. Desensitization procedures employing cognitive restructuring strategies were quite useful in Mary's case. It is important to note that Mary also learned how to distinguish those whom she could likely trust from those she probably could not. All too often, ACOA clients become "too" trusting and subsequently put themselves in positions where they are likely to be hurt.

Mary was also encouraged to begin sampling potentially enjoyable activities in order to increase opportunities for response contingent reinforcement. This procedure served several therapeutic purposes. First, it helped her see that she could find enjoyment in life. Second, it disputed her notion that she "is the kind of person" for whom the world offers no pleasure. Third, it helped Mary realize that she is good at things and is, in fact, competent. Finally, it helped her to establish opportunities for social interaction, which increased the likelihood of making friends and having activities in which she could partake when feeling depressed or bored. Activity scheduling, as such, is recommended as early intervention for depressed clients (Beck, 1967, 1975; Beck, Rush, Shaw & Emery, 1979).

Mary was encouraged to reward herself and better appreciate her efforts and personal value. She was challenged to separate evaluations of her behaviors from a self-evaluation and to increase her tendency for unbiased and unconditional self-appraisal.

Mary terminated therapy based on a collaborative decision. Treatment taught her how to identify problems, not to be afraid of them, to realize that they are approachable once clearly defined to challenge the irrational and distorted beliefs that either mediate or exacerbate her problems, and that with constructive and systematic efforts, she can overcome them.

References

Ackerman, R. J. (1983). *Children of alcoholics: A guidebook for educators, therapists, and parents* (2nd ed.). Holmes Beach, FL: Learning Publications.

Alberti, R. E., & Emmons, M. L. (1979). *Your perfect right: A guide to assertive behavior* (2nd ed.). San Luis Obispo, CA: Impact Press.

Bandura, A. (1982). Self-efficacy mechanism in human agency. *American Psychologist, 37*, 122-147.

Beck, A. T. (1967). *Depression: Clinical, experimental, and theoretical aspects*. New York: Hoeber.

Beck, A. T. (1975). *Depression: Causes and treatment.* Philadelphia: University of Pennsylvania Press.

Beck, A. T. (1976). *Cognitive therapy and the emotional disorders.* New York: New American Library.

Beck, A. T., Rush, A., Shaw, B., & Emery, G. (1979). *Cognitive therapy of depression.* New York: Guilford.

Billings, A. G., & Moos, R. H. (1982). Stressful life events and symptoms: A longitudinal model. *Health Psychology, 1,* 99-118.

Black, C. (1981). *It will never happen to me.* Denver: M. A. C.

Blane, H. T. (1988). Prevention issues with children of alcoholics. *British Journal of Addiction, 83*(7), 793-798.

Brickman, P., Rabinowitz, V. C., Karuza, J., Coates, D., Cohn, E., & Kidder, L. (1982). Models of helping and coping. *American Psychologist, 37,* 368-384.

Brophy, J. E., & Good, T. (1974). *Teacher-student relationships: Causes and consequences.* New York: Holt, Rinehart & Winston.

Brown, S. (1988). *Treating adult children of alcoholics: A developmental perspective.* New York: John Wiley.

Caudill, B. D., & Marlatt, G. A. (1975). Modeling influences in social drinking: An experimental analogue. *Journal of Consulting and Clinical Psychology, 43,* 405-415.

Cermak, T. L. (1984). The case for a new diagnostic category of co-dependency for children of alcoholics. *Alcohol Health and Research World, 8,* 30-38.

Cermak, T. L. (1985). *A primer on the adult children of alcoholics.* Pompano Beach, FL: Health Communications.

Cermak, T. L., & Brown, S. (1982). Interactional group therapy with the adult children of alcoholics. *International Journal of Group Psychotherapy, 32,* 375-389.

Claydon, P. (1987). Self-reported alcohol, drug, and eating-disorder problems among male and female collegiate children of alcoholics. *Journal of American College Health, 36*(2), 111-116.

Cole, D. A. (1991). Preliminary support for a competency-based model of depression in children. *Journal of Abnormal Psychology, 100,* 181-190.

Crawford, R. L., & Phyfer, A. Q. (1988). Adult children of alcoholics: A counseling model. *Journal of College Student Development, 29*(2), 105-111.

Darley, J. M., & Goethals, G. R. (1980). People's analyses of the causes of ability linked performances. In L. Berkowitz (Ed.), *Advances in experimental social psychology* (Vol. 13, pp. 1-37). San Diego: Academic Press.

Drake, R. E., & Vaillant, G. E. (1988). Predicting alcoholism and personality disorder in a 33-year longitudinal study of children of alcoholics. *British Journal of Addiction, 83*(7), 799-807.

Ellis, A., McInerney, J., DiGiuseppe, R. A., & Yeager, R. J. (1988). *Rational-emotive therapy with alcoholics and substance abusers.* Elmsford, NY: Pergamon.

Ellis, A., & Yeager, R. J. (1989). *Why some therapies don't work: The dangers of transpersonal psychology.* Buffalo, NY: Prometheus Books.

Fingarette, H. (1988). *Heavy drinking: The myth of alcoholism as a disease.* Los Angeles: University of California Press.

Fulton, A. I., & Yates, W. R. (1990). Adult children of alcoholics: A valid diagnostic group? *Journal of Nervous and Mental Disorders, 178,* 505-509.

Goodman, R. W. (1987). Adult children of alcoholics. *Journal of Counseling and Development, 66*(4), 162-163.

Haley, J. (1976). *Problem solving therapy.* San Francisco: Jossey-Bass.

Haley, J. (1980). *Leaving home: The therapy of disturbed young people.* New York: McGraw-Hill.

Hibbard, S. (1987). The diagnosis and treatment of adult children of alcoholics as a specialized therapeutic population. *Psychotherapy, 24,* 779-785.

Hibbard, S. (1989). Personality and object relational pathology in young adult children of alcoholics. *Psychotherapy, 26,* 504-509.

Higgins, R. L., & Marlatt, G. A. (1973). The effects of anxiety arousal upon the consumption of alcohol by alcoholics and social drinkers. *Journal of Consulting and Clinical Psychology, 41,* 426-433.

Higgins, R. L., & Marlatt, G. A. (1975). Fear of interpersonal evaluation as a determinant of alcohol consumption in male social drinkers. *Journal of Abnormal Psychology, 84,* 644-651.

Holmes, T. H., & Rahe, R. H. (1967). The Social Readjustment Rating Scale. *Journal of Psychosomatic Research, 11,* 213-218.

Jones, J. W. (1981). *The Children of Alcoholics Screening Test (C.A.S.T.).* Chicago: Family Recovery Press.

Lang, A. R., Goeckner, D. J., Adesso, V. J., & Marlatt, G. A. (1975). The effects of alcohol and aggression in male social drinkers. *Journal of Abnormal Psychology, 84,* 508-518.

Lange, A. J., & Jakubowski, P. (1980). *Responsible assertive behavior: Cognitive/behavioral procedures for trainers.* Champaign, IL: Research Press.

Latane, B. (1966). Studies in social comparison: Introduction and overview. *Journal of Experimental Social Psychology, 2*(Suppl. 1), 1-5.

Lied, E. R., & Marlatt, G. A. (1979). Modeling as a determinant of alcohol consumption: Effect of subject sex and prior drinking history. *Addictive Behaviors, 4,* 47-54.

Marlatt, G. A., Demming, B., & Reid, J. B. (1973). Loss of control drinking in alcoholics: An experimental analogue. *Journal of Abnormal Psychology, 81,* 223-241.

Marlatt, G. A., & Rohsenow, D. J. (1980). Cognitive processes in alcohol use: Expectancy and the balanced placebo design. In N. K. Mello (Ed.), *Advances in substance abuse* (Vol. 1). Greenwich, CT: JAI Press.

Marlatt, G. A., & Rose, F. (1980). Addictive disorders. In A. E. Kazdin, A. S. Bellack, & M. Hersen (Eds.), *New perspectives in abnormal psychology.* New York: Oxford University Press.

Meichenbaum, D. H. (1977). *Cognitive behavior modification.* New York: Plenum.

Meichenbaum, D. H., & Cameron, R. (1974). The clinical potential of modifying what clients say to themselves. *Psychotherapy Theory, Research and Practice, 11,* 103-117.

Miller, W. R. (1989). Increasing motivation for change. In R. K. Hester & W. R. Miller (Eds.), *Handbook of alcoholism treatment approaches: Effective alternatives* (pp. 67-80). Elmsford, NY: Pergamon.

Minuchin, S., & Fishman, H. C. (1981). *Family therapy techniques.* Cambridge, MA: Harvard University Press.

Moos, R. H., & Billings, A. G. (1982). Conceptualizing and measuring coping resources and processes. In L. Goldberger & S. Breznitz (Eds.), *Handbook of stress.* New York: Free Press.

Novaco, R. (1975). *Anger control: The development and evaluation of an experimental treatment.* Lexington, MA: D. C. Heath.

Parker, D., & Harford, T. (1988). Alcohol related problems, marital disruption, and depressive symptoms among adult children of alcohol abusers in the United States. *Journal of Studies on Alcohol, 49,* 306-313.

Piaget, J., & Inhelder, B. (1958). *The growth of logical thinking from childhood to adolescence.* New York: Basic Books.

Plescia-Pikus, M., Long-Sutter, E., & Wilson, J. P. (1988). Achievement, well-being, intelligence, and stress reaction in adult children of alcoholics. *Psychological Reports, 62,* 603-609.

Reich, W., Earls, F., & Powell, J. (1988). A comparison of the home and social environments of children of alcoholic and non-alcoholic parents. *British Journal of Addictions, 83,* 831-839.

Stipek, D. (1987). Emotional responses to objective and normative performance feedback. *Journal of Applied Developmental Psychology, 8,* 183-195.

Wallace, J. (1987). Children of alcoholics: A population at risk. *Alcoholism Treatment Quarterly, 4*(3), 13-30.

Werner, E. E. (1986). Resilient offspring of alcoholics: A longitudinal study from birth to age 18. *Journal of Studies on Alcohol, 47,* 34-40.

Yeager, R. J., DiGiuseppe, R. A., Leaf, R., & Resweber, P. J. (in press). A comparison of MCMI profiles among chronic residential substance abusers and a general outpatient population. *Psychological Reports.*

Yeager, R. J., DiGiuseppe, R. A., Olson, J., Lewis, L., & Alberti, R. (1988). Rational-emotive therapy in the therapeutic community. *Journal of Rational-Emotive Therapy, 6*(4), 1-25.

Yeager, R. J., & Miller, A. R. (1991, July). *Developing and instituting corporate wellness programs.* Paper presented at the University of Bridgeport Institute for Addiction Studies' Seventh Annual Issues in Addictions Conference: Beyond Tradition—Contemporary Approaches to De-Addiction.

Yeager, R. J., & Muran, J. C. (1991). *Endorsement of irrational thinking among substance abusers.* Unpublished manuscript.

Yeager, R. J., & Rothschild, B. (1990, June). *Irrational beliefs and addictive behavior.* Paper presented at the Annual Conference of the World Congress on Mental Health Counseling, Keystone, CO.

Yeager, R. J., Yeager, C. M., & Shillingford, J. A. (1990, June). *An examination of adult children of alcoholics.* Paper presented at the Annual Conference of the World Congress on Mental Health Counseling, Keystone, CO.

Using Rational-Emotive Therapy in Treating Pathological Gambling

VALERIE C. LORENZ

In 1976, the Congressional Commission on the Review of the National Policy Toward Gambling determined that 0.77% of the adult population, approximately 1.1 million people, could be labeled compulsive gamblers. In Nevada, at that time the only state in the country to have a total gambling climate, the incidence was more than double the national figures.

A review of the literature, both scientific and fictional, finds the compulsive gambler described typically as a white male businessman or professional, in his forties or fifties, who gambles in casinos, at race tracks, or on sports. Some compulsive gamblers eventually join Gamblers Anonymous (started in 1957) or seek professional treatment at a Veterans Administration Medical Center (Adkins, 1988; Custer & Custer, 1978; Lorenz, 1978).

AUTHOR'S NOTE: Valerie C. Lorenz, Ph.D., Executive Director of the Compulsive Gambling Center, Inc., is an internationally recognized expert on this disorder. For reprint requests, write Dr. Lorenz at 924 East Baltimore Street, Baltimore, MD 21202.

Societal and Attitudinal Changes

Since 1976, several factors have led to a dramatic increase in gambling and compulsive gambling in the United States: (a) expansion of the casino industry to Atlantic City; (b) legalization of bingo to remove the stigma of selective law enforcement; (c) implementation of state lotteries in lieu of raising taxes during a downward economy; (d) freedom of movement and access to money and credit cards by formerly disenfranchised groups as a result of the Civil Rights Movement and the Women's Liberation Movement; and (e) the advancing technology of computers, television, and telecommunications (Custer & Milt, 1984; Galski, 1985; Lorenz, 1990a).

Thus began a powerful, highly lobbied movement across the United States (and eventually the world) to legalize many forms of gambling, particularly state lotteries (Braidfoot, 1988). Lotteries were aggressively promoted as an act of civic responsibility (aid for the elderly, for education, or for other worthwhile causes) and as a means of exchanging poverty and boredom for dreams fulfilled. The advertising was geared to impulsive spending, immediate gratification, and big wins, all of which contribute to the development of potential gambling addiction.

Today there are many forms of gambling to be found in every state in the country. State lotteries, bingo, and horse racing are the most frequent forms of legal gambling. Other forms are private, charitable or floating casinos, card clubs, off-track betting, slot machines, poker machines, jai alai, dog racing, and pull tabs. Illegal in most states but nevertheless found with great regularity are sports betting, poker machines, after-hours clubs, dice, oriental games, cockfights, dogfights, paddle wheels or pushers, tip jars, punch boards, breakaways, and other small games of chance. In short, any form of gambling is available to virtually anyone, at any time, and for any amount of money. Each form of gambling is potentially addictive, and today's estimates of gambling addicts run from 1.5% of the adult population (Volberg & Steadman, 1988) to 4% or more, and up to 7% among teenagers (Jacobs, 1989; Lesieur et al., 1991; Lesieur & Klein, 1987).

Current Profiles of Compulsive Gamblers

Today, a compulsive gambler may be male or female, teenager or senior citizen, of any ethnic group or religious persuasion, from any socioeconomic level, a school dropout or postgraduate professional, employed or housewife. Compulsive gambling today is a truly democratic mental disorder.

Over time, the religious breakdown among gambling addicts has remained fairly constant. Among members of Gamblers Anonymous and those in professional treatment, 35% are Catholic, 30% Protestant, and 25% Jewish (Lorenz, 1981). Female gamblers were virtually unheard of in the 1970s. Now a female compulsive gambler typically is a woman who started gambling later in life (males tend to start in their teens), who has serious relationship problems, and who tends to be addicted to games of chance that initially cost comparatively little, such as lotteries, poker or fruit machines, bingo, or pull tabs (Lesieur, 1988; Lorenz, 1991).

Teenage or young adult compulsive gamblers were reported in the United States for the first time less than 10 years ago. Typically, they are addicted to horse racing or sports betting and also often to chemical substances (Lesieur & Heineman, 1988).

Elderly compulsive gamblers tend to be people who recently retired or became unemployed, who are unhappy in their marriages or are recently widowed, and who seek escape from loneliness and financial insecurity through bus trips to casinos or bingo parlors.

What has remained constant among all groups of compulsive gamblers is the extraordinarily high rate of suicide attempts—20% or higher in virtually every research study on compulsive gamblers. In a study undertaken by the Task Force on Gambling Addiction convened by the Maryland Department of Health and Mental Hygiene, which involved 91 members of Gamblers Anonymous, it was found that 65% had considered committing suicide, either by automobile, gun, pills, poison, gas, hanging, or butcher knife (Lorenz, 1990c).

Compulsive gambling is a high-stress activity that also impairs the addict's physical health, resulting in numerous psychosomatic problems, such as migraines, angina, back pain, dermatitis, or gastrointestinal complications (Lorenz & Yaffee, 1986, 1988, 1989; Roy et al., 1988).

Personality and Development

Common to compulsive gamblers, regardless of the type of gambling engaged in, is the etiology and development of the addiction (Custer & Milt, 1984; Lesieur, 1984; Livingston, 1974). Being good at gambling requires a knowledge of probabilities. Compulsive gamblers are above average in intelligence, good with numbers, highly competitive, and motivated to achieve (Custer & Milt, 1984; Lesieur, 1984; Lorenz, 1990a; Moravec & Munley, 1983; Taber & Boston, 1987). Prior to their addiction, they were honest, were conscientious about physical fitness, tended to avoid drugs or alcohol in early years, and typically did well in school and on the job. They are often workaholics.

The compulsive gambler is reared in a family environment in which there is a strong emphasis on money. There almost always is a history of alcoholism or pathological gambling in the family of origin. The gambler's childhood is marked with inconsistent, ineffective parenting and physical, verbal, and/or psychological abuse. Many compulsive gamblers have also been traumatized sexually. The gambler's family environment is one of deprivation of emotional nurturance and expression of love. The sense of self-esteem is devalued, and the gambler learns early on in life to be nonassertive about his or her own feelings or desires (Ciarrocchi & Richardson, 1989; Lorenz & Shuttlesworth, 1983; Shaffer, Stein, Gambino, & Cummings, 1989; Task Force, 1990; Yaffee, 1990).

The gambling addict has a history of exposure to painful, frightening, or anger-provoking events in childhood and in later stages of life. These traumas are unresolved and troublesome, often leaving the gambler in a state of dysphoria and vulnerability (Jacobs, 1986, 1988; Taber, McCormick, & Ramirez, 1987). Unresolved traumatic military experiences may add to the gambler's emotional stress.

Since early childhood, the future compulsive gambler is psychologically damaged. The gambler grows up to be emotionally immature and desperately wants the acceptance of a significant family member, most often the father. Since this is repeatedly denied, the gambler learns not to trust family members and to withdraw emotionally. This attitude eventually is generalized to outsiders, the community, and a higher power (Nakken, 1988). The gambler becomes a "loner" who is lacking in communication and coping skills, who has no self-esteem, who fears criticism and rejection, and who has poor impulse control and low frustration tolerance. The desire for relationships is thwarted by the fear of rejection. This fear of criticism and rejection leads to procrastination whenever something emotionally unpleasant comes their way. They develop systems of self-deception (Rosenthal, 1986).

Many compulsive gamblers suffer from an early onset (childhood or teens) of dysthymia, the result of dysfunctional family life and associated abuse, or other life stressors and trauma. Gambling, and winning, give this person a sense of action and excitement, a sense of confidence and of feeling good. Money and winning are seen as means of gaining attention and acceptance, especially from family members.

Gambling also provides the gambler with the opportunity to avoid facing the pain and discomfort of life for several hours or days at a time. Thus gambling not only adds excitement, challenge, and "action" to the gambler's life, but it also serves as an escape from past and immediate discomforts of life.

Continued gambling, reinforced by wins and attention from others, leads to irrational patterns of thinking, including beliefs of having superior gambling skills and luck (Gaboury & Ladouceur, 1987). As this irrational thinking is reinforced through more wins and becomes ever more fully developed, thought processes become more marked by denial, rationalization, self-deception, magical thinking, and obsessive thoughts of gambling. The gambler fails to recognize loss of control, seeks immediate gratification, and fails to consider the consequences of destructive or illegal behaviors (Brown, 1987; Lesieur & Klein, 1987; Lorenz, 1989a; Rosenthal & Lorenz, 1992).

As with other addictions, compulsive gambling follows a specific pattern of development (American Psychiatric Association, 1987; Lesieur & Rosenthal, 1991). First, the gambling becomes chronic and progressive, that is, gambling with more money, for longer periods of time, and more frequently. Second, an intolerance for losing develops. The competitive nature of compulsive gamblers will not permit the losses, which are seen as loss of esteem and acceptance and must be overcome at once or result in depression. Loss of funds must be recouped in order to cover up the gambling activity or to pay off gambling debts, all of which results in high stress and anxiety. Third, preoccupation with gambling urges and cravings emerges, resulting in the gambler setting up situations to make it possible to give in to those urges and cravings at any cost. Fourth, the gambler develops a disregard for consequences of gambling, which has led to such things as financial losses or indebtedness, loss of work productivity, absences from home, lies, the use of alcohol or drugs to avoid feelings of guilt and depression, and the commission of illegal acts to support the gambling. Fifth, efforts to stop gambling may result in withdrawal symptoms similar to those seen among substance abusers. These symptoms tend to be more common among the high-energy type of gamblers (casino/race track/sports bettor) than the depressed, escapist gamblers (slot or poker machines, lottery, and bingo). Sixth, relapse occurs. The gambler invariably attempts to abstain from further gambling and, while successful for a period of weeks or months, relapses in the absence of treatment and external support (Adkins, 1988; Gamblers Anonymous, 1984; Rosenthal & Lorenz, 1992).

By the time compulsive gamblers present for treatment, diagnoses may include affective disorders, personality disorders, and physical complications, all with severe psychosocial stressors. A Global Assessment of Functioning score will be in the 30s. Perhaps some 20% will also present with alcohol abuse or dependence and a lesser percentage with cocaine or marijuana abuse or dependence (Task Force, 1990).

RET and Other Treatment Considerations

Gamblers Anonymous (GA) is a self-help recovery group founded in 1957 that currently has more than 700 chapters in the United States. GA is based on the 12-step recovery program of Alcoholics Anonymous (AA). In practice there are many dissimilarities between GA and AA (Browne, 1991). For example, sponsorship is a strong component of the AA program, but not of the GA program. In AA, a sponsor teaches the newcomer the 12 steps of recovery. More typically in GA, a sponsor is someone a newcomer may call when an urge to gamble develops. Because gamblers are so fearful of rejection, they will not call the sponsor. In AA, a speaker may say, "My name is Joe, I am an alcoholic, and with the help of my Higher Power I have not taken a drink today." In GA, more typically the gambler says, "My name is Joe. I am a compulsive gambler. I have not made a bet in three years, eight months, and twenty-seven days."

Gamblers Anonymous has a high attrition rate, much of it due to the gambler's inability or unwillingness to accept the basic steps of the recovery or unity program. The First Step is practically always the most difficult one for the compulsive gambler to accept. Step One requires the gambler to admit powerlessness over gambling, a belief that is in strong conflict with two irrational beliefs held by virtually all compulsive gamblers: First, "*I must be in control* of all things at all times. Otherwise I will lose what is important to me, and that would be awful." Second, "*I must be fully competent* (or better than others) in everything I do at all times. In this manner, I will avoid criticism and rejection." These two beliefs will not allow for being powerless and turning one's life over to a Higher Power. Thus they will have repeated relapses in their attempts to be "controlled gamblers."

For further protection against criticism and rejection, the compulsive gambler develops additional beliefs that are dysfunctional.

1. *I must be accepted* (liked, loved, respected) at all times. If people knew who I really am, they would not accept me; therefore, I will behave the way I think they want to see me and not tell them what is really happening with me.
2. *Uncomfortable situations,* such as being assertive about my feelings or desires or admitting to losing money at gambling, *must be avoided* at all costs, through either lies or procrastination.
3. *Money will solve all my problems.* My childhood was all about money, society is all about money, and gambling is all about money. Without money in my pocket, I am nothing.
4. Because *I won in the past, I will win again in the future,* and this losing is just a temporary streak that is sure to change with the next bet.

These irrational beliefs (Ellis & Harper, 1975; Ellis & Knaus, 1977) result in much self-imposed pressure, and gamblers simply cannot fulfill the demands and expectations they have placed on themselves. Further, admitting to an out-of-control mental illness, such as is required in the First Step of the GA program, is very difficult for compulsive gamblers. They constantly struggle with this in the GA program, and often rationalize that they are not as bad as others in the room, and then attempt to maintain abstinence without attending GA or professional therapy. Since coping and effective communication skills are lacking, however, it is only a matter of time until good intentions are replaced by giving in to strong urges to return to gambling. These are the words of a gambler in treatment:

Case 1 (White married male, 31, businessman, who bet at casinos, on sports, and on race horses): When I first went to GA, I thought "Those guys are fucking sick, I don't belong here." I quit after the first meeting. It gave me an excuse to go back to gambling.

The basic thing in a compulsive gambler's life is money, the big score. If I couldn't bet football or baseball, I would bet on Wimbledon. I never even saw a tennis match, and I would bet on it.

It's self-torture. It is never enough. It is the challenge, you're there to beat them, and when you do, it still isn't enough. My dream used to be that the casino boss would say, "Sir, we can no longer handle your bet." You know what a thrill that would have been? It doesn't happen in real life, but if it had, I would have gone to the casino next door, and started all over again, winning and losing.

One time I won $30,000 and ended up borrowing $10 from the pit boss for gas to get home. Another time I ran $500 into $12,000 at the craps table. I hired a plane, flew over the Grand Canyon, and I saw a performance by Frank Sinatra. It was great. I had never been to a show before, and I loved it. Then, instead of taking that money and watching all these great shows with my wife, I went right back to the tables and lost it all.

You think your "good time" is gambling, that one good day is worth torturing yourself for 20 bad days. You remember the good days and ignore the bad. If I had money in my pocket, I would go to the track. If I didn't have money, my mind would go, "Where can I get $500? Who owes me a favor?" If I had a bad check out, I never thought the guy would prosecute, I only thought, I can't borrow from him. The other thought was, I gotta gamble.

I never realized I was escaping depression. I thought "the bills are due, I can't take the pressure, I've got to go to the track."

My last fling made me realize I needed help. I took a large wad of money, and put $500 in one pocket, the rest in the other. I wanted to prove to myself I could play with just $500. I did four races, $20 or $50, and thought, this is ridiculous. So I spent the whole wad on the next race, and lost it all. It was the same thing, just torturing myself. I remembered the doctor I went to the day before said compulsive gambling is chronic and progressive and that I was out of control. I knew then I couldn't just keep to the $500. I had a problem. I had to quit. The next day I started in intensive therapy. Now I go to GA to learn and to get help.

I wish I had known about compulsive gambling a lot sooner. Maybe I wouldn't have done so much damage. Now that I haven't gambled in two weeks, my head is starting to clear. I'm talking to my wife. I don't have to hide or lie. I'm beginning to think. I used to believe that my first thought was the only way. Now I know there are different ways of thinking and many options, not just one or the first. It's amazing, I had to be 31 and go through hell before I learned to think.

Common to compulsive gamblers after a short time of abstinence is the utter disbelief of their behavior while gambling. "I can't believe I did that" is a common reaction, which then is followed by tremendous guilt and remorse, often leading to major depression. Others may be facing legal charges, and their depression is complicated with major anxiety or panic attacks. Yet others speak of the tremendous sense of relief, even after an arrest. "At least the monkey is off my back, I don't have to lie or steal anymore." Virtually all are in agreement that the intervention of a strong external force was necessary before the gambler was able to admit to being out of control.

The Treatment Process

The belief that money will solve all the gambler's problems needs to be disputed early in the treatment process. In the gambler's mind, having money is equated with approval from others and as a measure of self-worth. Since money and acceptance can be obtained from diligent work, they tend to be very thorough on their jobs and put in long hours. Burns (1980) could have been thinking about gambling addicts when he wrote chapter 13, "Your Work Is Not Your Worth," in his book, *Feeling Good: The New Mood Therapy*. Disputation, then, would focus on the irrational beliefs and thought distortions within the compulsive gambler's schema. For example:

Patient: When I lose, it is just awful.
Therapist: What is so awful?
P: Not having any money in my pocket.
T: What are you telling yourself about that to make you feel so bad?
P: Well, if they knew I didn't have any money, they'd think I'm a no-good bum.
T: What evidence do you have that people know you have no money in your pocket?
P: Well, they don't really know, but I know it.

T: Suppose, for instance, that someone walking toward you actually knows you have no money in your pocket. What evidence do you have that he is actually thinking you are a "no-good bum?"

P: Well, I don't know that he is thinking it, but I am thinking it.

T: So you could change your way of thinking about that, couldn't you?

P: I could think, only I know I have no money in my pocket.

T: Good. Let's explore that further. I hardly ever have more than one or two dollars in my wallet. Does that make me a bum?

P: I see what you mean. But then, you're different. You're a doctor and you help people. So they like you.

T: I'm sure many people respect the work I do. But does that mean they like me?

P: Hum, no, not necessarily.

T: I did not always do this kind of work. Does that mean people did not like me before I started to do this, or that they will stop liking me when I retire?

P: I guess my thinking doesn't make much sense, does it? Work may get you some benefits, like respect for the job that you do, but that is separate from being liked.

Many compulsive gamblers admit working to excess not only to satisfy their approval and acceptance needs, but also because they fear emotional closeness with significant others. Being close to others means being more vulnerable to criticism and rejection, which is viewed as awful and to be avoided at all costs. As gambling losses increase, the gambler is faced with more bad feelings and relationship problems, which then tend to be avoided through lies and procrastination. "I must avoid bad feelings" is an irrational belief developed in early childhood and that is now reinforced as the gambling becomes out of control. Ultimately, however, the constant turmoil results in a feeling of numbness or constant depression, and the gambling addict is no longer able to experience the "high" or the "action." Many gambling addicts speak of initial feelings of strong elation, "being on top of the world" after a big win, and sinking into depths of depression after major losses. These feelings lose their strength eventually. A typical patient's statement is:

After all the wins and losses, you get numb. It's like being on automatic pilot. You just do it. Money becomes a piece of paper. You keep going as long as you have money. You can't stop, even though you tell yourself every morning, and all day long, "I'm not going to gamble today." Then something happens, like it rained today, and you're off, back to the tables. And you win again, and lose again, and you play all night, and the next night. Then when you drive home, you feel like a worm, and you think your wife and kids will be better off without you, and if you crash the car, the insurance will cover the accident, and all the bills will get paid. Maybe they won't hate me so much then.

Disputation of the gambling addict's irrational beliefs and correcting automatic thought distortions needs to be done repeatedly, until the thinking is more accurate (Ellis, McInerney, DiGiuseppe, & Yeager, 1988; Lorenz, 1989b, 1990b). In the above case, the breakthrough came when it was pointed out that the gambler was thinking about gambling all day, thereby putting pressure on himself constantly.

Patient: You're right. From the minute I get up, I think about gambling.
Therapist: What else could you tell yourself the first minute you get up?
P: I could think about anything, like I really slept well last night. I'll have the energy to work out, and jog a couple of miles.
T: Do you like working out or jogging?
P: I love it. I used to work out every day before work. It gets me going. I used to shoot baskets with the kids and to referee Little League. Once I started gambling, I didn't do any of that.
T: So now you have rediscovered some other things that are important to you, besides gambling?
P: You know, the whole crazy gambling started when I hurt my back at work. I had to stay in bed for two weeks. I couldn't stand the boredom. It was killing me. That's when I started calling the bookie, and then watching all the games on TV. Now I realize the gambling nearly killed me.

In treating compulsive gamblers, abstinence is considered essential. However, abstinence is only one goal in therapy. Invariably, other goals are finding exciting and meaningful substitutes for the gambling, improving relationships with family members and friends, learning more effective communication and coping skills, resolving financial and legal problems, and developing a life-style that provides quality and balance to the individual and the family (Adkins, 1988; Heineman, 1989, 1992; Hudak, Varghese, & Politzer, 1989; Lorenz, 1989c).

Cognitive/rational-emotive therapy has been found to be exceptionally effective. Disputation of irrational beliefs using the ABC model of RET tends to give the gambler not only a tremendous sense of relief and renewed sense of self, but it removes the internal pressure the gambler feels, such as the need to be in control of others or always be the best. The gambler no longer needs to escape into fantasies in order to feel good about him- or herself and can become part of the group instead of being the loner.

The Compulsive Gambling Center, Inc., in Baltimore, operates a residential and outpatient treatment program for compulsive gamblers and family members. Patients are taught to "think like a cop"; that is, they are urged to prove the accuracy of their thoughts and beliefs. Once they realize that no evidence exists for their beliefs, they are encouraged to alter their thinking. Therapists regularly point out when a patient's automatic thoughts are distorted or when beliefs are irrational. Large posters are prominently placed on walls, one with a dozen irrational beliefs, the other with automatic thought distortions. When the patient makes an illogical or inaccurate statement, the therapist disputes the statement verbally while also pointing to the specific thought or belief on the posters.

Another chart has a level-of-feeling scale. The therapist has the patient measure different levels of anger. Next, the therapist helps the patient identify the must and should statements and irrational beliefs that lead to the high level of anger and how that can be reduced through more accurate and less demanding statements.

Bibliotherapy is a required part of treatment. Reading assignments emphasize RET-based materials, especially those that are geared to overcoming addictions and strong negative feelings (Burns, 1980; Ellis, 1988; Lorenz, 1989b, 1990b). Gamblers and family members also use the library of RET tapes and educational materials that are geared to specific topics, such as overcoming procrastination, boredom, fear, guilt, low tolerance levels, learning to be more assertive, and sabotaging recovery. They are given daily mood logs (Burns, 1980) and the RET Self-Help form (Sichel & Ellis, 1984).

Gamblers respond well to numbers. It has thus been found helpful to give gamblers many short tests to identify levels of feelings or attitudes. The Novaco Anger Scale, the Dysfunctional

Attitude Scale (Burns, 1980), Bessell's Emotional Maturity Scale (1984), the Beck Depression Scale (Burns, 1980), and Robertson's Workaholic Scale (1989) are used regularly, not only with the gambler but also with the significant other in the gambler's life.

Rational Recovery (RR) groups provide a useful alternative for the recovering compulsive gambler who refuses to attend GA because of conflict with the First Step and with steps relating to a Higher Power. Similar to other self-help groups in that its basis is in the principles of the Alcoholics Anonymous program, RR nevertheless has some major distinctions from the AA concept (Trimpey, 1990). First, Rational Recovery focuses on short-term attendance rather than the lifetime attendance that is espoused by the more traditional 12-step groups. RR leaders teach new members the principles of rational-emotive therapy. Second, it appears that many compulsive gamblers have difficulty in accepting the spiritual principles of the AA or GA programs. Rational Recovery serves as an alternative to that concern in that it does not focus on powerlessness over the addiction or on a Higher Power, but rather on each individual's responsibility for his or her own behaviors and feelings. Third, Rational Recovery serves a useful purpose in that it is available in increasing locations, thus it may be the only group accessible to the compulsive gambler.

Spouses and Family Members

Spouses and other family members often act according to their own irrational beliefs or distorted thinking. Once aware of the gambling problem, they may quickly resort to "fortune telling" and "awfulizing." Their fear of the gambler's relapse often leads to excessive behaviors on their part as well as additional pressures they may put on the gambler. Spouses not only fear relapses themselves, but the consequences of going without food, having utilities shut off again, being evicted, and having credit cut off or bank accounts closed. Thus they might resort to such excessive spending as stockpiling food. They may insist on complete control over all monies in the family and how they are to be spent. It is not unusual for gamblers to experience additional guilt or anger about the family's response. Lacking coping skills, they may relapse into gambling as the only escape from these unwanted feelings. Family therapy, therefore, becomes important in the recovery process (Darvas, 1985; Heinemann, 1987, 1989, 1992; Lorenz, 1989c).

In therapy, the cognitive therapist would focus on competing messages of "I must be in control" and help the couple learn to cooperate and to work together on resolving issues of conflict. Early on in therapy, the following is typical:

Irrational Gambler: I earned the money. I am going to decide how to spend it. You haven't ever balanced a checkbook right. I always have to straighten it out. I hear what those wives do to the guys in GA. You expect me to beg you for an allowance? No way.

The spouse responds to that with her own sense of anger and resentment:

Irrational Spouse: For years you gambled the money away. You lied, you stole, we did without, and now we are over our heads in debt. If you hadn't gone to the track, we could own three houses by now. You want me to trust you? You SOB. You should be glad I'm still with you. I'll never trust you again. You either give me the whole paycheck, or get out.

The therapist would dispute the gambler's all-or-nothing thinking, overgeneralizing, should statements, negative predicting, need for control, fear of criticism, and fear of rejection. The therapist would also dispute the spouse's should statements, all-or-nothing thinking, labeling, and demand to be in control, so that revised statements might be:

Rational Gambler: I earn the money for the family, because we agreed that we want our children to be raised by their mother, not by a baby-sitter or day-care center. If I don't gamble, we will have more than enough money for you to stay home. Granted, you haven't been able to balance the checkbook, but that is because I did not enter checks or wrote in the wrong deposits, because I wanted to hide the truth from you when I was gambling. I hear in GA how

	some of the guys and their wives handle money, but that really scares me. I don't want to come to you for the rest of my life, asking for a dollar every time I need something.
Rational Spouse:	As much as I hate to learn about all of your gambling, at least now I have some facts and honest answers. I may not like it, but I can deal with reality, not with lies. It will take time, and proof, before I will trust you. Maybe I will never fully trust you again with money, but right now I am willing to work in that direction.

The therapist could then suggest a number of options for resolving financial difficulties. Gamblers Anonymous, for instance, has a financial pressure group for the gambler and spouse, during which all income and debts are budgeted and prioritized together. It is often helpful for the gambler in early stages of recovery to let the spouse or someone close actually handle the money and pay the bills, but with the full participation in the decision-making process and knowledge by the gambler of how the money is to be spent. Thus the therapist can help the gambler change irrational thinking ("She just wants the money. I can't stand being treated like a kid") to rational thinking ("For the time being, I will turn the money over to my wife. This will help her feel more secure, and I won't allow a pocket full of money to tempt me back to gambling").

Conclusion

Present research would suggest that a number of factors contribute to the development of pathological gambling. Family dynamics and emphasis on money, abuse, life stressors and traumas, exposure to gambling, and personality characteristics all play a role. While life events, stressors, and traumatic events cannot be changed or undone, certainly how one copes with these events and how one feels about oneself can be changed. Teaching gamblers or family members to identify and rid themselves of distorted thoughts and irrational beliefs leads to an improved sense of self-worth and improved coping skills. Once the clients have the tools for rational thinking, they no longer need to lead lives of silent pain and destruction. They can become masters of their thoughts and emotions. There is no further need to escape into dreams of fantasy and riches through compulsive gambling.

References

Adkins, B. (1988). Discharge planning with pathological gamblers: An ongoing process. *Journal of Gambling Behavior, 4*(3), 208-218.

American Psychiatric Association. (1987). *Diagnostic and statistical manual of mental disorders* (3rd ed., rev.). Washington, DC: American Psychiatric Association.

Bessell, H. A. (1984). *The love test.* New York: Morrow.

Braidfoot, L. (1988). Legalization of lotteries in the 1980s. *Journal of Gambling Behavior, 4*(4), 282-290.

Brown, R. I. F. (1987). Pathological gambling and associated patterns of crime: Comparisons with alcohol and other drug addictions. *Journal of Gambling Behavior, 3*(2), 98-114.

Browne, B. R. (1991). Selective adaptation of the Alcoholics Anonymous program by Gamblers Anonymous. *Journal of Gambling Studies, 7*(3), 187-206.

Burns, D. D. (1980). *Feeling good: The new mood therapy.* New York: Morrow.

Ciarrocchi, J., & Richardson, R. (1989). Profile of compulsive gamblers in treatment: Update and comparisons. *Journal of Gambling Behavior, 5*, 53-65.

Commission on the Review of the National Policy Toward Gambling. (1976). *Final report.* Washington, DC: Government Printing Office.

Custer, R. L., & Custer, L. F. (1978, December). *Characteristics of the recovering compulsive gambler: A survey of 150 members of Gamblers Anonymous.* Paper presented at the Fourth Annual Conference on Gambling, Reno, NV.

Custer, R. L., & Milt, H. (1984). *When luck runs out.* New York: Facts on File.

Darvas, S. (1985). *The spouse in treatment: Or, there is a woman behind every compulsive gambler.* Paper presented at the Fifth National Conference on Gambling and Risk Taking, Lake Tahoe, NV.

Ellis, A., & Harper, R. A. (1975). *A new guide to rational living.* North Hollywood, CA: Wilshire.

Ellis, A., & Knaus, W. J. (1977). *Overcoming procrastination.* New York: Institute for Rational Living.

Ellis, A., McInerney, J. F., DiGiuseppe, R., & Yeager, R. J. (1988). *Rational-emotive therapy with alcoholics and substance abusers.* Elmsford, NY: Pergamon.

Gaboury, A., & Ladouceur, R. (1987, August). *Irrational thinking and gambling.* Paper presented at the 7th International Conference on Gambling and Risk-Taking, University of Nevada/Reno.

Galski, T. (Ed.). (1985). *The handbook of pathological gambling.* Springfield, IL: Charles C Thomas.

Gamblers Anonymous. (1984). *Sharing recovery through Gamblers Anonymous.* Los Angeles: Gamblers Anonymous.

Heineman, M. (1987). A comparison: The treatment of wives of alcoholics with the treatment of wives of pathological gamblers. *Journal of Gambling Behavior, 3*(1), 27-40.

Heineman, M. (1989, Winter). Parents of male compulsive gamblers: Clinical issues/treatment approaches. *Journal of Gambling Behavior, 5*(4), 321-333.

Heineman, M. (1992). *Losing your shirt: Recovery for compulsive gamblers and their families.* Minneapolis, MN: CompCare.

Hudak, C., Varghese, R., & Politzer, R. (1989). Family, marital and occupational satisfaction for recovering pathological gamblers. *Journal of Gambling Behavior, 5*(3), 201-210.

Jacobs, D. F. (1986). A general theory of addictions: A new theoretical model. *Journal of Gambling Behavior, 2*(1), 15-31.

Jacobs, D. F. (1988). Evidence for a common dissociative-like reaction among addicts. *Journal of Gambling Behavior, 4*(1), 27-37.

Jacobs, D. F. (1989). Illegal and undocumented: A review of teenage gambling and the plight of children of problem gamblers in America. In H. Shaffer, S. Stein, B. Gambino, & T. Cummings (Eds.), *Compulsive gambling: Theory, research, practice* (pp.249-292). Lexington, MA: D. C. Heath.

Lesieur, H. R. (1984). *The chase: Career of the compulsive gambler.* Cambridge, MA: Schenkman.

Lesieur, H. R. (1988). The female pathological gambler. In W. R. Eadington (Ed.), *Gambling studies: Proceedings of the 7th International Conference on Gambling and Risk Taking* (pp. 230-258). Reno: University of Nevada, College of Business Administration, Bureau of Business and Economic Research.

Lesieur, H. R., Cross, J., Frank, M., Welch, M., White, C., Rubenstein, G., Moseley, K., & Mark, M. (1991, August). Gambling and pathological gambling among college students. *Addiction Behaviors and International Journal, 16,* 517-527.

Lesieur, H. R., & Heineman, M. (1988). Pathological gambling among youthful multiple substance abusers in a therapeutic community. *British Journal of Addictions, 83,* 765-771.

Lesieur, H. R., & Klein, R. (1987). Pathological gambling among high school students. *Addictive Behaviors, 12,* 129-135.

Lesieur, H. R., & Rosenthal, R. (1991). Pathological gambling: A review of the literature (Prepared for the American Psychiatric Association Task Force on DSM IV Committee on Disorder of Impulse Control Not Elsewhere Classified). *Journal of Gambling Studies, 7*(1), 5-39.

Livingston, J. (1974). *Compulsive gamblers: Observations on action and abstinence.* New York: Harper Torchbooks.

Lorenz, V. C. (1978). *Pathological gambling: Personality characteristics of the gambler, its impact on the family, and the effectiveness of GamAnon.* Unpublished master's thesis, The Pennsylvania State University, Middletown.

Lorenz, V. C. (1981, October). *Differences found among Catholic, Protestant and Jewish families of pathological gamblers.* Paper presented at the Fifth National Conference on Gambling and Risk Taking, Lake Tahoe, NV.

Lorenz, V. C. (1989a). Compulsive gambling and the expert witness. *Journal of Forensic Sciences, 34*(2), 423-432.

Lorenz, V. C. (1989b). *Releasing guilt.* Center City, MN: Hazelden Educational Materials.

Lorenz, V. C. (1989c). Some treatment approaches for family members who jeopardize the compulsive gambler's recovery. *Journal of Gambling Behavior, 5*(4), 303-312.

Lorenz, V. C. (1990a). *Overview of pathological gambling.* Baltimore, MD: National Center for Pathological Gambling.

Lorenz, V. C. (1990b). *Standing up to fear.* Center City, MN: Hazelden Educational Materials.

Lorenz, V. C. (1990c). Survey of Gamblers Anonymous members in Maryland. In Task Force on Gambling Addiction, *Final report* (pp. 90-111). Baltimore: Maryland Department of Health and Mental Hygiene, Alcohol and Drug Abuse Administration.

Lorenz, V. C. (1991). *Compulsive gambling hotline: Final report, FY91.* Baltimore, MD: National Center for Pathological Gambling.

Lorenz, V. C., & Shuttlesworth, D. E. (1983). The impact of pathological gambling on the spouse of the gambler. *Journal of Community Psychology, 11*(1), 67-76.

Lorenz, V. C., & Yaffee, R. A. (1986). Pathological gambling: Psychosomatic, emotional and marital difficulties as reported by the gambler. *Journal of Gambling Behavior, 2*(1), 40-49.

Lorenz, V. C., & Yaffee, R. A. (1988). Pathological gambling: Psychosomatic, emotional and marital difficulties as reported by the spouse. *Journal of Gambling Behavior, 4*(2), 13-26.

Lorenz, V. C., & Yaffee, R. A. (1989). Pathological gamblers and their spouses: Problems in interaction. *Journal of Gambling Behavior, 5*(2), 113-126.

Moravec, J. D., & Munley, P. H. (1983). Psychological test findings on pathological gamblers in treatment. *International Journal of the Addictions, 18,* 1003-1009.

Nakken, C. (1988). *The addictive personality.* Center City, MN: Hazelden Educational Materials.

Robertson, B. E. (1989). *Work addiction: Hidden legacies of adult children.* Deerfield Beach, FL: Health Communications.

Rosenthal, R. J. (1986). The pathological gambler's system for self-deception. *Journal of Gambling Behavior, 2*(2), 108-120.

Rosenthal, R. J., & Lorenz, V. C. (1992). *The pathological gambler as criminal offender: Comments on evaluation and treatment.* Philadelphia: W. B. Saunders.

Roy, A., Adinoff, B., Roehrich, L., Lamparski, D., Custer, R., Lorenz, V., Barbaccia, M., Guidotti, A., Costa, E., & Linnoila, M. (1988). Pathological gambling: A psychobiological study. *Archives of General Psychiatry, 45,* 369-373.

Shaffer, H., Stein, S., Gambino, B., & Cummings, T. (1989). *Compulsive gambling: Theory, research, practice.* Lexington, MA: D. C. Heath.

Sichel, J., & Ellis, A. (1984). *RET self-help form.* New York: Institute for Rational-Emotive Therapy.

Taber, J. I., & Boston, M. D. (1987, August). *Developmental vulnerability in the etiology of problem gambling and other addictions.* Paper presented at the 7th International Conference on Gambling and Risk-Taking, University of Nevada/Reno.

Taber, J. I., McCormick, R. A., & Ramirez, L. F. (1987). The prevalence and impact of major life stressors among pathological gamblers. *International Journal of the Addictions, 22*(1), 71-79.

Task Force on Gambling Addiction. (1990). *Final report.* Baltimore: Maryland Department of Health and Mental Hygiene, Alcohol and Drug Abuse Administration.

Trimpey, J. (1990). *Rational recovery from alcoholism: The small book.* Sacramento, CA: Lotus Press.

Volberg, R. A., & Steadman, H. J. (1988). Refining prevalence estimates of pathological gambling. *American Journal of Psychiatry, 146,* 1618-1619.

Yaffee, R. A. (1990). A profile of pathological gamblers in professional treatment programs. In Task Force on Gambling Addiction, *Final report* (pp. 154-191). Baltimore: Maryland Department of Health and Mental Hygiene, Alcohol and Drug Abuse Administration.

RET and Chronic Pain

BERTRAM H. ROTHSCHILD

Chronic pain is a phenomenon that staggers the imagination. Try to evoke a clear memory of the worst pain you have ever experienced. Then think of what life would be like if that pain persisted indefinitely, something to be experienced through your entire life with no hope of surcease. Unfortunately, that is the experience of tens of millions of people (Taylor & Curran, 1985).

Faced with that reality, the pale advice, "Learn to live with it," is both insufficient and incorrect. It is insufficient because it does not provide the training that is available for dealing with such pain. Worse, it is incorrect because it does not suggest an appropriate goal. Do not "learn to live with it." Rather, it is better to learn to enjoy life despite the pain, which is quite a different proposition in that it offers appropriate hope to those who struggle with the problem. This chapter offers information on how that goal might be accomplished using RET.

What Is Pain?

The topic of pain remains murky in that a satisfactory definition of pain has not been developed. Like obscenity, everyone knows the shock of encountering it, but it does not appear possible to establish a precise definition. There are, to be sure, words that can be used by the sufferer to describe the experience (Melzack, 1975), but there is no way independently to determine if someone else has it. What is it?

Understand that it is *not* synonymous with tissue damage and nerve conduction, though there is a close relationship between the two experiences. Nociception may provide a substrate for the experience, but it is not sufficient to produce what we call *pain.* Pain is a subjective experience usually, but not necessarily, associated with nociception (Gorsky, 1981).

It is well known that distraction has the effect of reducing the experience of pain. The more intense the distraction, the greater the reduction in experienced pain, even to the point where the individual becomes totally oblivious of any discomfort. Combat, football, or any experience that helps to refocus attention may be sufficient to accomplish this. Although distraction appears to be useful with low-intensity pain, it is not clearly useful with high-intensity pain (McCaul & Malott, 1984). Further, some research in cognition suggests that there is a rebound effect after efforts of focused distraction (Wegner & Schneider, 1989), so that it is possible that distraction may result in increased suffering.

It is well documented that some individuals experience pain in the absence of objective physical damage. Careful examination provides no clue to why the person should present with such "real" anguish. There may be mysteries of the body yet to be discovered that might account for such anomalous findings, but such a view goes against current understandings of how our bodies work. Depression may be the origin of a pain disorder (Blumer & Heilbronn, 1982), or it may only be a consequence of pain (Turk & Salovey, 1984). In any case, evidence suggests that antidepressants can significantly reduce pain (Clifford, 1985; Egbunike & Chaffee, 1990). Hysteria may (Merskey, 1965) or may not (Blumer & Heilbronn, 1982) be implicated. The idea that psychological state influences pain perception runs the gamut from dynamically oriented thinkers (Van Houdenhove, 1988) to psychophysiological theorists (Melzack & Wall, 1965).

Some years ago I fell and dislocated my elbow. I experienced no pain, including when it was being put back into place. Nevertheless, I was injected with Demerol and given 30 oxycodone tablets, the latter for anticipated pain. I was told it would "hurt like the devil," and I was not to try to be "brave." There was never any pain. A friendly physician came by and asked how I felt. "I feel no pain," I answered. "Of course not," he responded, "you just got a shot of Demerol." Why I did not experience pain surpasses my understanding. The curious thing was that the physicians refused to believe me. Based on their understanding of nociception, I should have been in pain throughout the event and for at least several days afterwards.

Still lacking a precise definition, I offer the following: *Pain is the individual's perception of an unpleasant state of the body that tends to motivate the person to reduce/eliminate it.* Granted, this definition is still vague: It does, however, focus our attention on the perception of the event, a psychological phenomenon.

Acute Pain

Acute pain comes as a result of some physical damage. If the sufferer acts appropriately (rests, gets treated, restricts use of the painful part), the pain goes away. The physician may prescribe medicines, including narcotics and/or bed rest. The important point is that, after a while, the pain is gone.

We generally learn that pain is good for us. It is a built-in system of warning that the body is being damaged and that some change is immediately necessary to keep the damage from becoming permanent. Without such a warning system, we could not have survived either as individuals or as a species (Pennebaker, 1982). Some individuals are born without the ability to feel pain. They need persistent observation and protection as children and as adults must be constantly vigilant to avoid unwitting body damage. One such young woman received severe burns because she rested her arm on a steam radiator. She had broken her bones many times without knowing it, and she finally died because of persistent infections of which she was unaware.

On a personal level, you might find it interesting to note how frequently acute pain touches you in daily life. Identify a time when you experienced pain. Now imagine the consequences of continuing the associated activity by ignoring how much it hurts. Up to a point, strength may be increased, but damage will eventually ensue. Even scratching an itch can become serious at some point.

As I sit and type this, minor pains suggest that I move my body to a more comfortable (pain free) position. But, alas, it will remain comfortable for only a short period, and I will again shift to another more comfortable position. The process, when not interrupted, is automatic. We rarely think of ourselves as in pain unless there is some constraint that forces us to remain in just the one position. Unless we move, our skin begins to break down and decubiti, commonly known as bed sores, appear. Upon closer inspection it becomes clear that pain is a daily friend that helps prevent damage to the body.

Chronic Pain

But what if the pain does not go away? What if the pain persists well beyond its body-protecting function and nothing can be done to eliminate it? Physician after physician is visited, and perhaps healers of different kinds as well. Yet the response remains and, after all their efforts, nothing can be done to eliminate the pain.

Chronic pain is different from acute pain; if the pain (more accurately, pain complaints) persists for three months (Merskey, 1986) after appropriate treatments have been tried, chronic pain is diagnosed. Ideally, the chronic pain then becomes the focus of interventions, and the futile effort to eliminate the cause is ended. Complexities arise, however, because not all chronic pain sufferers are the same.

There are, first, patients who have identifiable damage to a part of their body appropriate to the pain. Examination provides evidence that something is wrong but beyond our power to correct.

Then there are those who have such damage, but it is not commensurate with the level of their pain complaints. The physician may comment that the amount of degenerative joint disease should produce only some minor complaints but not the anguish presented.

Still others have no identifiable damage but still complain of persistent, significant pain in such a way as to convince the observer that real damage has occurred.

There is, finally, pain that is purely psychological in nature. Some patients complain in such manner that it is almost certain that nothing is wrong physically, yet they are often in great discomfort. The complaints are vague and diffuse, as if the entire body is in pain. Such patients are most likely depressed, as pain is a common complaint associated with that problem. Such individuals are most appropriately treated for their depression.

Reinforcement

It is obvious that malingering may become a crucial issue in some settings because of the secondary gain when the pain does not go away. Such reinforcers serve as reasons to struggle against giving up the pain (Fordyce, 1976). As a chronic pain patient stated with a burst of insight during a discussion of such reinforcers: "Wait a minute, you mean if my pain goes away I have to get a job? Forget it! I haven't worked in 11 years. What could I do?" From his point of view, and perhaps accurately, the loss of his pain would produce even more intense hardship than he currently suffered. For those 11 years he had been unaware that he needed his pain to preserve his life-style; the result was failed treatment. If he could have at least learned not to complain, his life might have been somewhat better, but he persisted in thinking that complaining validated his experience.

Some people regard their pain as protecting them from further damage. A patient, upon noticing that his pain was slight or totally gone, would purposely stress that part of his body to make sure the pain was really there. He was frightened that, without the pain, he might do something too strenuous and worsen the damage that was already there. His justification was that as long as he had the pain, he could know when to rest. A variation of this theme is the patient who becomes convinced that experiencing pain provides evidence that nothing worse is going on.

For some patients, the development of a "sick role" is a pathway to what they consider to be an improvement in their social relationships (Gallagher & Wrobel, 1982). Loving and caring people provide services that were never provided before. Less and less is expected of the sufferer, who then becomes more demanding as the process spirals downward. It is an insidious process because there is no doubt that injured loved ones do require our care until they recover. But if there is no recovery and the process of invalidism develops, the helper is expected to devote more time and energy to serve the needs of the patient, who, gradually, becomes sensitized to any withdrawal of care. Getting people better means expecting them to do more for themselves, which may produce much household anguish. The patient may complain bitterly of being unable to do any more and may accuse the spouse of not caring. Actually, caring behavior often means some withdrawal of overt assistance so that the sufferer can develop a greater capacity to be independent.

Another, and more insidious, reinforcement involves escalating the use of chemicals. This problem is sometimes created by physicians in their attempt to reduce the pain, but it may also occur when the patient drinks or uses street drugs to reduce the pain. Curiously, when drugs are used under appropriate supervision the likelihood of escalation because of increased tolerance is small. Still, narcotics are powerful reinforcers and the patient must be carefully monitored when they are used (Friedman, 1990; Melzack, 1990).

Levels of Pain

A standard procedure is to have the patient rate the level of the pain experience on a 10-point scale, with 10 being the worst pain imaginable. If the pain barely enters consciousness, it can easily be either ignored or eliminated by an over-the-counter medicine. Perhaps you move a bit more slowly because of it. Sometimes you might even use a heating pad to give yourself some relief. It is there, but you can enjoy life in spite of it. It is no more than a 3 on the scale.

Suppose it goes up to a 5 or 6. Now it is more intrusive. You get a sense of great discomfort. Still, you can get your work done and take care of household chores. People have great sympathy for you but, because you look healthy, they may feel irritated that you move a bit more slowly and retard their progress toward a common goal. Perhaps your spouse, noticing that he or she is doing more of the work around the house, begins to wonder how much you really hurt. You look so damned comfortable sitting and reading. Does it really hurt so much that you can't wash the dishes? Feeling guilty, you push yourself to do more of the chores, only to discover that you experience increased pain and later can do less than before. Life seems to revolve around the experience.

Now consider an intensity in the 7-to-10 range, a level that is tough to accept. There is no longer an issue of your ability to do much; you are held in a vise that keeps you almost immobile; if you move, it is very slowly and with grimaces and sometimes curses. It is hard not to be irritable at interruptions when you devote your being just to moving from here to there. You may still look healthy in repose, however, and a question lingers in the minds of well-wishers and loved ones about your real pain, particularly because there are times when you can do more. Under such circumstances, for example, men have built their own homes by working two or three hours per day over a period of years. If you watch them working, you might be enraged that they can do so much. Why are they not employed? If they can build a house, their pain just isn't that bad! What you don't see is how much pain they are in during those few hours of labor, nor how much they suffer for the rest of the day. That they can do work is not an issue; they are not employable because they are unreliable. They can sometimes work a full day, at other times only a few hours, and at other times not at all. There are few employers who could tolerate such uncertainty.

At this level of pain, and perhaps earlier, you have probably been to several physicians. Tests have been done and the final statement is: "I'm sorry. I don't know why you have all that pain, and I don't know what to do about it. There are limits to medical science. Learn to live with it." What a staggering message—one that is usually followed by a sense of great outrage. You have gone to physicians in a reasonable attempt to care for your body, and you are told that they also are helpless. Your body has failed you, as have the physicians, and you are left with the awareness that you are stuck, mired in a never-ending struggle to find some comfort in life. You are in touch with chaos.

Pretty bad? There's more if your income depends on your ability to use your body. If you ordinarily work at sedentary occupations, you might still be able to do so, though with some difficulty. If you need to move your body, lift things, push things, change positions, and the like, your problems are only just starting. Economic disaster may be your fate. If you have been a homemaker, with such responsibilities as running the household, taking care of the children, shopping, cooking, and doing laundry, your ability to carry on these activities is almost gone. Just getting out of bed is miserable and only the strictly necessary things are accomplished. Employees may at least have the potential to change their way of earning a living, but if homemakers can't do the job, it just doesn't get done. Again, uncomprehending observers may be secretly wondering if some of it isn't put on.

So far I have discussed the consequences of chronic pain somewhat narrowly. While such consequences are not absolutely inevitable, they remain a grim potential for the unwary and tend to test the strength of all relationships. Many individuals transcend such problems, not only learning to live with them but rediscovering that pleasure in life is still available despite the losses.

Chronic Pain Syndrome

It is important to understand that whatever final knowledge we may come to about the pathophysiology of pain, Chronic Pain Syndrome (CPS) is a purely psychological phenomenon. Many people with chronic pain remain fairly stable and successfully readjust their lives. Others are treated successfully by their physicians. Many others' lives deteriorate, however, as they find less pleasure in life and become more demanding in seeking treatment from their physicians (Black, 1975; Chapman, 1977; Rothschild & Storaasli, 1990; Sanders, 1985).

In a word, they *suffer*, which produces psychological changes that alter almost every aspect of their lives. These changes are not inevitable. When they do occur, however, it is as if the sufferer has become an alien separated from all others in the universe, angrily yearning for identification with the rest of humanity while remaining in forced isolation. Everyone else seems to be free to exist fully; the sufferer enviously assumes that others are happy and no longer have any time for or interest in him or her. Minority status is discovered. "How can they possibly like me now that I am like this?" Perhaps having learned even in childhood that the physically disabled are "lesser human beings" and only to be tolerated, that lesson is turned against one's self. "I must be no good. That's why people shun me. I hate it, but I understand, because I have become useless and deserve to be shunned."

Adding to the isolation is the dismal reality that looking healthy can further destroy relationships. Imagine living on a meager social security income, watching every penny, and then struggling to keep up your morale when a new friend asks why you don't work. "I have chronic pain," you explain. "Work is impossible for me. I can do some things, but I can't be reliable because sometimes I just can't move." "Gee, that's a shame," responds your friend. "You look so healthy. Are you sure?" The temptation is great to groan and complain in exaggerated ways. Rather than be rejected, it is far better to overstate the problems so that people will take you seriously. This attempt to protect relationships may become a habit that the sufferer comes to believe is necessary, which brings further isolation from general society. The sad truth is that increased complaining results in fewer relationships.

CPS problems are compounded by using alcohol or short-acting narcotics to relieve the pain experience. Narcotics, which are so useful in reducing acute pain, are often a disaster for the CPS patient. There is a natural sequence of events in which tolerance for the substance goes up, so that the person needs more of the chemical to produce the same effect. The pain experience is reinforced by the pleasure of the substance experience, which produces an oceanic sense of well-being. The consequence is an increased focus on the pain and a lowering of tolerance for its experience.

Further, such short-acting narcotics as oxycodone peak in about 90 minutes. There is some relief (more likely psychological) for a short period of time and then discomfort begins to accelerate, not only because of the reduced amount of the drug but because of withdrawal effects. Thus the experience becomes worse and the patient has a tendency to take the next dose somewhat earlier than prescribed. As this process continues, the patient increases demands for more medication, insisting that life would be normal with just a slightly larger dose. With further increases in the dosage, other effects of the narcotics become more noticeable. The patient becomes incapable of doing anything in this drug-induced semistuporous state other than to feel terrible.

Why RET?

RET, by promoting a general philosophy of life (Ellis, 1962, 1977; Ellis & Dryden, 1987), is perhaps the only therapeutic system that directly tackles our confrontation with reality. It is obvious that reality, ubiquitous and indifferent to our desires, is at the core of the development of our psychological experience. We are always faced with the truth that we have little or no control over the events around us—even with enormous expenditures of energy. We are as likely to fail as the ancient English king who commanded the tide to stop. We tend to be preoccupied with our demands that reality change to serve our preferences. If you are not aware of this, consider your behavior in a traffic jam, or note how much effort you expend to get your loved ones to alter their behavior. Punishment of others always has a pedagogical intent: This will teach you a lesson, you uncooperative (wife, child, etc.). How we confront reality is the essence of our lives.

The ancient Stoics (Dennett, 1984) understood this quite well. Imagine a dog tied to the end of a carriage that goes according to the dictates of the driver, the dog having no choice in the matter. Perhaps the road is dusty and filled with stones; perhaps the wagon crosses streams and drags the dog through them. The dog must follow, either barking and whimpering or with grace and dignity. That is the freedom we all have, the freedom to choose our response. Epictetus (A.D. 78/1955) has argued that the only things we should be concerned with are the things we have control over. Those being our inner experiences, there is clear evidence that detaching ourselves from pain reduces the experience (Pennebaker, 1982; Kabat-Zinn, Lipworth, & Barney, 1985).

Irrational Beliefs

It is curious that, while human beings perceive themselves to be in contact with reality and as learning from it, an examination of human behavior suggests quite the opposite. We don't often understand the source of either our behaviors or our emotions and, when things go wrong, hold rigidly onto our beliefs while blaming external events for the problem. Even when those beliefs cause us extreme distress, we may desperately clutch them to us and strongly defend their validity in the face of objective evidence that things are getting worse.

There are a number of important irrational beliefs (iBs) that transform a person with chronic pain into someone with CPS.

Ciccone and Grzesiak (1990) have discussed four iBs often associated with chronic pain: awfulizing, demandingness, lowered self-worth, and externalizing. Such ideas certainly contribute to the problem, but the issue seems more complicated than that. Consider the following seven irrational beliefs regarding chronic pain.

1. I Must Feel Good All the Time. It is important to reflect on the reality that we all behave in accordance with a conception of what is best for us. Socrates noted that no person errs willingly. There may be objections based on the idea that people willingly do bad things, but such arguments miss the point. If someone attacks another, it is instructive to question the purpose. In such cases the malefactor did in fact have a reason that *at the time* was sufficient to justify the attack. At the moment of the act, there was a purpose to be accomplished that was believed to be in the best interests of the person acting.

An unthinking perspective tells us that feeling good is best for us. Anything that interferes with that experience is to be avoided. Certainly much of the motivation for substance abuse is based in that irrationality. While most of us do not take it that far, we nevertheless exaggerate its importance. The general population overeats, smokes cigarettes, and avoids exercise in a vain attempt to feel good or to avoid feeling bad. Pain avoidance is taught to us by our parents and by a society that rushes to provide a multitude of remedies for feeling bad. If we look around us, however, there are numerous examples of the wonders that can be performed when there is a willingness to accept pain. We see people with strong bodies, who are well-educated and productive and who constantly experience pain. We could learn from the lesson they provide us if we refused to believe that pain must be avoided and we must feel good.

The experience of persistent pain is a crushing blow to many people, particularly those who see pain as violating a basic law of the universe: They believe that pain is evil and must be eliminated. At best, they are perplexed; at worst, they are outraged that the universe should have done them such wrong. With righteous indignation they see themselves as "entitled" to special consideration from the rest of humanity.

This irrational belief can be challenged by helping the individual to look realistically at the nature of the human experience and to relinquish the Garden of Eden myth that we were created to exist in a benign universe in which pain was never part of the bargain. It is much better to think of ourselves as problem-solving human beings capable of accepting and dealing with things as they are, rather than whining about life not being to our liking.

In addition to disputing the iB that the person must feel good all the time, it is extremely useful to give homework that requires that the patient experience some increased pain while performing a task that has some meaning to him or her. The discussion centers around weighing the relative merits of feeling good as opposed to getting something accomplished. When the patient accomplishes the task, more painful homework can be given while continuing to challenge the iB that feeling good all the time is an appropriate way to organize one's life. Getting initial compliance is the hardest part of the therapeutic task, but once the patient performs some task that increases his or her pain, it becomes simpler after that.

2. The Pain Is the Most Important Thing in My Life. As noted above, we live in a society that emphasizes pain avoidance. A quick examination of the shelves in any drugstore will reveal how much space is devoted to remedies for discomfort: Slight differences are emphasized in each category, so that each kind of pain has its own remedy. Even such ailments as the common cold must be assaulted because the discomfort is too important to ignore. Our major sources of entertainment (perhaps a bit less now than in the past) show how tension can be reduced by a cigarette or a quick drink. For many, then, it is no surprise that pain becomes the only "proper" focus in their lives. It seems obvious to the patient that nothing else is worth talking about; only the pain is important.

It can be of great value to teach the sufferer to put the pain into proper perspective by examining the significance of the pain in the overall context of the person's life. For example, the following self-talk provides a simple way to deal with ordinary pains, such as headaches, that is likely to work for anyone. "There are more important issues in my life than the discomfort I'm experiencing, so I had better focus on them. The pain is unimportant." This self-talk formula can be used again and again.

If this example seems trivial, perhaps the following anecdote might be more convincing. Initially, the pain patient either remained in his home or came to the hospital for physical therapy.

The pain was reported to be too great to allow other activities. As he learned that the experience of pain was not that important, he began to ride his motorcycle again, got married, and even did a parachute jump. Afterward, the pain was so great that he was forced to stay in bed for a few days, but, as he put it, "I've always wanted to parachute. It was worth it."

A useful technique is to discuss the variety of things the patient values, and then ask which of them he or she would be willing to give up in service of getting rid of the pain. If the iB is correct, that the pain is the most important thing in the patient's life, it would follow that loved ones would be discarded to get relief from the pain, but few are willing to make that trade-off. Once the patient understands that there are more important things than pain, the therapist insists that he or she focus on them. As that process moves along, the patient's insistence that the pain be the focus of the patient's life diminishes.

3. I Must Never Be Thwarted. Much of what we observe in adult behavior is nothing more than the socialized demandingness of children who will brook no interference with their desires. A child lies screaming in the supermarket as if being tortured by red-hot pincers, its howls piercing the ears of the customers, with a distraught and terrified mother hovering nearby. What's wrong? A cookie was requested and denied.

Low frustration tolerance is a function of the internal statement: "If I want something, I must have it immediately and with no discomfort on my part. If I am denied, the world is a horrible place, and you are a total wretch for not cooperating." The CPS patient says: "If I want the pain to be gone, it must be gone immediately and totally. If not, the world is a horrible place, and you are a total wretch for not cooperating." Further, like the child screaming, there are no compromises. The pain must be totally removed; nothing else is permitted. Such a belief permits bursts of emotion. Rage, crying, and desperation are all in the response repertoire of the sufferer who does not see that refusing to give up his or her desperate attempt to control only leads to worse anguish.

By focusing on the demand for relief, the patient remains fixed on the pain. It is by far wiser for the patient to focus on the remaining possibilities in life, the kinds of activities that can provide interest and pleasure. Patients learn that by accepting the pain, by not endlessly demanding that it be taken away, they become free to find other ways of self-expression.

It is extremely important to insist to the patient that the good life does not depend on getting desires gratified, and to get the patient to accept the reality that one is not a god whose every wish is gratified. The patient is given homework that will lead to frustration, that is, asking strangers for $100 and rejecting anything less. The discussion then deals with how the patient's life is only marginally affected by the disappointment.

4. *I Must Never Be Helpless.* Perhaps the most extraordinary belief that we humans have is that we can run our lives so as to minimize the degree to which we are helpless. We have a powerful sense that if we are the right kind of person and if we act correctly, we will have control over the events around us. We take special pains around life-threatening situations, of course, but the conceit goes further than this. Much of our covert daily planning is designed to keep us in control of all events around us, particularly the behavior of other people.

We have noted that human beings tend not to be as closely in contact with reality as they fancy. The general belief that we can be in control of the behavior of other human beings seems ubiquitous to all cultures, and it clearly persists in the face of significant disconfirming evidence. Reflect for a moment on the sense of frustration you experience when others do not follow your dicta and how frequently you become emotional when faced with that reality. Examine how you attempt to resolve the situation. Most people don't calmly say: "OK, if that's what you want to do. I don't like it, but you have your right to run your life the way you choose." Instead, we upset ourselves and angrily struggle against the other person's wishes, *knowing* he or she is wrong and hating the reality of our helplessness. Suppose the other person acquiesces and goes along with your game. Have you then disproved your helplessness? Not at all. You have deluded yourself by concluding, because the other person has changed behavior to suit you, that you have caused it. The other person has chosen your desired behavior for *his or her* own reasons. In reality you have expressed your desire and described or demonstrated the consequences of not getting your way: emotionalism, aloofness, rejection, violence, or withdrawal of reinforcers. You have the freedom to react in any way you choose to the other person's behavior, but that person also has the right to ignore you, regardless of the consequences.

We tend to invent ways to deny the reality of helplessness when faced with extreme circumstances. Consider how men deal with the experience of combat, an activity that gets as close to chaos and helplessness as possible. Remaining in combat violates basic rules about staying alive and unmaimed, yet men do so. To a large extent, this is possible because they delude themselves about the nature of reality by developing fantasies in which they are invulnerable. Men in combat often come to believe that (a) they can read the enemy's mind, (b) they are so competent that nothing bad can happen to them, (c) their bodies become shielded in some mysterious way, (d) they are dead, so nothing worse can happen to them, or (e) carrying magic talismans will ward off danger. The ancient Greeks hallucinated the gods fighting on their side. What better antidote to fearful reality than that?

The frustrations of life can become so great that we prefer not to accept them but invent beliefs about personal control as a way of avoiding their reality. We cringe when proven wrong, which is often what happens in CPS. Many of us are aware that the aging process brings with it a certain amount of decrepitude, though most of us don't examine the possibilities too closely. Still, when things go wrong and the physician explains that it is the "aging process," we seem to derive some comfort from that understanding. Such things, even though unpleasant, are going the way we expect them to go.

When severe pain becomes part of our daily lives, especially before we think it appropriate, the situation is quite different. We have to face our helplessness but resent it mightily. Even worse, we confront our physician's helplessness. After visits to experts of every kind, we are finally told that nothing can be done to ameliorate the pain. Not only are we helpless, but the people we depend on are also helpless. There is literally nothing to do except to face life with the knowledge of unremitting pain.

This an outrageous situation for many individuals, and they rage against the health-provider's "incompetence." Some, in their attempt to avoid helplessness, *discover* that their physician (or the hospital, or the system) has it in for them and will not "fix" them. By maintaining that belief, at least something *could* be done; it is just a matter of persuading the doctor. Others rail against the universe with their complaints of "Why me?" Such a response to the reality of their lives only serves to make their lives worse.

The most useful therapeutic intervention is to point out our ultimate helplessness in all things, especially that we will, in spite of our best efforts, all die. That being the reality, it is far better to focus on how to have inner control rather than decry the reality that events occur without our permission.

5. I Shouldn't Be in Pain. The notion that we shouldn't be in chronic pain is another example of how we manage to remain remote from reality. The ancient Stoics understood quite well that what is, should be. For any individual to take seriously the notion that he or she should not be in pain flies against all logic, yet it is a common phenomenon in CPS. A variation of this is the belief that the doctor should know what is wrong and should be able to fix it. Patients are astonished when it is pointed out to them that they "should" have the pain and that the doctor "shouldn't" know what is wrong. Most people misunderstand this notion of "should," thinking of it as a command rather than a state of being.

People should be in pain if that is the state of their body. Doctors should not know how to help and should not know the cause of the problem if that is the current state of medicine. To argue otherwise is analogous to insisting that pigs should fly because one wants them to fly, and then to complain over the self-evident reality that they do not fly. Faced with the helplessness of their situation, individuals may insist that it should not be so but, in the process, rediscover how helpless they are and cycle into tighter coils of misery.

The therapist insists on the *shouldness* of the pain, that things are as they are, insisting that the patient's demand that he or she should not be in pain is a delusion that keeps him or her in more misery than the pain itself. As the patient accepts this reality, he or she realizes that the pain is only bad luck rather than a major dislocation in the nature of reality.

6. I Can Never Be Happy With This Pain. Approximately 2,000 years ago, Epictetus (1955) pointed out that we do not own our bodies and that, while all sorts of bad things can happen to them, we can learn to accept such misfortunes by focusing on that which is in our control—our inner selves. While the Stoics were not concerned with being in a state of happiness, it is clear that they would accept the notion that happiness is largely self-created and that there are not many conditions that mitigate against it. This is such a counterintuitive idea that it is perhaps the most difficult of the irrational ideas to combat.

The CPS sufferer who believes that unhappiness is caused by the pain itself produces a profound sense of loss of something that can never be regained. The reality is that happiness is a by-product of active lives, in which we tackle projects and work hard at them without concerning ourselves greatly with the attendant frustrations. Another way to say this is that we are more effective when involved with the process of our lives more than our goals.

The patient keeps demanding: "How can I be happy with this pain?" The therapist responds: "How can you not be happy, even with the pain?" It is important for the patient to understand that happiness is neither a function of external events nor is it ratable. The therapist listens for descriptions of pleasurable experiences and then helps the patient understand how much of the experience was internally generated. This becomes a model for creating happiness in other kinds of situations. It is important that the therapist be alert for the range of iBs not related to pain that can produce emotional distress. Unless these are dealt with, the patient will continue to feel miserable and continue, incorrectly, to assert that it is the pain.

7. It Is Awful to Have to Change My Life-Style. Many people with chronic pain have no choice but to change their life-style, especially if their income is reduced to the point that they become poor. Those who are already poor complain bitterly about thwarted chances to gain economic success. In a society in which the good life is identified with doing more, doing better, and never sliding back, the self-induced consequences of a forced reduction in lifestyle can be devastating. Regardless of the reason for an economic loss, many individuals become so helpless as to be incapable of reorganizing their lives around diminished resources. If we have learned early in life to hold economic failures in contempt, we may develop contempt for ourselves for being in the "awful" situation. As long as the situation does not change, emotional suffering seems a natural outcome.

Obviously there is no point in trying to do therapy with someone whose economic life is unstable. Given an economically stable (though now much poorer) patient, the therapist demands proof that poverty directly causes emotional misery. Further, the therapist challenges the notion that poor people are to be held in contempt because of their poverty. The patient learns to accept limited resources as a challenge rather than a blight and accepts him- or herself in spite of reduced circumstances.

Therapeutic Issues

Resistance to the Mental Health Approach

CPS patients are often astonished when they are referred to a mental health expert. They experience the pain in their bodies and resent any hint that it is all in their heads. While they are not told this directly, they quickly get the message that there is something psychologically awry with them, especially when there are limited objective findings to account for their pain. A major part of the therapist's responsibility is to help the patient understand that there are significant things to be accomplished by a therapeutic collaboration.

Patients are often frightened that their pain will be called "psychological," which they interpret as meaning that it is not real. It Is important to accept overtly that the pain is real and that it is indeed located where it is felt. The purpose of psychotherapy is to help CPS patients reorganize their lives around the reality that nothing much can be done directly to reduce or eliminate the pain while expanding their perspective such that life values transcend the pain experience. It is around such issues that the philosophical concerns of RET can have great impact. Successful outcomes depend on very small shifts in the above iBs, but it is a major task to get the individual to accept the notion that treatment needs to focus less on pain than on beliefs about life.

Relevance of Psychotherapy

Another treatment challenge involves the idea many clients have that psychotherapy is trivial to the task at hand, that it is only a minor palliative offered because all else has failed. There is, of course, some truth to the complaint. It is obvious that the preference would be to get rid of the pain. In the absence of that possibility, the notion that one might reorganize one's mental life to attain some degree of comfort makes therapy much less trivial. Nevertheless, most CPS patients have little understanding that much of their misery is self-inflicted in the form of their thoughts about the pain. Therapy does not offer the promise that the pain will go away, but it suggests that life can be better. In this manner, therapy provides a reasonable goal that most CPS patients can understand and accept, even though it seems paradoxical to become involved in the process of their thinking instead of the pain itself.

Well-Meaning Physicians

It is important to keep in mind that the CPS patient properly maintains a relationship with a physician who does want to help. A problem arises when the physician also believes that the pain itself is the major cause of the patient's unhappiness. Such physicians sense that telling patients simply to live with the pain is akin to asking their patients to accept something so awful that they doubt they could handle it themselves. Such physicians tend not to give up but to continue medication and to consult with surgeons in an attempt to find a solution for the patient. Unfortunately, such well-meaning efforts interfere with the therapy process because they offer hope that the situation can be changed. The data on pain reduction from multiple back surgery are clear. By the time of the fourth surgery, the chances are remote that any significant change will occur. Still, some surgeon can be found who is willing to take the chance. It is also well known that amputation of painful limbs may result in such complications as stump problems and phantom pain, which simply replace the original pain.

Therapy can be enhanced by developing a working relationship with the physician, so that the purposes of therapy are understood. This is not to say that new medical interventions should not be tried if they seem plausible. Such treatments are best presented to the patient with the understanding and knowledge of the therapist so that important therapy issues can be dealt with in advance.

Realistic Consequences

There are some consequences to developing chronic pain. There is an increased probability of economic dislocation and consequent lower standard of living. There may be a loss of a number of pleasurable behaviors, along with a reshuffling of social contacts. It is often not easy to get patients to focus attention on more productive areas. Treatment strategies are designed to help patients accept the limitations imparted by their pain so that they can make the best of what they can do.

Treatment Strategies

The use of RET with CPS patients follows the usual procedures of identifying and disputing irrational beliefs and replacing them with more effective rational ideas. There are certain problems in working with CPS patients, however, that call for special attention.

A major endeavor in working with CPS patients is to help them transform their identification of the problem as being an external event (the pain) to identifying it as an internal event (beliefs). It must be clearly established, before psychotherapy is considered, that there are no solutions to eliminating the pain. It is also essential to help the patient understand that life has not now become a matter of "hanging in there," which invokes an image of the sufferer hanging on the edge of a cliff, fingernails desperately dug in to keep from slipping to doom. Patients must be relieved of the notion that the physicians can stop the pain but refuse to do so. Altering these three beliefs provides a foundation for a sound RET treatment approach.

In beginning treatment, it is important to accept that the pain is real and located where the patient says it is. It is helpful as well to identify problems that have existed separate from the pain. A poor work history before the pain started not only will not be resolved by pain-focused treatment but might complicate such treatment by providing a powerful secondary gain to not getting better.

At a very early stage it is important to introduce the notion that chronic pain not only has psychological consequences but that these consequences actually *add to the experience of pain,* so that eventually it becomes difficult to distinguish between physical and emotional pain. While the pain itself cannot be taken away, the psychological consequences can be altered so that the pain becomes less intrusive and the person can move in new directions. Little can be accomplished until the patient accepts this notion. Consider the following example.

Patient: I don't get it. My pain hurts. Of course I feel lousy because of the pain. If there were no pain, I'd feel great.

Therapist: Can you see the difference between you now, with depression and anger, and a you, still with pain but calmer and friendlier?

P: Yeah. My wife would sure like that.

T: How about you? A calmer and more relaxed you, still in pain, but just feeling better.

P: That makes sense, but how can I do that? The pain will always be there.

T: Probably, but what happens is that your upsetness makes the pain feel worse. Don't you feel even worse when you are depressed about what's happened to you?

P: Yes.

T: If we can help you reduce your emotional reaction to the pain, you'd be better off, right?

P: Yes.

T: OK, then. Let's work on how you can reduce your emotions that get out of hand, because anything we do that can help you feel better will be all to the good.

P: Yeah.

The patient, now accepting that it makes sense to work on the problem, may still believe that not much can be done about his or her emotional responses because they are "natural" consequences of the pain.

Therapist: Suppose you were the sort of person who loved pain. Do you think that you would be depressed and angry? Not at all.

Patient: That would be crazy.

T: Perhaps, but the point is that different people could have different reactions to the pain. Reactions to it seem to be in the person, not the pain.

P: Well, I see your point, but I'm the kind of person who hates pain.

T: Sure, but that might be the problem. Perhaps you get so busy hating whenever you notice it that you inadvertently produce the emotional discomfort.

Case Study

Charlie had been coming to the hospital for whirlpool treatments twice a week for two years. Otherwise, he remained in his darkened apartment, living on his pension and decrying his fate. An automobile accident had left him with a damaged back and such chronic pain that he had to give up any employment. Before the accident he had worked in construction. He had moved around the country and lived a fairly boisterous and robust life. No longer being the "man he used to be," he preferred to remain isolated from others.

Patient: God damn it! How can I enjoy life with this Goddamned pain?
Therapist: Is the pain that stops you or is it that you think that you can't be happy because of it?
P: Hell, I can't even get out of the house.
T: Nonsense. You get out of the house twice a week for whirlpool treatments because they seem worth it to you. Your problem is that you keep talking yourself into misery rather than getting out and doing things.
P: That's different.
T: No way. Getting out is getting out. In one case, you talk yourself into it in spite of the pain. In the other case, you talk yourself out of it, not because of the pain, but because you talk yourself out of it.

Charlie gradually accepted the idea that his attitude about happiness was a major problem for him but, seeing where that would lead, he switched to the following stance:

Patient: I shouldn't have this pain, I'm a decent guy and there is no reason for it. I shouldn't have it.
Therapist: That's a crazy idea. We know that you do have it. To say that you shouldn't have it only gets you to focus on its permanence and then you feel even worse.
P: That's true. Once I get myself worked up, I really feel lousy. It's like there's nothing left for me.
T: Sure, because all you do is wind up focusing on how you shouldn't have it. The truth is, given the state of your body, you should have the pain. It's not nice, but that's the reality of it. Once you accept the reality, you can give up your fight against it and focus on other things. What would you prefer to do?
P: Go drinking like in the old days.

T: So?
P: Yeah, I guess I could do that.
T: You're guessing?
P: Ok, damn it. I'll go.

Treatment proceeded in this vein for several more sessions. Then the patient missed a session because his pain overwhelmed him. To my surprise, he was cheerful at the following session.

Patient: You'll never believe what I did.
Therapist: Oh?
P: I always wanted to go skydiving, so after our last session I did it. What a thrill. Of course the landing put me in bed for a few days, that's why I missed last week, but it was worth it.

After a few more sessions, the patient stated that he would be visiting relatives in another state. The next session was about three months later.

Patient: Wild trip, I went down on my motorcycle, had a ball with my relatives and then came back with two women on my motorcycle. After a few weeks, one of them went back and it looks like I'm marrying the other one.
Therapist: Pain?
P: Sure. Hurts like a son-of-a-bitch, but what the hell, that's not the most important thing in the world.

This truncated description of what happened with Charlie is not atypical of others, though perhaps a bit more dramatic in outcome. It was the philosophical change that made the difference in his life.

Afterword

It should be obvious that the chronic pain sufferer is no different from the rest of us. The RET credo is as appropriate for them as for the rest of humanity. We all have to struggle with the truth that the universe does not give a damn. In reality, we can always make the best of our bad situations. As Epictetus (1955) said to a man who wished to understand his maladaptive behavior: "Come, study philosophy."

References

Black, R. G. (1975). The chronic pain syndrome. *Surgical Clinics of North America, 55*, 999-1011.

Blumer, D., & Heilbronn, M. (1982). Chronic pain as a variant of depressive disease: The pain-prone disorder. *Journal of Nervous and Mental Disorders, 170*, 381-406.

Clifford, D. B. (1985). Treatment of pain with antidepressants. *American Famlily Physician, 31*, 181-185.

Chapman, C. R. (1977). Psychological aspects of pain patient treatment. *Archives of Surgery, 112*, 767-772.

Ciccone, D. S., & Grzesiak, R. C. (1990). Chronic musculoskeletal pain: A cognitive approach to psychophysiologic assessment and intervention. *Advances in Clinical Rehabilitation, 3*, 197-231.

Dennett, D. C. (1981). *Elbow room.* Cambridge: MIT Press.

Egbunike, I. G., & Chaffee, B. J. (1990). Antidepressants in the management of chronic pain syndromes. *Pharmacotherapy, 10*, 262-270.

Ellis, A. (1962). *Reason and emotion in psychotherapy.* New York: Lyle Stuart.

Ellis, A. (1977). The basic clinical theory of rational-emotive therapy. In A. Ellis & R. Grieger (Eds.), *Handbook of rational-emotive therapy.* New York: Springer.

Ellis, A., & Dryden, W. (1987). *The practice of rational emotive therapy.* New York: Springer.

Epictetus. (1955). *The handbook of Epictetus* (N. P. White, Trans.). Indianapolis: Hackett. (Original work published circa A.D. 78).

Fordyce, W. E. (1976). *Behavioral methods for chronic pain and illness.* St. Louis: C. V. Mosby.

Friedman, D. P. (1990). Perspectives on the medical use of drugs of abuse. *Journal of Pain and Symptom Management, 5*(Suppl.), S2-S5.

Gallagher, E. B., & Wrobel, S. (1982). The sick role and chronic pain. In R. Roy & E. Tunks (Eds.), *Chronic pain: Psychosocial factors in rehabilitation* (pp. 36-52). Baltimore, MD: Williams & Wilkins.

Gorsky, B. (1981). *Pain: Origin and treatment.* New York: Medical Examination Publishing.

Kabat-Zinn, J., Lipworth, L., & Barney, R. (1985). The clinical use of mindfulness meditation for the self-regulation of chronic pain. *Journal of Behavioral Medicine, 8*, 163-191.

McCaul, K., & Malott, J. (1984). Distraction and coping with pain. *Psychological Bulletin, 95*(3), 516-533.

Melzack, R. (1975). The McGill pain questionnaire: Major properties and scoring methods. *Pain, 1*, 277-299.

Melzack, R. (1990). The tragedy of needless pain. *Scientific American, 262*, 27-33.

Melzack, R., & Wall, P. D. (1965). Pain mechanisms: A new theory. *Science, 150*, 971-979.

Merskey, H. M. (1965). Psychiatric patients with persistent pain. *Journal of Psychosomatic Research, 9*, 299-309.

Merskey, H. M. (1986). Classification of chronic pain syndromes. *Pain, 3*(Suppl.), S1-S225.

Pennebaker, J. W. (1982). *The psychology of physical symptoms.* New York: Springer.

Rothschild, B. H., & Storaasli, R. (1990). The referral of chronic pain patients to a pain clinic. *Pain Management, 3*, 347-352.

Sanders, S. H. (1985). Advances in chronic pain management. *Annals of Behavioral Medicine, 7*, 3-5.

Taylor, H., & Curran, N. M. (1985). *The Nuprin report.* New York: Louis Harris.

Turk, D., & Salovey, P. (1984). Chronic pain as a variant of depressive disease: A critical appraisal. *Journal of Nervous and Mental Disorders, 172*, 398-404.

Van Houdenhove, B. (1988). Hysteria, depression and the nosological problem of chronic pain. *Acta Psychiatrica Belgica, 88*, 419-431.

Wegner, D., & Schneider, D. (1989). Mental control: The war of the ghosts in the machine. In J. Uleman & J. Bargh (Eds.), *Unintended thought* (pp. 287-305). New York: Guilford.

5

Traumatic Incident Reduction: A Cognitive-Emotive Treatment of Post-Traumatic Stress Disorder

ROBERT H. MOORE

Problem Profile

In recent years, significant media attention has been given to the Post-Traumatic Stress Disorders (PTSD) of Vietnam veterans, whose postwar "nervous" problems (i.e., sleep disturbances, hypervigilance, paranoia, panic attacks, explosive rages, and intrusive thoughts) were known to veterans of earlier campaigns as "battle fatigue," "shell shock," and "war neurosis" (Kelly, 1985). As any number of mugging, rape, and accident victims have testified, however, one need not have been a casualty of war to experience PTSD (American Psychiatric Association [APA], 1987). An equal opportunity disabler, PTSD occurs in children as well as adults (Eth & Pynoos, 1985) and has been attributed to abuse, abortions, burns, broken bones, surgery, rape, overwhelming loss, animal attacks, drug overdoses, near drownings, bullying, intimidation, and similar traumata.

The PTSD reaction is most easily distinguished from emotional problems of other sorts by its signature flashback: the involuntary and often agonizing recall of a past traumatic incident. It can be triggered by an almost limitless variety of present cognitive and perceptual cues (Foa, Steketee, & Rothbaum, 1989; Kilpatrick, Veronen, & Best, 1985). Lodged like a startle response beyond conscious control, the reaction frequently catapults its victims into a painful dramatization of an earlier trauma and routinely either distorts or eclipses their perception of present reality. Although we can't confirm that any of the countless animal species with which researchers have replicated Pavlov's (1927) conditioned response ever actually flashed back to their acquisition experiences, the mechanism of classical conditioning is apparent in every case of PTSD. As salivation is to Pavlov's dog, so PTSD is to its victims.

Like emotional problems of other sorts, however, PTSD is not accounted for solely in terms of antecedent trauma and classical conditioning. In order to provoke a significant stress reaction (C), as Ellis (1962) and others observe, an experience (A) must ordinarily stimulate certain of an individual's preexisting irrational beliefs (iBs). Veronen and Kilpatrick (1983) confirm that the rule holds for trauma as well as for more routine experience. Errant beliefs—related to the tolerance of discomfort and distress; performance, approval, and self-worth; and how others should behave—"may be activated by traumatic events and lead to greater likelihood of developing and maintaining PTSD symptomatology and other emotional reactions. Individuals who premorbidly hold such beliefs in a dogmatic and rigid fashion are at greater risk of developing PTSD and experiencing more difficulty coping with the resulting PTSD symptomatology" (Warren & Zgourides, 1991, p. 151). Also activated and often shattered by trauma are assumptions regarding personal invulnerability; a world that is meaningful, comprehensible, predictable, and just; and the trustworthiness of others (Janoff-Bulman, 1985; Roth & Newman, 1991). Such preexisting beliefs and assumptions, plus the various conclusions, decisions, attitudes, and intentions specific to a particular traumatic incident (especially when held as imperatives), constitute the operant irrational cognitive components (iBs) of PTSD.

PTSD is as diverse in its symptomatic expression as in its experiential origin. It manifests as a wide range of anxieties, insecurities, phobias, panic disorders, anger and rage reactions, guilt complexes, mood and personality anomalies, depressive reactions, self-esteem problems, somatic complaints, and compulsions

(Dansky, Roth, & Kronenberger, 1990). Because of the considerable breadth of its symptomatology, "PTSD" alone does not constitute a fully adequate diagnosis. The current PTSD-related diagnostic lexicon allows us to designate a case only as either chronic/delayed or acute (see Table 5.1). It does not enable us to communicate either the specific features or the psychodynamics of a case. Assuming, for example, that a tell-tale flashback or some other clinical indicator properly identified them, each of the following case presentations could easily qualify as PTSD:

1. The father who explodes in violent rages at his two-year-old's spills and messes *(Vietnam war veteran)*;
2. The graduate student who gets so panicky at exams and interviews that he can barely function *(severe childhood sports injury)*;
3. The housewife who is bored to tears by her dull routine but can't get motivated to start a new activity *(physically abused as a child)*;
4. The college co-ed who desperately makes and breaks love relationships at the rate of three or four a semester *(date-raped in her teens)*;
5. The 10-year-old who gets nauseated and faint at the mere suggestion that he get into a car *(parents killed in an auto accident)*.

The designation "PTSD," then, is not associated with any particular symptom, symptom cluster, or stressful current circumstance but denotes, instead, the historic mechanism by which any of a broad range of emotional disturbances or conditioned responses, along with their supporting irrational beliefs, were incorporated into a client's repertoire.

Primary and Secondary Trauma

What makes PTSD a particularly persistent and pernicious variety of disturbance is the occurrence, at the time of its acquisition trauma, of significant physical and/or emotional pain. Such pain, in association with the other perceptual stimuli, thoughts, and feelings (As, Bs, and Cs) one experiences at the time, constitutes the *primary* traumatic incident. One's composite memory of the primary incident, therefore, contains not only the dominant audio/ visual impressions of that moment, but also one's mind-set (motives, purposes, intentions, rBs, and iBs) and visceral (emotional

Table 5.1 Diagnostic Criteria for 309.89 Post-Traumatic Stress Disorder

A. The person has experienced an event that is outside the range of usual human experience and that would be markedly distressing to almost anyone, e.g., serious threat to one's life or physical integrity; serious threat or harm to one's children, spouse, or other close relatives and friends; sudden destruction of one's home or community; or seeing another person who has recently been, or is being, seriously injured or killed as the result of an accident or physical violence.

B. The traumatic event is persistently reexperienced in at least one of the following ways:
  (1) recurrent and intrusive distressing recollections of the event (in young children, repetitive play in which themes or aspects of the trauma are expressed)
  (2) recurrent distressing dreams of the event
  (3) sudden acting or feeling as if the traumatic event were recurring (includes a sense of reliving the experience, illusions, hallucinations, and dissociative [flashback] episodes, even those that occur upon awakening or when intoxicated)
  (4) intense psychological distress at exposure to events that symbolize or resemble an aspect of the traumatic event, including anniversaries of the trauma

C. Persistent avoidance of stimuli associated with the trauma or numbing of general responsiveness (not present before the trauma), as indicated by at least three of the following:
  (1) efforts to avoid thoughts or feelings associated with the trauma
  (2) efforts to avoid activities or situations that arouse recollections of the trauma
  (3) inability to recall an important aspect of the trauma (psychogenic amnesia)
  (4) markedly diminished interest in significant activities (in young children, loss of recently acquired developmental skills such as toilet training or language skills)
  (5) feeling of detachment or estrangement from others
  (6) restricted range of affect, e.g., unable to have love feelings
  (7) sense of a foreshortened future, e.g., does not expect to have a career, marriage, or children, or a long life

D. Persistent symptoms of increased arousal (not present before the trauma), as indicated by at least two of the following:
  (1) difficulty falling or staying asleep
  (2) irritability or outbursts of anger
  (3) difficulty concentrating
  (4) hypervigilance
  (5) exaggerated startle response
  (6) physiologic reactivity upon exposure to events that symbolize or resemble an aspect of the traumatic event (e.g., a woman who was raped in an elevator breaks out in a sweat when entering any elevator)

E. Duration of the disturbance (symptoms B, C, and D) of at least one month.

Specify delayed onset if the onset of symptoms was at least six months after the trauma.

NOTE: Reprinted with permission from the *Diagnostic and Statistical Manual of Mental Disorders* (3rd ed., rev.). Copyright 1987 American Psychiatric Association.

and somatic, C) reactions. Thus, whenever one subsequently encounters a "restimulator"—any present-time sensory, perceptual, cognitive, or emotive stimulus similar to one of those contained in the memory of an earlier trauma—one is likely to be consciously or unconsciously "reminded" of and, therefore, to reactivate its associated pain or upset. It is this subsequent painful reminder, the involuntary "restimulation" of the primary trauma, that constitutes the painful *secondary* experience we recognize as PTSD (Foa et al., 1989).

In the Pavlovian model, the occurrence of the restimulator (current stimulus-event, A) equates to the ringing of the bell; the stress reaction itself (C) equates to salivation. The mechanism is almost indefinitely extendable by association. Once the dog has been conditioned to salivate to the ringing of the bell, for example, the bell may be paired with a new perceptual stimulus—say, the flashing of a light—so that the dog will then salivate to the light as well as to the bell. If one next flashes the light and pulls the dog's tail, the dog will learn to salivate when its tail is pulled (Hilgard, 1962). By sequencing stimuli so as to create a "conditioned response chain" in this manner, we expand the domain of stimuli that will elicit the salivation response.[1]

Since the laws that govern the construction of the conditioned response chain in the laboratory are exactly those that govern the development of the post-traumatic stress disorder in vivo, this simple mechanism—the expansion of the secondary restimulator (toxic A) domain by association—has very significant implications for clinical practice. It is responsible for the longevity of many PTSD cases, for the persistence of PTSD symptoms in the absence of flashbacks (Moore, 1990), for many apparent compulsions (Goodman & Maultsby, 1974), and for the fact that *any secondary PTSD experience can itself be restimulated and thus function as a traumatic incident* (Kilpatrick et al., 1985).

This process may be illustrated by the following example: A veteran originally injured in an artillery attack (primary A) will often tend to be restimulated, even years later, by such things as smoke and loud noises (secondary As). So it's no surprise when he panics, postwar, in response to fireworks. However, should he happen to be triggered into a full-blown panic reaction by a fireworks display *while eating fried chicken one day at a picnic in the park*, he is likely thereafter, as strange as it seems, to get panicky around fried chicken (whether he flashes back to the park at the time or not). In such a circumstance, fried chicken gets added to the domain of toxic secondary restimulators of his war experience, and the "picnic in the park" incident acquires secondary trauma status and is itself subject to later restimulation. If, for instance, fried chicken subsequently gets (or previously had gotten) associated with his mother-in-law (who prepares it for his every visit), his contact with her also becomes subject to PTSD toxicity by association. The dynamic effect of such repeated reactions over a period of time is a gradual increase in the client's toxic "secondary A" domain. The cumulative associated evaluative cognitions then produce a corresponding reduction of his day-to-day rationality and an inability both to comprehend and to break out of his increasingly volatile reactive pattern (see Hayman, Sommers-Flanagan, & Parson, 1987).

The more reactions one experiences, the more new toxic stimuli develop. The more new toxic stimuli there are, the more reactions one has, which suggests that those experiencing PTSD would eventually come to spend most of their time with their attention riveted painfully on past trauma. In point of fact, that does happen. The longer and more complex the chains or sequences of secondary incidents become over time, however, *the less likely one is to flash all the way back to the primary trauma*. This is why so many PTSD clients who appear to succeed in getting their attention off their primary traumata nevertheless withdraw from many of the life activities they previously enjoyed. Because they flash back to "the big one" a lot less, their PTSD cases are presumed to have abated. In reality such clients are in worse shape overall because a lot of little things in their traumatic incident networks (all the secondary restimulators or "cues" they picked up in the years following their primary traumata) bother them much more than they did in the past (Gerbode, 1989).

As neatly applicable as it appears to be, the basic Pavlovian mechanism does not adequately display the cognitive aspects of the human conditioning experience as manifest in PTSD. Warren and Zgourides (1991) observe, in this connection, that:

> Classical conditioning (stimulus-response [S-R] model) easily accounts for most of the PTSD symptomatology. However, RET posits that while conditioned stimuli may remind one of the trauma (stimulus-stimulus

[S-S] model), the emotional response is not entirely conditioned, but rather it is mediated by one's current appraisal of these stimuli as well as by preexisting irrational beliefs. The importance of information pertaining to meanings in the fear structure is consistent with RET, and *the theory that meaning, stimuli, and response information is stored in long-term memory provides an account of the mechanism by which one's beliefs are sustained and activated.* (p. 151) (author's emphasis)

Gerbode (1989) concurs and points out that such long-term storage of the cognitive-emotive content of a traumatic incident is virtually assured by most PTSD clients' understandable reluctance to mentally unsuppress and reexamine their traumata. He posits, moreover, that some of the key cognitions contained in the memory of any traumatic incident that later cause trouble when they are restimulated are those specific conclusions, decisions, and intentions the individual generated during the incident itself in order to cope emotionally with the painful urgency of the moment. In such a circumstance, not only would certain preexisting beliefs govern one's reaction to a traumatic event but also the traumatic event itself would give rise to the formulation of new, potentially errant cognitions. Viewed in this light, PTSD is very much a cognitive-emotive disorder and not nearly so simply Pavlovian as it at first appears to be. Accordingly, an effective cognitive-emotive approach is called for in its remediation, in which the errant cognitions formed under the duress of the trauma are located and corrected.

PTSD and the Cognitive Therapies

Secondary Approaches

PTSD is one of the few terms in the diagnostic lexicon that reliably suggests the etiology of the disturbance to which it refers. In so doing, ironically, it focuses attention on an area that rational-emotive therapists have generally chosen to ignore. In actual fact, RET is not entirely oblivious to the historic roots of emotional disturbance and generally acknowledges that stress reactions get programmed in somewhere along the way. Dryden and Ellis (1986) point out that some emotional disturbance is directly attributable to such background traumata as natural disasters and personal tragedies. But recognizing that the cognitive processes responsible for a client's *current* disturbance are frequently preconscious and therefore accessible in present time, rational-emotive and most other cognitive therapists have traditionally favored challenging a client's *current* disturbance-causing belief system over directly confronting the earlier experience(s) responsible for its acquisition (Ellis, 1962, 1989).

Which of us, for instance, wouldn't prefer to challenge whatever *present* errant cognition (iB) we could find that would compel an otherwise competent and loving father to whip (C) his two-year-old child viciously for spilling something (A) instead of probing such a client's own childhood abuse for the acquisition of his punitive mind-set? And who among us hasn't employed a "counter-conditioning" relaxation or quieting routine to desensitize a client to the specific *current* social situation in which he invariably chokes up and can't speak? In so doing, we manage to avoid having to address the POW experience he flashes back to whenever he chokes up. These, after all, are basic procedures in the cognitive therapist's repertoire (see Saigh, 1991).

Anxiety management techniques, such as Beck's (1976) cognitive therapy, Meichenbaum's (1977) Stress-Inoculation Training (SIT) and Lazarus's (1976) multimodal approach, are similar in this regard. They combine the monitoring/stopping of automatic thoughts and assumptions, cognitive restructuring, and guided self-dialogue with such techniques as covert modeling, role playing, relaxation, breath control, and various desensitization procedures. But the overall focus is nevertheless almost exclusively on a client's *current* (secondary) experience, cognition, and symptomatology (Olasov & Foa, 1987). The following "coping self-statements" used in SIT to deal with an anger-provoking situation reveal the present, situational/symptomatic focus typical of the secondary, reaction-management approaches:

> This is going to upset me, but I know how to deal with it. . . . Try not to take this too seriously. . . . Time for a few deep breaths of relaxation. . . . Remember to keep your sense of humor. . . . Just roll with the punches; don't get bent out of shape. . . . There is no point in getting mad. . . . I'm not going to let him get to me. . . . Look for the positives. Don't assume the worst or jump to conclusions. . . . There

is no need to doubt myself. What he says doesn't matter. . . . I'll let him make a fool of himself. . . . Let's take the issue point by point. . . . My anger is a signal of what I need to do. . . . Try to reason it out. . . . I can't expect people to act the way I want them to. . . . Try to shake it off. Don't let it interfere with your job. . . . Don't take it personally. (Meichenbaum, 1977, p. 166-167)

A therapist's decision to focus an intervention mainly on a client's responses to day-to-day stressors is most understandable when the client does *not* report flashing back at the time of the upsets. Most non-PTSD clients, after all, have no special awareness of their early acquisition experiences and, therefore, have little or nothing to say about them. Their attention is fixed on a steady stream of disturbance-provoking current events (As) for which both we and they realize they *do* need more rational coping skills.

In the clear-cut PTSD case in which flashback is evident, the client not only puts the acquisition experience (the primary trauma) in focus right at the start but also often seems virtually obsessed by it. Flashback content, which is often concurrent with the client's upset over something in present time, is so painfully "charged" that he or she is either barely able to shift attention from it or else must regularly struggle to resist attending to it (Solomon, Mikulincer, & Arad, 1991). In such a circumstance, the therapist who focuses intervention exclusively on the client's dramatic overreactions to current (secondary) events (on the restimula*tor*, rather than on what is being restimula*ted*) bypasses the opportunity to address directly and resolve the core of the client's PTSD case. Such attention mainly to the present-time "cueing effect," according to Goodman and Maultsby (1974, p. 62), "explains many failures or partial successes in psychotherapy, despite the best intentions of patient and therapist."

Given the extreme volatility of the memory of a trauma, though, it's really no wonder that many therapists and their PTSD clients (tacitly) agree *not* to confront such incidents head on. To understand why this is so often the case, consider the following:

1. It is nearly impossible to get PTSD clients to perceive or appraise objectively a traumatic experience they are in the midst of dramatizing;
2. It is usually difficult, even when they are not dramatizing, to sell PTSD clients on the idea of de-awfulizing a traumatic event that has given them nightmares for the last 15 or 20 years;

3. Cognitive restructuring, thought stopping, and stimulus blunting techniques give PTSD clients little or no control over their tendency to flash back spontaneously and go into restimulation; and

4. Helping PTSD clients minimize the disruptive impact of their intrusive thoughts and teaching them not to down themselves over the persistence of their symptoms is better than nothing.

It becomes understandable, then, that many therapists choose to assist clients in their ongoing struggles to distance themselves from the memories of their traumata in an attempt simply to limit the frequency and intensity of their post-traumatic episodes.

Therapists may actually bring superb rational-emotive therapeutic skills to bear on clients' overreactions to a variety of contemporary stimulus-events (e.g., rage over a spill, anxiety at a meeting), but unless they help PTSD clients to resolve the prior trauma (e.g., auto accident, childhood abuse, war experience) that actively supports their current disturbance and to revise the irrational ideation associated with that primary experience, they have elected not to address the PTSD at all. The result of such a purely secondary intervention is that clients' unresolved primary traumas continue intermittently to intrude into consciousness, and clients are left to struggle alone to secure a sense of rationality against the influence of these traumas.

Warren and Zgourides (1991) report that a combination of rational-emotive therapy (RET), relaxation training, imaginal exposure to the trauma, in vivo desensitization to toxic external stimuli, behavioral rehearsal, and role-playing helped a PTSD client ("Eva," a 60-year-old woman traumatized when a truck crashed into her house). Their report includes the observation that toward the *end* of her therapy, "Eva and her husband decided to remodel parts of their house so that less time would need to be spent near the part of the house where the accident occurred. This appeared to increase Eva's sense of future safety" (p. 163).

Eva's need to escape a persistently restimulative environment indicates that her post-traumatic stress response was still quite active at the end of her therapy. The report ends with this observation: "Even more debilitative than the phobic reactions to truck stimuli was Eva's difficulty accepting herself as more emotional, less confident, and no longer the rock of the family. RET was helpful with this secondary disturbance. At termination of therapy, however, this problem remained an ongoing challenge for Eva" (p. 163).

This unfortunate and all too familiar outcome of an intervention too heavily focused on secondary issues is made more poignant by the following considerations:

1. The client, although in somewhat better control, was actually terminated with her PTSD case still active (suggesting the therapist didn't know what else to do for her) and with no mention of follow-up;
2. The client was encouraged to continue working on *"accepting herself* as more emotional, less confident, and no longer the rock of the family" (suggesting that she should never again expect to be *less* emotional, *more* confident, and once again the rock of the family);
3. The authors chose Eva's case as most illustrative of the application of RET and related cognitive therapies to PTSD!

The acceptance of such a dismal outcome for PTSD clients is not confined to the cognitive-behavioral domain. A report by Scurfield, Kenderdine, and Pollard (1990) reveals a similar outlook at the American Lake Veterans Administration Medical Center Post-Traumatic Stress Treatment Program (PTSTP). According to Scurfield et al.:

> It appears that a number of traumatic memories will never be completely or even perhaps mostly forgotten; after all, a number of war-related experiences truly are unforgettable. If so, it becomes imperative, then, for the veteran in effect to develop a "better attitude toward," and less toxic reaction to, intrusive symptoms. The development of such an improved "coexistence" with still continuing intrusive symptomatology seems to be a very important and relevant stress recovery phenomenon (and one that we teach in the PTSTP). (p. 198)

The indication here is that if a traumatic experience is truly unforgettable (which most of them are), it must also be permanently and painfully intrusive. This simply is not the case. A *fully resolved* traumatic experience is neither completely nor mostly forgotten. It is, by definition, simply benign and incapable of intrusive restimulation (Fairbank & Nicholson, 1987). But the message from the VA to the veteran with persistent flashbacks— "You're just going to have to learn to live with them!"—couldn't be clearer. It sends an unmistakable signal that some of our colleagues have not yet begun to employ the more robust cognitive-emotive techniques of primary PTSD case resolution.

Primary Approaches

Because a traumatic incident is, by definition, exceedingly unpleasant, there is an understandable tendency, at the moment one is occurring, to resist and protest it as best one can. It is at just such moments of extreme physical and/or emotional pain, according to Gerbode (1989), that one's thinking (evaluative cognition, B) is least likely to be well-reasoned and objective and most likely to be irrational. There is, moreover, a subsequent tendency to suppress and/or repress the memory of such an incident so as not to have to reexperience the painful emotional "charge" its restimulation carries with it. Unfortunately, suppression/repression of the memory of a traumatic incident effectively locks its irrational ideation and painful emotion away together (along with the incident's sensory and perceptual data) in long-term storage. Thus, the stage for PTSD is set. Fortunately, however, when accessed with the specific cognitive-imagery procedure described later in this chapter, a primary traumatic incident can be stripped of its emotional charge permitting its embedded cognitive components (iBs) to be revealed and restructured. With its emotional impact depleted and its irrational ideation revised, the memory of a traumatic incident becomes innocuous and thereafter remains permanently incapable of restimulation and intrusion into present time (Gerbode, 1989).

It may seem a bit unorthodox to RET practitioners to assign more clinical significance to the irrational beliefs associated with events that traumatized clients in the past than to beliefs associated with present events. If only PTSD clients' present disturbances weren't so tightly tied to and governed by their past traumata, we could forgo such apparent unorthodoxy. The connection is inescapable, however, and neither orthodox (present-focus) RET nor any other theoretical framework presently provides as thoroughly workable an approach to PTSD as one that directly addresses both the cognitive and emotive components of a client's *primary* trauma. Irrational ideation is irrational ideation wherever *or whenever* it is found.

Support for the necessity of dealing directly with the primary trauma to resolve a PTSD case comes from many corners of the profession. In their review of theoretical and empirical issues in the treatment of PTSD, Fairbank and Nicholson (1987) conclude that, of all the approaches in use, only those involving some form of direct imaginal exposure to the trauma have been successful. Roth and Newman (1991) describe the ideal resolution process as one involving "a reexperiencing of the affect associated with the trauma in the context of painful memories" (p. 281). Such a process, the authors point out, brings the individual "to both an emotional and cognitive understanding of the meaning of the trauma and the impact it has had . . . and would lead to a reduction in symptoms and to successful integration of the trauma experience" (p. 281).

References to the use of "imaginal" procedures and to the "integration" or "assimilation" of past trauma may also seem unfamiliar to the RET practitioner who has relied mainly on the standard present-time iB-challenge to carry interventions to completion. As Ellis (1973) and others periodically remind us, however, RET (if not all practitioners of RET) employs a variety of cognitive, emotive, and behavioral techniques to help clients identify, dispute, and revise their irrational points of view about themselves and their world. We are not confined in RET to addressing our clients' most immediately obvious and easily accessible beliefs about their experience. The beliefs they most need to revise, after all, are those that actually underlie their disturbances, whether such beliefs happen to be immediately obvious and easily accessible or embedded in one or more painful past traumata. Neither are we limited only to the use of didactics, Socratic dialogue, reason, and logic in the revision of our clients' thinking.

For PTSD clients, in other words, there is a *literal and clinically significant, trauma-based answer* to the usually rhetorical therapist's question, "*Where is it written?*" Many if not most of the irrational beliefs that support today's PTSD reactions were "written" into our PTSD clients' cognitive-ergo-emotive repertoires during various acutely painful past experiences. This is what makes PTSD-related ideation so difficult to access and reformulate by ordinary rational-emotive means. It is encapsulated, so to speak, in an area of memory that erupts like Vesuvius the moment the therapist (or anyone else, for that matter) so much as brushes against it. Only the skillful use of a specific cognitive-imagery process, at this point, can access and revise it successfully.

Additional support for the efficacy of cognitive-emotive imagery procedures is found in Beck's (1970) observation that "When a patient has an unpleasant affect associated with a particular situation, the unpleasant affect may sometimes be eliminated or reduced with repeated imagining of the situation." Grossberg and Wilson (1968) and Blundell and Cade (1980) independently confirm that repeated visualization of an anxiety-provoking situation produces a significant reduction in the physiological (GSR) response to the threatening image. MacHovec (1985) finds that hypnotic regression can help a client to recall and revivify the trauma, permitting a venting of emotions and reintegration of the experience. Frederick (1986) maintains that a frame-by-frame imaginal review of a traumatic experience is essential to the dissipation of its associated anxiety.

Speaking specifically to the use of cognitive-imagery procedures in the rational-emotive treatment of PTSD, Warren and Zgourides (1991) report that:

> In fact, exposure is most often effective in facilitating the types of cognitive restructuring described earlier. Keane et al.'s (1989) implosive therapy, Horowitz's (1986) gradual dosing, and Foa and Olasov's (1987) prolonged imaginal exposure are methods that help clients work through their traumatic event, discover and revise meanings, and develop more adaptive responses to the traumatic event. In RET, we incorporate imaginal exposure to the traumatic event . . . [and] . . . while conducting the imaginal exposure and in reviewing imagined and behavioral exposure homework assignments, we are on the lookout for clients' cognitive and emotional reprocessing of the trauma that may relate to the issues of meaning of the event, shattered assumptions, irrational beliefs, and so on. (p. 161)

It is important to note, however, that cognitive imagery and visualization procedures, including "systematic desensitization" (Turner, 1979), "flooding" (Keane & Kaloupek, 1982), "implosion" (Lyons & Keane, 1989; Stampfl & Lewis, 1967), "repetitive review" (Raimy, 1975), and "direct therapeutic exposure" (Boudewyns, Hyer, Woods, Harrison, & McCranie, 1990), are neither all alike nor all equally effective. Boudewyns et al. (1990), for instance, describes direct therapeutic exposure (DTE) as "encouraging the patient to experience repeated or extended exposure, either in reality or in fantasy, to *objectively harmless*, but feared stimuli for the purpose of reducing (extinguishing) negative affect" (p. 365) (author's emphasis). Reference to its focus on "objectively harmless" stimuli identifies DTE as a procedure used here to desensitize a client to *secondary* (present-time) trauma. No such procedure should be equated with one that directly addresses *primary* trauma. Neither can any procedure that is confined to the 50-minute hour (as was the case in the Boudewyns study) be considered flexible enough to handle the average primary traumatic incident.

The cognitive-emotive procedure best suited to the task of thorough PTSD resolution must also accommodate the predictable complexities and specific peculiarities of a given traumatic incident network. As Manton and Talbot (1990) observe, "traumatic events . . . can bring into consciousness unresolved prior situations (with similar themes) such as incest, child abuse, or the death of an important person in the victim's life" (p. 508). When clients have more than one trauma in their history, the only completely effective procedure is one that traces each symptom of the composite post-traumatic reaction back through sequence(s) of related earlier incidents to each of the contributing primaries. Interestingly, a very similar observation was made by one of our earliest colleagues, Freud (1984), who wrote:

> What left the symptom behind was not always a *single* experience. On the contrary, the result was usually brought about by the convergence of several traumas, and often by the repetition of a great number of similar ones. Thus it was necessary to reproduce the whole chain of pathogenic memories in chronological order, or rather in reversed order, the latest ones first and the earliest ones last. (p. 37)

Although we must wind the clock back to give PTSD clients the opportunity to confront the pain and cognitions associated with their prior traumas, we have not abandoned our interest in remediating their current response repertoires in favor of some quasi-analytic or purely cathartic approach. The fact is that (a) PTSD clients generally have to work through some intense emotional and/or physical pain simply in order to get in touch with the *beliefs* they formulated during their traumatic experiences, and (b) the beliefs they formulated during their traumatic experiences control their current PTSD response repertoires. For these reasons, we remain as interested in seeing clients identify and restructure the irrational elements of their thinking about past traumatic experience as we do about any of their day-to-day concerns. As Raimy (1975) puts it:

> Many current therapies attempt primarily to relieve the client or patient of his pent-up emotion, either in cathartic episodes or over longer periods of time in which emotional release takes place less dramatically. If we examine catharsis more closely, however, we can readily discover several cognitive events which have significant influence on the experience. If these cognitive events do not occur, no amount of "emotional expression" is likely to be helpful. (p. 81)

The simple fact is that in order to deal effectively with past trauma, we must guide the client through to its resolution in imagery. The imagery process itself, however, is just the means by which we help PTSD clients get through their residual primary pain. It is by revising the errant cognition associated with that pain that they are freed from the grip of their PTSD.

Traumatic Incident Reduction

The most thorough and reliable approach to the resolution of both long-standing and recent disaster PTSD currently in use is Traumatic Incident Reduction (TIR), a guided cognitive imagery procedure developed by Gerbode (1989).[2] A high-precision refinement of earlier cognitive desensitization procedures, TIR effectively resolves the outstanding trauma of the majority of the PTSD clients with whom it is used when carried out according to the strict guidelines detailed below.

TIR appears to be more efficient and more effective than other cognitive-imagery or desensitization procedures, as such procedures frequently focus mainly (and most often incompletely) on secondary episodes. By tracing each traumatic reaction to its original or primary trauma(ta) and by taking each primary trauma to its *full resolution or procedural "end point" at one sitting* (a *crucial* requirement), the TIR process leaves clients observably relieved, often smiling, and no longer committed to their previously errant cognitions. At that point, the traumatic incidents, their associated irrational ideation, and consequent PTSD have been fully handled, and clients are able to reengage life comfortably in ways they might not have been able to do since their original trauma(ta).

Done one-on-one, the core TIR procedure may be completed in as little as 20 minutes or it may require two or three hours (average: 1½ hrs) of "viewing" per incident.[3] The therapist needs to be willing to take the time necessary to guide the client back through the relevant trauma, carefully following TIR procedural guidelines, to permit the client to work through the painful memories of the experience in order to restructure its cognitive content (primary iBs) as needed for full resolution.

Ideally, PTSD clients correctly identify their active primary incidents during intake. Clients who have regular flashbacks generally do this with ease. Such clients may be briefed on TIR the same day and, if not on drugs, scheduled for viewing the next day. Their PTSD problems can often be alleviated within the week. It is not unusual for a TIR *narrative* procedure to resolve an "unoccluded" (obvious) primary traumatic incident in as little as two or three hours. Case resolution then would depend mainly on how many primary and secondary traumata needed to be addressed to restore full functioning.

More commonly, however, PTSD clients do not correctly identify all their active primary incidents at intake. A war veteran, for instance, may at first report with conviction that it all dates back to Vietnam; he's only had the problem since then, and that is the content of his flashbacks. Once he gets into it, however, he is sometimes surprised to discover that his wartime experience was actually secondary to some previously occluded or less memorable earlier trauma.[4]

In chronic cases, including some phobias and panic disorders in which flashbacks are absent, clients often have no clue at intake as to where or when their reaction patterns were actually acquired. Although technically not classified as PTSD, many such clients have had a significant number of stressful experiences over the years. Yet they cannot, at first, identify any one incident as having been much more significant than any other. They are often thoroughly frustrated and discouraged, as well as genuinely baffled, about the persistence of their symptoms. Those among them who lead otherwise comfortable lives and seem not to think much less rationally, day-to-day, than the majority of the population frequently come to the usually erroneous conclusion that their problems must be genetic in origin ("run in the family").[5] (Needless to say, such cases are not resolved within the week.) They are not generally a problem for TIR, however, as they may be handled to resolution very adequately by the *thematic* approach, a variation of the narrative procedure. Thematic TIR does not require clients to be aware of or to identify correctly the relevant historic components of their cases right at the start of their intervention. Instead, the thematic procedure simply traces each manifest (present-time) emotional and somatic symptom (theme) back through its chain(s) of secondary incidents, one at a time, until the originally occluded primaries come into awareness and can be dealt with routinely.

Toward clients' understanding of the TIR routine, which assuredly will be new to them, it is often useful to draw upon the illustrative value of the Pavlovian example mentioned earlier and with which they may already be familiar. One may point out, in this connection, that when the dog's salivation response to the bell (primary A) is extinguished, the light (secondary A) loses its restimulative potential automatically (Hilgard, 1962). Likewise, once a primary incident is completely resolved, none of the stimuli that had later become associated with it as secondary restimulators is capable of triggering any further reaction (Gerbode, 1989). This means that when the veteran fully resolves his "artillery attack" (and any other related primary incidents), he will no longer be vulnerable to restimulation triggered by the various secondarily toxic stimuli associated with that experience. At that point, fried chicken and mother-in-law are back to representing nothing more than fried chicken and mother-in-law.

This may seem like a rather classical Pavlovian explanation and leave the RET therapist wondering how it relates to the "A, B, C" model of RET. The TIR approach actually arrives at the same place as RET, but through the "back door." Once clients realize that it was the cumulative effect of their traumatic incident networks (As) on their cognitive-emotive response sets (Bs) over a period of time that is responsible for the persistence of their PTSD symptoms (Cs), and once they understand that there is a way to shut down the networks' active components permanently, they'll be happy to use the TIR approach, even if you've already gotten them well indoctrinated in the standard use of A, B, and C. Then, even thoroughly frustrated and discouraged chronic and absent-flashback PTSD clients will begin to feel hopeful.

The lexicon of TIR reflects its purpose and procedure. The client is called a "viewer" because his or her primary function is to confront, via the viewing process, past trauma. The person conducting the session is called a "facilitator" because his or her purpose is simply to facilitate the viewer's process of viewing (Gerbode, 1989). Just as "physician" and "patient" become "analyst" and "analysand" or "surgeon" and "organ donor," based on the requirements of their respective roles, the designations "facilitator" and "viewer" are reserved for those whose interaction is governed by the singular requirements of the TIR process.

TIR, like other cognitive-imagery processes, differs somewhat from orthodox RET. Although it is guided by the same basic philosophy and purpose—in that it holds errant cognition to be the root cause of emotional disturbance and in need of revision—unlike standard RET, TIR carries the revision process back to the specific experience(s) that originally produced and enforced such errant cognition. In this regard, TIR is a bit more "personal" than RET. Instead of relying mainly upon the therapist's application of rational therapeutic principle to establish a client's probable irrational viewpoint (the standard B for a given C), as is common in RET, TIR guides clients in the discovery and revision of their own original disturbance-causing cognitions.

What makes such a procedure both necessary and possible is the fact that, in PTSD, the disturbance-causing cognitions (except for the preexisting ones) were originally generated in response to, and in order to cope with, a traumatically painful and/or upsetting experience. Moreover, the offending cognitions are still being kept in force by the long-term residual impact of the incident. In other words, if it hadn't been for the specific circumstance of the trauma, as subjectively experienced by the client—for example, A: *"Oh my God, I've been shot! I'm gonna die!"*—the client wouldn't have formulated the response—for example, B: *"I should never let my guard down, even for a minute!"* Moreover, if the incident hadn't been so emotionally and/or physically painful, making it extremely difficult for the client to confront, its attendant cognition would be a great deal more accessible to routine rational revision.

So, while it remains very useful to be able to infer with reasonable certainty that an anxious client is "awfulizing" while an angry client is "shoulding" about something (pardon the reductionism), these are just some of the more obvious "common denominator" cognitions RET associates with their respective disturbances. What we *cannot* infer but what TIR reveals to clients who have experienced trauma is exactly what happened (at a subjective/cognitive-emotive level) that so overwhelmed them that they would come away from their experience stuck in an involuntary, out-of-date, and irrational mind-set constructed, among other things, of numerous fairly obvious "awfuls" and "shoulds."

In a certain respect, TIR adds a new dimension to our understanding of the relationship between cognition and emotion. While RET has long observed that irrational thinking tends to promote upset feelings, TIR suggests that one's (traumatically) upset feelings also tend to promote irrational thinking. Dodging the "Which came first?" (chicken or egg) question, it is probably safe to say that, on the face of it, the causal equation appears to be reversible. That is, not only does cognition significantly influence emotion but emotion appears to significantly influence cognition.

Even more critically significant, at least in cases of PTSD, the remedial equation seems to be reversible as well. Whereas orthodox RET routinely demonstrates that the restructuring of one's irrational thinking produces a corresponding reduction of emotional disturbance, TIR confirms Ellis's (1990) observation that a reduction of primary traumatic emotional disturbance produces a corresponding restructuring of one's irrational thinking! In short, the client whose trauma has been fully reduced and resolved *and who has become able to talk (and think) freely and painlessly about it* (a TIR goal) almost immediately and self-directedly begins to display a substantively rational (moderate, tolerant, objective) viewpoint regarding that previously painful experience. As always, the client who succeeds in embracing a more rational viewpoint about an experience, regardless of how unfortunate or traumatic that experience once seemed, is no longer disturbed over it or unwittingly under its control. As a consequence, secondary restimulation and flashbacks cease, life's energy and interest revive, and self-esteem rebounds.[6]

What is particularly remarkable about the cognitive restructuring that takes place in TIR is that it takes place so obviously and spontaneously during the course of a given session. Equally remarkable is the fact that it takes place—and truly *must* take place—without didactic or corrective facilitator input. The facilitator's role in TIR (detailed below) is mainly to so conduct the session and guide the viewer in "repeated review" of the selected trauma that the viewer will be able rationally to restructure his or her own "misconceptions" about it (Raimy, 1975). Bear in mind that at this level of intervention the viewer is truly the only one who can decipher (by patient and careful reexamination of the cognitive images stored in memory) what actually happened or appeared to happen in the incident, what its significance was, what he or she was thinking at the time, why it was so extraordinarily painful, how he or she coped with that pain, and what trauma-related conclusions and/or decisions (probable iBs) were made at the time. So, as the viewer reviews this highly sensitive and very painful material repeatedly in imagery in order to discharge the emotional impact holding the irrational cognitions in place, the facilitator *says not a word.*

Although in TIR's handling of PTSD the operant trauma-related irrational cognitions virtually self-correct once the inordinate emotional distress of the traumatic experience is relieved, viewers frequently want to follow a completed TIR session with some discussion or review of some of the ways in which certain of their newly surrendered trauma-related irrational beliefs and attitudes had affected them since the occurrence of their original trauma! Most practitioners find this discussion one of those truly rewarding moments in clinical practice. It is not only confirmation of a successfully completed specific intervention. It is reconfirmation of what RET therapists have asserted all along about the relationship between cognition and emotion—with the additional suggestion that that relationship may be even more interesting than we had originally supposed.

TIR Viewing Procedure

In order to handle the demands of viewing successfully, the viewer must be able to maintain a high degree of concentration throughout the viewing session. The viewer must also be made to feel secure and safe from interruptions, critical judgments, and the like. It is the facilitator's responsibility to create such a "safe space" for the viewer. It is also the facilitator's responsibility to acknowledge and handle all viewer communication and to guide the viewer through the steps in the procedure in such a way that the viewer is not distracted from the task of viewing. A facilitator, therefore, would *minimally* need to become thoroughly acquainted with both the TIR Viewing Procedure and the Rules of Facilitation sections of this chapter. (Better yet would be to review the TIR Workshop Manual [French, 1991] and/or Demonstration Video before plunging in. Best of all would be to attend a TIR facilitation training workshop.[7])

Before undertaking a viewing session with a PTSD client, the facilitator takes time to familiarize the inexperienced viewer thoroughly with the following:

1. *The nature and purpose of the overall procedure, as it relates to the client's case.* Most clients find the description of TIR's conceptual framework interesting, if only because it makes clear to them—often for the first time—how PTSD really works. Occasionally clients are either so trusting or so impatient they seem not to want to bother hearing about it, but to get on with it. Both of these latter types will give you headaches unless you ultimately get them to take responsibility for understanding what PTSD and TIR are all about before getting involved.[8]

2. *The procedure's specific prerequisite conditions related to the viewer's physical condition.* Viewers need to know not to expect to do TIR when they are tired, hungry, or under the influence of alcohol or psychotropic medication (see section on Rules of Facilitation).

3. *The meaning of each of the instructions in the viewing process.* It's best to have them repeat back to you their concept of what each instruction means and what they are to do in response to it, until they've got it. Do not introduce any of their case material (traumatic incidents) into the instruction phase. Use made-up and benign examples of incidents (e.g., "The time when you brushed your teeth") to illustrate what the instructions mean.

4. *The purpose of each step in the viewing process.* Again, without reference to their case material and without predicting what specific insight they might achieve by addressing an incident with viewing, explain whatever they need to know to comprehend what the procedure will require of them. Question: "How many times will I have to review a given incident before I'm done?" Answer: "As many as it takes to

accomplish its resolution, which is why session length won't be guided by the clock."

5. *The concept of a proper viewing procedural end point.* It is most important that the facilitator have a clear concept of exactly what constitutes the proper procedural end point, as described later in this section, so as not to permit the process to end prematurely and so as not to overrun it. It is initially only important that the viewer understand that viewing is not necessarily accomplished within a 50-minute hour and that the facilitator is going to hang in there every step of the way until a given incident has been "completely resolved." In speaking at any point of the process outcome, use a phrase like "completely resolved," or something similarly general, in lieu of any specific advance reference to how they will "feel better about it" or "think more rationally about it."

6. *Anything else the viewer wants or needs to know in order to agree, before getting started, that the procedure sounds like an appropriate one to use in his/her case and that he/she intends to follow it through to a proper procedural end point.* TIR is not kid stuff. It addresses the nitty-gritty reality of life's most excruciating pain. Clients ought to be properly prepared, although not alarmed, in order to confront it. They can note, as well, that since they survived their original traumata, there's really no way they can't survive the "replay." And only by replaying it are they going to be able to resolve it and put it behind them once and for all. All but the most nonconfrontive (and drug-inclined) will see it through.[9]

The facilitator ensures that session preconditions are met and follows the procedural guidelines for viewing exactly as outlined below. Incidents are always addressed in the order of the viewer's sense of their importance. Viewers unable to recommend a specific incident for viewing may be candidates for the thematic approach to TIR, if they can identify a specific outstanding symptom (theme) they wish to address. During the viewing session, the facilitator does not tell the viewer what to view nor the meaning of what is being viewed. Likewise, the rightness of the viewer's feelings and attitudes about what is being viewed is not judged.

The TIR viewing procedure for "running" a narrative traumatic incident proceeds as follows: ("F" denotes the facilitator's instruction and "V," the viewer's response)[10]

1. F: Have the viewer select an incident to be run. *(Viewers* always select the incident to be run. If in doubt about which incident

to select, they can be encouraged to choose any incident to which they tend to flash back, one that was outstandingly traumatic whether they flash back to it or not, or simply one in which they find they have an especially high level of interest. If they say that several incidents are of equal importance, invite them to select the earliest one. How do you know whether the incident selected is a primary or a secondary? You don't. The procedure itself sorts that out, so you don't need to know in advance. Viewers who are ultimately unable to choose an incident, for any reason, may be candidates for the thematic approach to viewing.)[11]

	V:	(Chooses an incident.)
2.	F:	*"When did it happen?"* or *"When was it?"* (If the incident was dated in the response to Step 1, skip this step.)
	V:	(Gives date, age, grade in school, or *any* other reference.)
3.	F:	*"How long does it last?"* (You are asking the viewer to give you any finite period of seconds, minutes, hours, days, or weeks. Durations longer than a month usually can and should be broken up into separate incidents. An incident's duration may also be expressed nonquantitatively, e.g., "It seemed like a hell of a long time.")
	V:	(Gives the duration of the incident.)
4.	F:	*"Move to the start of the incident and tell me when you're there."* (When viewers haven't already closed their eyes, the facilitator adds the instruction, "Close your eyes," but doesn't insist on it. Some viewers acknowledge having heard the instruction for Step 4, before acknowledging having completed the instruction. The facilitator must distinguish between these two possible responses and make sure that the instruction has been completed before moving on to Step 5.)
	V:	(Nods, says "Okay," or says that he/she is there.)
5.	F:	*"What are you aware of?"* (Meaning: viewer's visual or other sensory impression from wherever the viewer is at the start of the incident.)
	V:	(Describes the immediate surroundings at the start of the incident.)
6.	F:	*"Move through to the end of the incident."* (Meaning: *silently* re-view the incident from beginning to end. Facilitator waits, in complete silence, as long as necessary for the viewer to finish.
	V:	(Silently re-views the incident; indicates when finished.)
7.	F:	*"Tell me what happened."* (Meaning: ". . . in the broadest sense." The instruction is intentionally open-ended, so as not to limit

the viewer's account of an incident solely to a recitation of its visual content or "plot-line." The properly briefed viewer will feel free to include in his or her feedback events, sensory impressions, thoughts and feelings of all sorts—not only those experienced during the incident but those experienced while viewing the incident as well. [Note: viewing-related feedback anticipates Step 8.] The facilitator listens attentively, but without comment, question, correction, or "active listening," and gives a one-word acknowledgement when viewers indicate that they have completed the step, before going on to the next instruction.)

	V:	(Recounts aloud the incident just silently re-viewed.)
4.	F:	*"Move to the start of the incident and tell me when you're there."* (As mentioned above, the viewer may or may not acknowledge having *heard* the instruction, before acknowledging having *completed* the instruction. The facilitator must be certain that the instruction has been completed, before moving on to Step 6.)
	V:	(Nods, says "Okay," or says that he/she is there.)
6.	F:	*"Move through to the end of the incident."* (Facilitator waits.)
	V:	(Silently re-views the incident; indicates when finished.)
7.	F:	*"Tell me what happened."* (Facilitator listens without comment; gives acknowledgement of completion.)
	V:	(Recounts aloud the incident just silently re-viewed.)

The facilitator patiently continues to loop the viewer through Steps 4, 6, and 7 (4-6-7, 4-6-7, 4-6-7, etc.). The viewer may become visibly intense or restimulated—which can happen right at the start or after a number of times through the loop—as he or she contacts the incident's most highly charged parts. The facilitator will notice that the viewer's account of the incident being viewed changes—sometimes substantially—from one time through to the next. Aspects of the incident that were originally very significant to the viewer may seem less so after a few repetitions. Important new content may emerge later that hadn't been remembered at all at the start. Changes of this sort may continue through many repetitions of the incident. They indicate that the procedure is working properly and that the cyclic repetition of Steps 4, 6, and 7 should continue.

Eventually, the facilitator will observe one of two things happening. One possibility is that the intensity of the viewer's reaction to the incident will seem to have peaked at some point and to have begun to lighten, leaving the viewer looking and feeling at least somewhat relieved. Another possibility is that the intensity of the viewer's reaction to the incident will seem to have stabilized at some level of heaviness or discomfort (even if lower than peak level), leaving the viewer looking and feeling persistently upset and/or frustrated.

In the instance of diminishing intensity, the indication is that the viewer is working his/her way successfully through a primary incident. The facilitator's only appropriate response is to continue cycling through Steps 4, 6, and 7. The end point of the procedure isn't reached until the viewer looks and reports feeling *completely* relieved, comfortable, and not interested in further review of the experience, having discovered and spontaneously corrected the irrational ideas (distortions, overgeneralizations, misevaluations, etc.) associated with the incident's previously inordinate emotional charge. The viewer will indicate that the incident no longer has any restimulative power.

Persistent heaviness or discomfort indicates that the viewer (a) has not completed viewing the primary incident and may need to find an earlier beginning to the incident before continuing with Steps 4, 6, and 7 of the procedure, or (b) is actually viewing a secondary incident and needs to identify and to begin to view the associated primary or whichever earlier incident has already gone into restimulation.

Unless a viewer has spontaneously reported either flashing back to or remembering an earlier similar incident while recounting the incident being viewed, the facilitator cannot yet know with certainty whether the viewer is currently viewing a primary or a secondary incident. If at any point the viewer spontaneously comes up with an earlier similar incident, it indicates that the current incident is a secondary trauma instead of the primary one. When this happens, the facilitator must direct the viewer's attention to that earlier incident (which may either be the sought-after primary or an earlier secondary), by resuming the process at Step 2 (2-3-4-5-6-7, 4-6-7, 4-6-7, etc.).

A persistently uncomfortable viewer who *does not* spontaneously mention either flashing back to or remembering an earlier similar incident is handled as follows. Immediately following the viewer's response to Step 7, the facilitator inserts Step 8:

8.   F: *"Is the incident getting lighter or heavier?"*[12]
     V: (Indicates lighter, heavier, the same, or comments in detail.)

If the viewer says that the incident is now getting lighter (the emotional or physical pain in it is weaker, fading)—indicating that it is still changing—it appears to be a primary. Even though the viewer had *looked* persistently uncomfortable, the facilitator must believe the viewer's assertion that the incident is still changing and continue cycling through Steps 4, 6, and 7. If the viewer indicates that the incident has either remained at the same uncomfortable level for a while or has gotten heavier (i.e., the pain is stronger, more vivid), the incident still may be either a primary or a secondary. The facilitator then proceeds as follows.

Given the possibility that the incident currently being viewed may yet be found to be a primary (in which case it will ultimately resolve), the facilitator invites the viewer to consider expanding the duration of the incident by looking for an *earlier beginning* to it. This next "earlier beginning" step (Step 9) ensures that the viewer has not overlooked some of the incident's significant earlier aspects, the viewing of which may be essential to the resolution of the trauma.

9.   F: *"Does the incident we are running actually start earlier?"*
     V: (Looks, thinks, or comments, and ultimately says yes or no.)

If the viewer says "yes" in response to Step 9, indicating that there is something worthy of his attention related to the incident and preceding its previously established starting point, whether by minutes, hours, days, or weeks, the facilitator resumes the process with the following slightly modified form of Step 4.

4a. F: *"Move to the new start of the incident; tell me when you're there."*
     V: (Acknowledges the instruction and/or having completed the instruction.)

The facilitator then continues cycling through Steps 4, 6, and 7, as before.

If the viewer says "no" in response to Step 9, indicating that there is nothing worthy of his attention preceding the incident's previously established beginning point, the facilitator moves on to a consideration of the possibility that the incident is actually a secondary. To explore that possibility, the facilitator inserts Step 10 immediately after the viewer's "no" response to Step 9:

10. F: *"Is there an earlier incident similar in some way to this one?"*
     V: (Introspects, may comment, ultimately decides yes or no.)

If the viewer answers "yes" in response to Step 10, the fact that an earlier similar incident exists confirms that the viewing was of a secondary incident. The facilitator's appropriate response is to direct the viewer's attention to that earlier incident, which may or may not be the sought-after primary, by resuming the process at Step 2 (2-3-4-5-6-7, 4-6-7, 4-6-7, etc.). A "no" in response to Step 10 suggests that no earlier incident exists. Thus, the facilitator resumes the process of viewing the current incident at Step 4 and continues cycling through Steps 4, 6, and 7.

From this point on, the facilitator continues to insert Steps 8, 9, and 10 into the repetitive cycle of Steps 4, 6, and 7 every couple of repetitions until either the current incident begins to diminish in intensity or the viewer detects an earlier similar incident.

During the repetition of Steps 4, 6, and 7, as the incident being viewed continues to get lighter, the facilitator must remain alert for any indication that its reduction is complete, which is the proper end point of the viewing process. If the viewer indicates that the incident no longer triggers a response or is of minimal interest, or if the incident is recounted very rationally, dispassionately, or matter-of-factly, it is time for the facilitator to insert Step 11 immediately after such a response to Step 7 in that cycle.

11. F: *"How does the incident seem to you now?"*
     V: (Indicates completely reduced or still getting lighter.)

If the viewer's response to Step 11 is "still getting lighter," the facilitator resumes the process at Step 4 and continues cycling through Steps 4, 6, and 7, as before. Step 11 is thereafter inserted after Step 7 every few repetitions, until the viewer indicates that the incident is completely reduced.

If the viewer's verbal response to Step 11 is "completely reduced," and (a) the irrational cognitive components of the incident have undergone substantial review and revision, (b) the emotive components of the incident have undergone thorough reduction, and (c) the viewer appears totally relieved, the facilitator moves directly to Step 13.

If the viewer's verbal response to Step 11 is "completely reduced" (or words to that effect) but he/she does *not* appear totally relieved, the facilitator moves immediately to Step 12—even if the cognitive and emotive components of the incident have undergone revision and reduction.

12.   F: *"Did you make any decisions or come to any conclusions at the time of that incident?"* (Note that this step solicits *original incident* cognitions, as distinguished from those observations or insights resulting from the viewing procedure. In response, viewers frequently report both original and "revised" cognitions—especially when they are near the end of the process. The facilitator accepts and acknowledges whatever a viewer offers, without correction or comment. Viewers who had already articulated some of their incident-related decisions and conclusions during Step 7 may be asked instead, "Did you make any *additional* decisions or come to any *other* conclusions at the time of that incident?")

This step directly addresses the cognitive content of the incident. It may elicit any number of rational and irrational cognitions derived from and evaluative of the viewer's traumatic experience. At the end of the procedure, it also almost invariably elicits the spontaneous repudiation of the incident's irrational thought content in favor of the rational. This is a key indicator that the incident has been resolved.

V: (Reveals original and/or revised cognitions, brightens up, and appears totally relieved and content.)

13.   F: *"Okay, then we'll leave it at that."* (Or something similarly brief and final. The facilitator then moves on to another topic, for example, "Let's take a break," or "Let's schedule our next session." Avoid the temptation to debrief, analyze, or evaluate the session except as encouraged by the viewer.)

V: (Whatever . . .)

At that point, whether it took just 20 minutes or the better part of three hours to get there, the proper end point has been reached

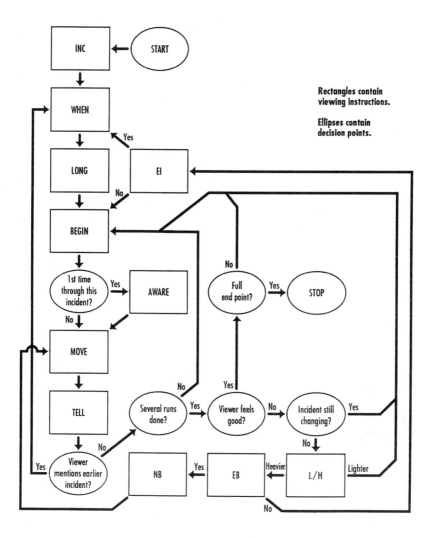

Figure 5.1. Flow Chart for Narrative TIR

and the viewing session is over. The viewer has thoroughly unrepressed and discharged the incident and has identified and revised the incident's irrational cognitive components. The viewer, visibly relieved, often appears amazed and delighted to have

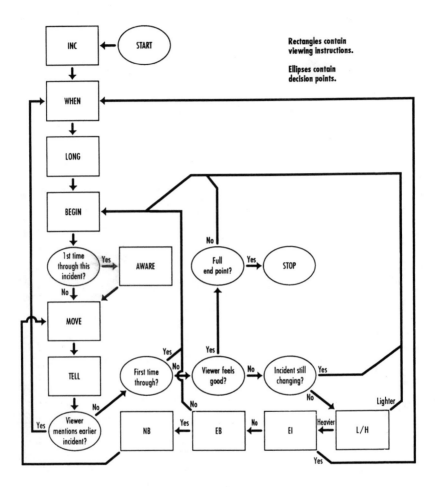

Figure 5.2. Flow Chart for Thematic TIR

achieved a new, comfortable, rational view of a previously traumatic incident, one that is now completely restructured and incapable of subsequent restimulation. This is the only resolution that should be regarded as a proper end point for any TIR session.

Rules of Facilitation

Much of the skill of facilitation has nothing to do with one's knowledge of PTSD or of the theory or technique of either TIR or RET. The facilitator's greatest challenge is to create an environment suitable for viewing and to conduct the session according to the strict rules governing the procedure. In order to bring a viewing session to a proper end point, the facilitator must observe the following rules (taken from Gerbode, 1986a):

1. *Ensure that the viewer is in optimum physical condition for the viewing session.* Ensure that the viewer is not hungry, tired, physically ill, or under the influence of alcohol or psychoactive drugs (except when drugs are prescribed as an absolute medical necessity). If at all possible, get the viewer to avoid tranquilizers, antidepressants and painkillers altogether or, at the very least, to refrain from taking a dosage that would block either physical or emotional sensation, without which effective viewing becomes difficult.[13]

2. *Ensure that the session is being given in a suitable place and at a suitable time.* Ensure that the viewing environment is secure, private, clean, quiet, and environmentally comfortable. Support personnel and colleagues should understand that, *other than for a true emergency,* the session is not to be interrupted. Telephones, intercoms, and pagers are to be turned off and personal physical needs attended to before the session begins. Assure that the time frame for the session is *inviolable.* Neither the viewer nor the facilitator should have conflicting appointments or be under any time pressure. The classic 50-minute hour used in many therapies is inadequate for the purpose of viewing because 50 minutes may not be sufficient to complete the viewing procedure. A viewer should *never* be sent home with a procedure left incomplete and/or in a state of restimulation.

3. *Do not interpret for the viewer.* Do not tell the viewer anything about the material being viewed, including what it means or how to think or feel about it. Facilitators differ radically from therapists, who feel free to interpret a client's personal experience. In TIR, viewers must be regarded as the ultimate authority on their own experiences. The facilitator acknowledges all

viewer communication and unconditionally accepts it as accurately representing their own subjective experience.

4. *Do not evaluate for the viewer.* Avoid indicating, in any way, that what the viewer has said or done is right or wrong. Do not judge, criticize, disparage, or invalidate the viewer or the viewer's perceptions, assumptions, conclusions, values, reactions, thoughts, feelings, or actions. Also, do not *validate* the viewer because such praise may lead the viewer to sense a judgmental atmosphere and to anticipate that the next judgment might not be so favorable. The use of extrinsic reinforcements of this sort might be appropriate when one is trying to reshape a client's thinking or behavior, but it is counterproductive when facilitating a client's confrontation with the often painful subtleties of a personal trauma.

5. *Control the session and take complete responsibility for it without dominating the viewer.* This makes it unnecessary for the viewer to be concerned about what comes next in the viewing procedure and allows total attention to be placed on the viewing.

6. *Be sure to comprehend what the viewer is saying.* A viewer knows right away when the facilitator does not comprehend and then feels alone and unsupported. The facilitator who does not comprehend must seek clarification and, at the same time, take responsibility for the need to do so. The facilitator might say, *"I'm sorry. I didn't get what you said. Could you give it to me again?"*, and would *not* say, *"You are being unclear,"* or even, *"Please clarify what you mean."* Do not use Rogerian or "active listening" skills to restate what the viewer has said.

7. *Be interested in the viewer and in what the viewer is saying instead of being interesting to the viewer.* A viewer generally knows immediately whether or not the facilitator is really interested. If the facilitator becomes interest*ing* (and *most violations of the Rules of Facilitation will seem interesting to the viewer!*) the viewer's attention will be pulled away from the viewing itself. The facilitator's interest supports the viewer's willingness to view and report on the material being viewed.

8. *Act in a predictable way so as not to surprise or distract the viewer.* It is not appropriate for a facilitator to disclose personal

feelings during a viewing session. The viewer has enough to do when confronting the traumatic past without having to deal with extraneous actions, remarks, or displays of emotion on the part of the facilitator.

9. *Do not try to work with someone against that person's will or in the presence of any protest.* Sometimes a relative, friend, or employer will succeed in persuading a person to do viewing when he/she does not really want to. In such a circumstance, viewing does not work well or at all. Accordingly, the facilitator must be guided only by the viewer's interest and priorities and must never try to coerce or manipulate the viewer into running a particular procedure when the viewer is not really interested in doing so. The facilitator must never rush the viewer. Instead, allow the viewer to take as much time as it takes to answer each question and/or to execute each instruction. The viewer who senses that a quick response is being demanded will not take time to do the major beneficial action in viewing, the act of viewing itself.

10. *Carry each viewing action to success for the viewer.* Be certain not to end a viewing procedure at a point of failure or incompleteness. This is the main reason sessions must not be fixed in length. One of the major functions of a facilitator is to help the viewer find the courage and confidence to confront difficult material that he/she has not been willing or able to confront alone. When viewing becomes painful, difficult, or embarrassing, the viewer may feel like ending the session. Should this occur, the facilitator's job is to encourage the viewer to stick with it and to confront and handle the difficulty to a point of resolution. Fortunately, the TIR procedure is sufficiently powerful and effective to warrant such confidence on the part of an experienced facilitator.

11. *Maintain a firm and primary intention to help the viewer.* As obvious as it may seem, a facilitator who is mainly interested in improving clinical skills or in making money, even if he/she also intends to help the viewer, will tend to lose a viewer's trust. In order to maintain the level of viewer/facilitator confidence required to preserve the viewer's sense of session security, the viewer's interests must be preserved at all times.

The facilitator must agree not to reveal or use anything the viewer says for any purpose except to help the viewer and to enhance the process of viewing. If session content is to be used as an illustration to train or educate others, the consent of the viewer must first be obtained, and steps must be taken to protect the privacy of the viewer. If the viewer feels that certain material would be potentially damaging or embarrassing, then that material should not be recorded (Gerbode, 1986b).

Thematic TIR in Application: A Case Illustration

The tidiest example of TIR in application to PTSD would be of a straightforward narrative procedure on a one-of-a-kind trauma to which the client has been flashing back regularly and that resolves in due course without the involvement of earlier incidents or complexities of any sort. A more typical example illustrates the interesting and often hidden connection of a client's current complaint with some aspect of the trauma history. Given that Tom didn't report actively flashing back when he first appeared for therapy, his case provides such an example.[14]

Tom was preparing to become a first year law student and presented for therapy with severe test anxiety. He'd had the problem at least since junior high school, but it didn't really catch up with him until he got to college. He controlled his most disruptive thoughts with alcohol and/or a mild tranquilizer and sometimes actually did well enough in his studies to be exempt from the feared final exams. But he was clean when he sat for the LSAT, and he choked up and "bombed" the test. Unable to see how he would get into—much less through—law school if he couldn't take a test without his "chemical courage," he went for help.

It didn't take more than 10 or 12 sessions of biofeedback-based (EMG) relaxation training and cognitive reorientation to bring his test-related anxiety, which included palpitations, throat constriction, and nausea, under control. At that point, he was able to confront the LSAT again and scored well enough the second time to get into law school. The demands of his first semester, however, put Tom into a panic he couldn't completely shake. His image of himself as a student eroded steadily with each successive challenge.

He barely survived his midyear exams by alternating periods of study with periods of cassette-guided relaxation. By the time he came to see me, with final exams approaching, he was on academic probation and in dread of flunking out.

To give him a bit of breathing space, I first reinforced the relaxation and quieting routines he'd learned in college. Then I set about to discover just what was happening cognitively to push his buttons so badly in connection with being tested. He had always felt, he said, as though his respectability hung on the outcome, as though each test were a rite of passage, and that he would forever be "consigned to hell" if he didn't do well. Although he had usually done well at whatever he tried, he was haunted by the cumulative evidence of his inadequacy. He approached every test, audition, and interview with fear and dread, throbbing nauseatedly throughout as though he were on trial for his life. (This is not an unfamiliar presentation for a test anxiety case.)

We know that dramatic reactions in nondangerous circumstances are frequently secondary to earlier trauma, regardless of whether the client reports actively flashing back or simply a feeling of "haunting inadequacy." My attention was "hooked" by his description of the way he "had always felt" in testing situations. I briefed Tom on the essentials of PTSD and TIR and invited him to take a look at the problem in retrospect. He agreed. As he had no special interest in any particular past trauma, I took the thematic approach. His choice of themes was anxiety, "Not just *any old* anxiety," he made it clear, but *"that throat-clutching, nauseating kind of anxiety"* peculiar to the threat of a testing situation. He had no trouble recalling the several occasions on which he'd had it most acutely.[15]

The first incident he selected was the bombed LSAT, which restimulated very shortly after he began viewing it. His pulse raced noticeably, and he reported that waves of nausea punctuated the memory of this trial by entrance exam. By his fourth time through Steps 4, 6, and 7, the persistence of his discomfort made it clear we should look for an earlier incident containing anxiety. His major comprehensive exam as a senior in college was, indeed, such an incident. He had passed the test, but he choked up badly doing it. Thus, we had a similar circumstance and a similar emotional reaction. It took only two or three repetitions to give him a headache and to confirm our need to look for yet an earlier incident.

It took him a little while to spot the next one, because he was expecting it to be—and was, at first, looking for—an earlier testing situation of some sort. But the thematic question in Step 10 is unequivocal. *"Is there an earlier incident (of any sort) containing anxiety?"* [11] So it surprised him for a moment when he recalled suffering the same excruciating anxiety after school one day in the tenth grade. He had gotten so nervous while auditioning for a part in a play that he threw up right there on stage in front of God and everybody. I thought for a moment we had perhaps found a primary, but as a viewer's verbal feedback and nonverbal "indicators" *always* take precedence over a facilitator's *unspoken* personal speculation about what's going on in the session, I was soon convinced otherwise. After five repetitions, Tom's embarrassment, now added to his earlier discomforts, was still unabated. So there must have been an even earlier incident containing that kind of anxiety.

Several minutes passed, during which Tom silently reviewed memories of his early years, his tightly squinting eyes reflecting the urgency of his need for relief from the cumulative discomforts of the incidents he had now been viewing for nearly an hour. Abruptly, his squint intensified momentarily, his head jerked back, and he dissolved into anguished and uncontrollable sobbing. The impact of whatever he had recalled was such that Tom sobbed and gagged continuously for nearly five minutes before he could so much as speak, and when he did speak, it was in the desperately rasping, tearful voice of a 10-year-old Little League infielder who had just taken the full force of a line drive square in the face during his first game. He'd had just a fleeting look at the ball as it leapt off the bat in his direction faster than he could bring his glove up to meet it. The next thing he knew he was on his back and gagging painfully on what was left of his front teeth and gums. Add to that a splitting headache, nausea, embarrassment, the rigors of reconstructive surgery and, with it all, the certain knowledge that *by displaying such complete incompetence as he had done—JERK THAT HE WAS!—the respect he had so yearned to win from his peers had been lost forever.*

It wasn't an easy incident for Tom to confront. His first several times through (Step 6, as reported in Step 7) were nothing more than a blinding, consciousness-obliterating flash. Only gradually, over the next 10 to 15 agonizing repetitions, did the incident open up and reveal the brutality of its impact to his conscious inspection. And only gradually, thereafter, did it lighten to the point at which he could recount its traumatic detail without gasping in pain. But it did completely discharge, as primary traumata inevitably do if one is diligent and patient. *"I caught it right in the teeth,"* Tom said dryly at the end, *"and I made a big deal out of how bad it made me look. It hurt like hell, that's for sure! But I blew it out of all proportion. And that's all there is to it!"* Two and a half hours into the session, thoroughly exhausted but amazed and exhilarated, he added, *"I thought since I'd stopped reverberating over that mess while I was still in high school, that it was history. I'd never have believed it could still affect me that way. Boy, was I wrong about that! That was unbelievable!"*

Note that, as is typical for TIR, the cognitive restructuring occurred spontaneously.

Tom reported at his next, and last, session that he'd "had a smile that wouldn't quit" for several days following his TIR and that, although he hadn't yet been put to the test, he couldn't imagine why he should ever again be shaken by any exam or interview. He was to call me without hesitation if he had the slightest recurrence of his test-related discomfort. When I hadn't heard from him by the end of the year, I put him on the list to receive our follow-up "Counseling Effectiveness Questionnaire." Felt-tipped boldly across his reply, right beneath the heading that identified his presenting problem, Tom's brief response said it all:

"TEST ANXIETY? WHAT TEST ANXIETY?"

Notes

1. Since this classic example of the conditioned response is not of one energized by trauma, the magnitude and persistence of the salivation response will tend to diminish as the number of chain-linked secondary stimuli increases. The highly charged and painful PTSD response, on the other hand, demonstrates considerable strength and persistence through an almost indefinitely long chain of associated secondary stimuli.

2. Emergency relief workers, paramedics, and trauma teams find TIR a highly effective procedure for use with survivors of natural disasters, violent crimes, and the like. It may be used as soon after the trauma as survivors are physically/medically able to receive it. It enables them to emerge from their ordeals without residual PTSD symptomatology.

3. The actual length of a TIR session is dictated largely by the number and complexity of the incident(s) being viewed and by the ability of the viewer to confront them.

4. Of course, some PTSD vets are completely correct when they identify their wartime experience as primary.

5. Regarding the paradox of those who suffer emotionally yet seem to think just as rationally, day-to-day, as the majority of the population, and vice versa, Meichenbaum (1977) makes a provocative observation:

> It may not be the *incidence* of irrational beliefs that is the distinguishing characteristic between normal and abnormal populations (since) nonclinical populations may also hold many of the unreasonable premises that characterize clinical populations. . . . The *nonpatient* may be more capable of "compartmentalizing" (upsetting) events and be more able to use coping techniques such as humor, rationality, or what I have come to call "creative repression." (pp. 190-191)

In this connection, it may very well be worth investigating the traumatic backgrounds of patient and nonpatient populations matched as to their *incidence* of irrational beliefs. Perhaps the unsuspected secondary impact of past trauma has something to do with the patient population's apparent inability to "creatively repress" the activation of their faulty thinking.

6. "All theorists are faced with a dilemma in trying to explain how inappropriate affect can be severed from cognition. The same events can be interpreted as cognitive reorganization, as 'expression' of affect, or as extinction of a conditioned emotional response by nonreinforcement or counterconditioning. The cognitive explanation has a major advantage for psychotherapists in that its referents—the conceptions and misconceptions of the patient—are more accessible to direct observation" (Raimy, 1975, p. 83).

7. The *TIR Workshop Manual,* Demonstration Video (available in American [VHS] and European [PAL & SECAM] formats) and a schedule of TIR training workshops in the United States and Western Europe are available from Frank A. Gerbode, M.D., Institute for Research in Metapsychology, 431 Burgess Drive, Menlo Park, CA 94025. Phone: 415-327-0920; fax 415-325-0389. **(The need for precision in application of TIR is such that prior clinical training is *strongly* recommended.)**

8. Other clients with whom it would not immediately be appropriate to use TIR, even if they very obviously were PTSD cases, are:

a. *Psychotics.* They can get stuck in the dramatization of an incident and temporarily lose whatever objectivity and grip on reality they might have started with. They are not outpatients, as a rule. They're mentioned here in case you work with that very special inpatient population.

b. *Severely Repressed.* They sometimes have no memory of and can't get in touch with the picture even of a fairly recent trauma. Or if they do remember the incident, they can't get in touch with their feelings about it (flat affect) even though they claim it must hurt deep down inside. They constitute a very small percentage of the outpatient population. They have a "wooden" presentation, and no client who displays any emotional upset fits this category.

c. *Acutely Preoccupied.* They're overburdened and distracted by problems in the present. Their attention is too compromised by pressing day-to-day concerns to have any left to give to their old business. Some people seem to be in this fix all of the time. Almost everybody feels like this once in a while. The general procedure is to get them to handle as many of the present time concerns as necessary to free up sufficient attention and energy to address the underlying PTSD case.

d. *Current Drug/Alcohol Abusers.* Mood-altering drugs (licit or illicit, prescription or over-the-counter) and alcohol compromise the viewer's ability to concentrate on the material being viewed. They also either dull or block the very emotional and physical sensations the viewer needs to work through in order to resolve a trauma. Even occasional users of psychotropics or street drugs may have to abstain in order to profit by TIR. Those who are serious about handling their PTSD problems and who *can* abstain generally will not object to this requirement. Those who cannot abstain are in need of detox or addiction services before beginning TIR.

9. Experience indicates that some new PTSD clients—even some of those who know exactly which of their traumata most need to be addressed—require as many as three or four hour-long sessions during which to get acquainted with TIR and the viewing procedure before they are ready to address their first incident. It pays not to rush them into viewing. In the event a viewer does pause during the running of an incident to ask a procedural or other viewing-related question, reply with enough information to keep the procedure moving forward but defer any further discussion until after the end of the session. While running TIR, take care not to let clients divert you into unproductive dialog. A very distraught client who whines painfully in the middle of Step 7, *"How many times must I do this!"* is not usually asking a question (the literal answer would be, *"Until the incident [or thematic chain] is resolved."*). He or she usually means something more like, "This hurts like hell and I want to stop!" Since Step 7 is not a dialog between the two of you, no response is called for. If the client makes a serious bid to stop because the process is upsetting, give only as much reassurance as is necessary to convey firmly but caringly that *the two of you are going to see it through together.* The client's original briefing should convey that the viewing of a given incident (like an appendectomy) is not something we "try." It is something we either do or don't do.

10. In order to completely reduce a traumatic incident using the TIR *Narrative Viewing Procedure*, one must know exactly which procedural steps to use following a given viewer response and be thoroughly familiar with the rules of facilitation.

11. The TIR *Thematic Viewing Procedure* is the variation to use when the viewer cannot, for whatever reason (e.g., no flashbacks, can't choose), select a specific traumatic incident to address with the TIR Narrative Viewing Procedure. The thematic procedure begins with the *viewer's selection* of a theme (symptom) for the session: one *specific* unwanted emotion, feeling, or sensation (e.g., "sadness," "rage," "nervous stomach," "stabbing pain in the throat," etc.). It is usually, though not always, the feeling that has been dominant most recently, but the viewer need not actually be feeling it at the beginning of the session. The chosen theme is used by the facilitator to guide the viewer retrogressively in selection of incidents that contain it. The procedure begins as follows:

a. Have the viewer select a *theme* to run. (encourage specificity)

1. "Select an incident containing (exact theme)." (viewer selects) (Then Steps: 2-3-4-5-6-7, 4-6-7, as in narrative procedure.)

8. "Is the incident getting lighter or heavier?" (If lighter: Steps 4-6-7, 4-6-7, etc. If heavier: Step 10a)

10a. "Is there an earlier incident containing (exact theme)?" (If yes: 2-3-4-5-6-7, 4-6-7, etc., on the earlier incident. If no: Step 9.)

9. "Does the incident we are running actually start earlier?" (If yes: 4a-6-7, 4-6-7-8, etc. If no: 4-6-7, 4-6-7-8, etc.)

You'll note that in *thematic* viewing, narrative Steps 9 and 10 are interchanged. This is because the client usually moves back through a sequence of secondaries before locating a primary that will reduce completely. In this connection, the procedure anticipates that each secondary in turn will more likely lead back to a separate earlier incident than just to an earlier starting point of its own. Procedural logic is otherwise the same as that for narrative viewing, except that you wouldn't go through each incident as many times until you do, in fact, finally reach the primary. In thematic TIR, when the current incident is getting heavier, it is time to look earlier.

Note also that procedurally speaking, "All roads lead to Rome." When the incident you're running seems to be a secondary because it's not getting lighter, both the narrative and thematic TIR procedures direct you to look earlier. When the incident you're running seems to be a primary because it is getting lighter, both procedures tell you to "Stay with this one!" So you can't really go wrong in your choice of procedures. Just be sure to schedule enough time to handle whatever comes up.

12. In *narrative* TIR, this is *not* a question you would ask until you had run the incident *many* times. Depending on the length and complexity of an incident and on the number of details of interest to the viewer, it is not uncommon to have to make 10 or 15 passes. Complete resolution of a narrative incident may occasionally require as many as 20 or more passes.

13. Sometimes a person must delay viewing for a period of from one day to two or three weeks until the effects of drugs, medication, illness, or exhaustion have fully worn off. In most cases, the effects of alcohol will have worn off in 24 hours. Some psychotropics have much longer-lasting effects, depending on their dosage and on the viewer's idiosyncratic reaction to them.

14. A sufficient number of clinically insignificant details in this case illustration have been altered to ensure the anonymity of the client.

15. Correct thematic TIR procedure requires the selection and running of one very specific theme at a time. In this case, although Tom describes his "anxiety" in terms that make it sound like a *cluster* of themes, the facilitator was persuaded that "that kind of anxiety" in fact represented one well-defined theme. Had it turned out to be only one of several individually distinguishable and separable themes (e.g., anxiety, constricted throat, nausea, embarrassment, etc.), each with a chain and primary of its own, the appropriate procedure would have been to address and run as many of them separately as held Tom's interest.

References

American Psychiatric Association. (1987). *Diagnostic and statistical manual of mental disorders* (3rd ed., rev.). Washington, DC: American Psychiatric Association.

Beck, A. T. (1970). Role of fantasies in psychotherapy and psychopathology. *Journal of Nervous and Mental Disease, 150,* 3-17.

Beck, A. T. (1976). *Cognitive therapy and the emotional disorders.* New York: New American Library.

Blundell, G. G., & Cade, C. M. (1980). *Self-awareness and E.S.R.* London: Audio Ltd.

Boudewyns, P. A., Hyer, L., Woods, M. G., Harrison, W. R., & McCranie, E. (1990). PTSD among Vietnam veterans: An early look at treatment outcome using direct therapeutic exposure. *Journal of Traumatic Stress, 3,* 359-368.

Dansky, B. S., Roth, S., & Kronenberger, W. G. (1990). The trauma constellation identification scale: A measure of the psychological impact of a stressful life event. *Journal of Traumatic Stress, 3,* 557-572.

Dryden, W., & Ellis, A. (1986). Rational-emotive therapy (RET). In W. Dryden & W. L. Golden (Eds.), *Cognitive-behavioral approaches to psychotherapy.* London: Harper & Row.

Ellis, A. (1962). *Reason and emotion in psychotherapy.* New York: Lyle Stuart.

Ellis, A. (1973). *Humanistic psychotherapy: The rational-emotive approach.* New York: McGraw-Hill.

Ellis, A. (1989). The history of cognition in psychotherapy. In A. Freeman, K. M. Simon, L. E. Beutler, & H. Arkowitz (Eds.), *Comprehensive handbook of cognitive therapy* (pp. 5-19). New York: Plenum.

Ellis, A. (1990). *The revised ABC's of rational-emotive therapy (RET).* Paper presented at The Evolution of Psychotherapy Conference, Anaheim, CA.

Eth, S., & Pynoos, R. S. (Eds.). (1985). *Posttraumatic stress disorder in children.* Washington, DC: American Psychiatric Press.

Fairbank, J. A., & Nicholson, R. A. (1987). Theoretical and empirical issues in the treatment of post-traumatic stress disorder in Vietnam veterans. *Journal of Clinical Psychology, 43,* 44-55.

Foa, E. B., & Olasov, B. (1987). *Treatment of post-traumatic stress disorder.* Workshop conducted at Advances in Theory and Treatment of Anxiety Disorders, Philadelphia, PA.

Foa, E. B., Steketee, G., & Rothbaum, B. O. (1989). Behavioral/cognitive conceptualizations of post-traumatic stress disorder. *Behavior Therapy, 20,* 155-176.

Frederick, C. J. (1986, August). *Psychic trauma and terrorism.* Paper presented at the annual meeting of the American Psychological Association, Washington, DC.

French, G. D. (1991). *Traumatic incident reduction workshop manual.* Menlo Park, CA: IRM.

Freud, S. (1984). Two short accounts of psychoanalysis. In J. Strachey (Trans.), *Five lectures on psychoanalysis* (p. 37). Singapore: Penguin.

Gerbode, F. A. (1986a). Assistance without evaluation. *Journal of Metapsychology, 1,* 7-9.

Gerbode, F. A. (1986b). A safe space. *Journal of Metapsychology, 1,* 3-6.

Gerbode, F. A. (1989). *Beyond psychology: An introduction to metapsychology.* Palo Alto, CA: IRM.

Goodman, D. S., & Maultsby, M. C. (1974). *Emotional well-being through rational behavior training.* Springfield, IL: Charles C Thomas.

Grossberg, J. M., & Wilson, H. K. (1968). Physiological changes accompanying the visualization of fearful and neutral situations. *Journal of Personality and Social Psychology, 10,* 124-133.

Hayman, P. M., Sommers-Flanagan, R., & Parsons, J. P. (1987). Aftermath of violence: Posttraumatic stress disorder among Vietnam veterans. *Journal of Counseling and Development, 65,* 363-366.

Hilgard, E. R. (1962). *Introduction to psychology* (3rd ed.). New York: Harcourt, Brace & World.

Horowitz, M. (1986). *Stress response syndromes* (2nd ed.). Northvale, NJ: Jason Aronson.

Janoff-Bulman, R. (1985). The aftermath of victimization: Rebuilding shattered assumptions. In C. R. Figley (Ed.), *Trauma and its wake* (p. 18). New York: Brunner/ Mazel.

Keane, T. M., Fairbank, J. A., Caddell, J. M., & Zimering, R. T. (1989). Implosive (flooding) therapy reduces symptoms of PTSD in Vietnam combat veterans. *Behavior Therapy, 20,* 245-260.

Keane, T. M., & Kaloupek, D. G. (1982). Imaginal flooding in the treatment of a posttraumatic stress disorder. *Journal of Consulting and Clinical Psychology, 50,* 138-140.

Kelly, W. E. (Ed.). (1985). *Post-traumatic stress disorder and the war veteran patient.* New York: Brunner/Mazel.

Kilpatrick, D. G., Veronen, L. J., & Best, C. L. (1985). Factors predicting psychological distress among rape victims. In C. R. Figley (Ed.), *Trauma and its wake* (pp. 113-141). New York: Brunner/Mazel.

Lazarus, A. (1976). *Multi-modal behavior therapy.* New York: Springer.

Lyons, J. A., & Keane, T. M. (1989). Implosive therapy for the treatment of combat-related PTSD. *Journal of Traumatic Stress, 2,* 137-152.

MacHovec, F. J. (1985). Treatment variables and the use of hypnosis in the brief therapy of post-traumatic stress disorders. *International Journal of Clinical & Experimental Hypnosis, 33,* 6-14.

Manton, M., & Talbot, A. (1990). Crisis intervention after an armed hold-up: Guidelines for counsellors. *Journal of Traumatic Stress, 3,* 507-522.

Meichenbaum, D. (1977). *Cognitive-behavior modification.* New York: Plenum.

Moore, R. H. (1990, October). *Absent flashback/covert PTSD: A video case report.* Paper presented at the annual meeting of the International Society for Traumatic Stress Studies, New Orleans.

Olasov, B., & Foa, E. G. (1987). *The treatment of post-traumatic stress disorder in sexual assault survivors using stress inoculation training (SIT).* Paper presented at the annual meeting of the Association for the Advancement of Behavioral Therapy, Boston.

Pavlov, I. P. (1927). *Conditioned reflexes.* New York: Oxford University Press.

Raimy, V. (1975). *Misunderstandings of the self.* San Francisco: Jossey-Bass.

Roth, S., & Newman, E. (1991). The process of coping with sexual trauma. *Journal of Traumatic Stress, 4,* 279-297.

Saigh, P. A. (1991). *Posttraumatic stress disorder: A behavioral approach to assessment and treatment.* Elmsford, NY: Pergamon.

Scurfield, R. M., Kenderdine, S. K., & Pollard, R. J. (1990). Inpatient treatment for war-related post-traumatic stress disorder: Initial findings on a longer-term outcome study. *Journal of Traumatic Stress, 3,* 185-201.

Solomon, Z., Mikulincer, M., & Arad, R. (1991). Monitoring and blunting: Implications for combat-related post-traumatic stress disorder. *Journal of Traumatic Stress, 4,* 209-221.

Stampfl, T. G., & Lewis, D. J. (1967). Essentials of implosive therapy: A learning-theory-based psychodynamic behavioral therapy. *Journal of Abnormal Psychology, 72,* 496-503.

Turner, S. M. (1979). *Systematic desensitization of fears and anxiety in rape victims.* Paper presented at the annual meeting of the Association for the Advancement of Behavior Therapy, San Francisco.

Veronen, L. J., & Kilpatrick, D. G. (1983). Stress management of rape victims. In D. Meichenbaum & M. E. Jaremko (Eds.), *Stress reduction and prevention.* New York: Plenum.

Warren, R., & Zgourides, G. D. (1991). *Anxiety disorders: A rational-emotive perspective.* Elmsford, NY: Pergamon.

Overcoming Performance Anxiety: Using RET With Actors, Artists, and Other "Performers"

MITCHELL W. ROBIN

Anxiety can be defined as a pervasive experience of dread typically accompanied by, or sometimes preceded by, somatic disturbance. This experience of dread is behaviorally manifested as avoidance, inhibition, sleeplessness, and decrements in problem-solving skills. RET practitioners typically classify any experience of anxiety as a dysfunctional emotion because it so often interferes with the client achieving his or her goals. The client is believed to have endorsed irrational beliefs about possible dire consequences that might occur. Overwhelming anxiety about the possibility of encountering unimaginably dire consequences can be characterized as "fear in search of a cause." RET's conceptualization of anxiety is, there-

AUTHOR'S NOTE: A version of this chapter was presented at the *World Congress on Mental Health Counseling* held in Keystone, CO, on June 14, 1990. It is based on my work with actors, artists, and "civilian" performers at the Institute for Rational-Emotive Therapy in New York.

I would like to thank my research assistant, Caroline Chernowski, for her help in the preparation of that earlier draft. I would also like to express my appreciation to Albert Ellis and Rochelle Balter, colleagues and friends, for their editorial advice and support in the development of this version of the chapter.

fore, characterized by the concept of "What if . . ." (Wessler & Wessler, 1980) and postulates two additional forms of anxiety: ego anxiety and discomfort anxiety (Ellis, 1979, 1980).

Ego Anxiety

The client suffering from ego anxiety anticipates with apprehension the possible damage to his or her self-worth in a given situation. Thus, ego anxiety is the direct result of global-rating, one of four core irrational beliefs.[1] Clients perceive the given situation as threatening to their self, soul, or essence and, therefore, want to avoid it. Those clients suffering from ego anxiety typically equate their behavior with their self-worth: good behavior equals good or enhanced personal worth, while poor behavior equals poor or diminished personal worth. They also tend to fear the world will rate them as harshly as they rate themselves. Paradoxically, they expect the world to engage in this form of rating at the same time that they make demands that the world should not/must not do this to them.

Discomfort Anxiety

Those clients suffering from discomfort anxiety anticipate with apprehension the level or intensity of the *hassles* that either will be or might be experienced in a given situation. They may also anticipate with apprehension the degree of physical stress or discomfort that either will be or might be experienced as a result of these hassles. Thus discomfort anxiety is the direct result of low frustration tolerance (LFT), another core irrational belief. People who suffer from LFT perceive the physical or social discomfort they have experienced or *expect to experience* in a given situation as unbearable and intolerable. They demand that the world not provide them with this or any other form of discomfort. They may additionally have low expectations of being able to master, or of even being able to learn how to master, this discomfort. Consequently, they typically attempt to avoid any situation associated with this "intolerable" discomfort.

The Anatomy of Performance Anxiety

Performance anxiety, commonly known as stage fright, is generally conceived of as anxiety that arises when an individual is called upon to perform (Burton, 1988; Chiu, 1985; Cooper & Wills, 1989; Matthews & Burnett, 1989; Steptoe, 1989). The specific situational referent could be such "civilian" (nonprofessional) activities as public speaking, meeting a new person, engaging in sexual activities, making a "cold call," or trying out for the team. It could also be the more esoteric performance situations experienced by actors, musicians, artists, athletes, and other performers involving such things as auditioning, rehearsing, performing, showing the portfolio, or playing in the "big game."

The performance setting could be either familiar or novel, and it could, objectively, be within the client's current ability level or at a new and challenging level. Clients typically experience some degree of performance anxiety when they

1. are either in a novel situation or are in a familiar situation that has been experienced previously as stressful;
2. perceive a situation as producing intolerable discomfort;
3. are in a situation or expect to be in a situation that challenges their efficacy or current level of ability;
4. perceive the situation as a threat to their ego or self-worth.

Performance anxiety includes both ego anxiety and discomfort anxiety. The *specific* performance situation is experienced by the person as *both* intolerably uncomfortable *and* as threatening to the self. Additionally, clients may doubt their ability to cope effectively with the performance situation. The net behavioral result of performance anxiety to any client, whether he or she is a civilian or a professional performer, tends to be either poor performance or nonperformance.

A brief examination of the four components of performance anxiety (see Table 6.1) leads us to hypothesize possible alternative consequences (Cs in RET's model) for the client. The hypothesis matrix presented in Table 6.2 examines the following components and hypothesizes potential behavioral and emotional outcomes.[2] In this new formulation of performance anxiety, behavioral outcomes range from nonperformance to *improved* performance for those clients who experience moderate levels of stress, who perceive their efficacy as adequate to the task at hand, and whose ego or self is *not* on the line. In effect, these latter individuals are

Table 6.1 Variables Within the Hypothesis Matrix

A. Quality of Situation (Empirical)
    1. Familiarity
        a. Familiar
        b. Unfamiliar
    2. Difficulty
        a. Hard
        b. Easy
B. Perceived Intensity of Stress/Discomfort
    1. High
    2. Moderate
    3. Low
C. Perceived Challenge to Self-Efficacy
    1. Efficacy is adequate to task
    2. Efficacy is inadequate to task
D. Perceived Threat to Self
    1. Self is "on the line"—Threatened
    2. Self is "not on the line"—Unthreatened

nonanxiously stressed. They experience a form of stress, called *eustress,* that is accompanied by pleasure and enhanced performance. Emotional outcomes can vary from eustress to distress. Eustress is accompanied by feelings of joy and elation, when the task is perceived as reasonably difficult (stress levels are moderate to high, and both self-worth and self-efficacy are *not* on the line). Distress is typically accompanied by ego or discomfort anxiety and panic or phobic-like avoidance at the other extreme.

As can be seen in Table 6.2, clients who present performance anxiety issues are not simply suffering from a physical disturbance "caused by" their having to perform but rather from a syndrome of disturbances based on irrational cognitions or "screwy thinking." It is my contention that mental health practitioners who treat only one or two of these components run the risk of ineffective treatment or frequent relapse.

Treatment Models

Traditionally, there have been a number of methods for treating performance anxiety. These methods have demonstrated efficacy,

Table 6.2 Performance Anxiety Hypothesis Matrix

Situation	Intensity	Efficacy	Self	Result*
Familiar/ Easy	High	Adequate	Threatened	Perf/wEgoAnx
			Unthreatened	Perf
		Inadequate	Threatened	*PerfAnx*
			Unthreatened	Perf/wDiscAnx
	Moderate	Adequate	Threatened	Perf/wEgoAnx
			Unthreatened	Perf+
		Inadequate	Threatened	PerfAnx
			Unthreatened	Perf/wDiscAnx
	Low	Adequate	Threatened	EgoAnx
			Unthreatened	Bored
		Inadequate	Threatened	Perf/wDiscAnx
			Unthreatened	Perf/wDiscAnx
Familiar/ Hard	High	Adequate	Threatened	EgoAnx
			Unthreatened	Perf−
		Inadequate	Threatened	*HiPerfAnx*
			Unthreatened	DiscAnx
	Moderate	Adequate	Threatened	PerfAnx
			Unthreatened	Perf+
		Inadequate	Threatened	PerfAnx
			Unthreatened	Perf−
	Low	Adequate	Threatened	EgoAnx
			Unthreatened	Bored
		Inadequate	Threatened	Perf−
			Unthreatened	Perf−
Unfamiliar/ Easy	High	Adequate	Threatened	Perf/EgoAnx+
			Unthreatened	Perf−
		Inadequate	Threatened	*HiPerfAnx*
			Unthreatened	DiscAnx
	Moderate	Adequate	Threatened	EgoAnx
			Unthreatened	Perf+
		Inadequate	Threatened	PerfAnx
			Unthreatened	Perf/wDiscAnx
	Low	Adequate	Threatened	EgoAnx
			Unthreatened	Concerned
		Inadequate	Threatened	Perf−
			Unthreatened	Perf−
Unfamiliar/ Hard	High	Adequate	Threatened	EgoAnx+
			Unthreatened	Perf−
		Inadequate	Threatened	*HiPanic*
			Unthreatened	DiscAnx+
	Moderate	Adequate	Threatened	Perf
			Unthreatened	Perf
		Inadequate	Threatened	*Panic*
			Unthreatened	Perf−
	Low	Adequate	Threatened	Perf−
			Unthreatened	Concerned
		Inadequate	Threatened	Perf−
			Unthreatened	Perf−

*Perf = perform or performance; Perf+ and Perf− = enhanced or diminished performance; /w = with; Anx = anxiety; Disc = discomfort.

but many of them examine only one aspect of the problem and may, therefore, "miss the boat" with a particular client by attending only to one element of the syndrome to the exclusion of all others.

Medical Models

As with other problems, the medical model assumes that the client's difficulties stem from some chemical imbalance or other physical disturbance. Thus medication is provided in an attempt to ameliorate debilitating physical symptoms of stress and to reduce the unpleasant emotions experienced in the performance situation (Bennett, Bernard, Amrick, & Wilson, 1989; Gershon & Eison, 1987; Neftel et al., 1982).

Stress Reduction Models

Stress reduction models assume that the physical experience of stress is the major component of performance anxiety. Clients are trained in such activities as controlled breathing, meditation, progressive relaxation, and biofeedback to help them reduce their own stress prior to or during a performance situation (Crocker, 1989; Fried, 1990; Neiss, 1988).

Behavioral Models

Behavioral models essentially use flooding, behavioral retraining, stress inoculation, and other stress management techniques to provide an incompatible response to stress in commonly stressful situations.

Cognitive Models

Cognitive models use cognitive restructuring to alter the client's thoughts about the specific situation in which performance anxiety occurs (Bryant & Zillmann, 1988; Burton, 1988; Emmite & Diaz-Guerrero, 1983).

Cognitive/Behavioral Models: RET

Cognitive/behavioral models address all the major components by:

1. providing training in physical stress reduction using traditional stress management techniques, disputation, and behavioral retraining.
2. disputing dysfunctional thoughts associated with the performance situation.
3. conducting behavioral training or retraining in the specific social coping skills or performance skills needed for the specific performance situation (Dendato & Diener, 1986; Kendrick, Craig, Lawson, & Davidson, 1982; Nagel, Himle, & Papsdorf, 1989; Warren, Deffenbacher, & Brading, 1976).

Using RET With Performance Anxious Clients

RET's cognitive/behavioral approach provides a full armamentarium for mental health practitioners who work with performance anxious clients. The therapist may use cognitive restructuring, stress reduction, social-skills training and other CBT methods. The intervention(s) selected depend on the nature of the presenting problem and an assessment of the client's goals. (As part of my initial assessment procedures when working with performance anxious clients, I usually give a series of questionnaires that I have developed.[3])

Many clients, however, equate feeling better with getting better and may be reluctant to do anything that they perceive might increase their current level of discomfort. They may merely wish "not to shake *so* much" or "not to feel *so* uncomfortable." The initial strategy for such clients may be stress management or relaxation techniques rather than active and vigorous disputing or the giving of "shame attacks" as homework. For such clients, the accomplishment of this initial goal may require a didactic component, one that provides the client with information about the stress he/she is experiencing and the possible alternative consequences. Table 6.3 provides a brief summary of the information that I typically provide to performance anxious clients at some point in therapy.

As with all therapeutic interventions, timing and pacing is an important consideration. It is usually best to present this didactic component early and often for clients who present with strong LFT/discomfort anxiety issues.

Using vigorous evocative techniques, I try to help them draw a number of conclusions:

Table 6.3 Stress

I. Stress Defined
    A. It is *normal!*
    B. It is the body's automatic response to novelty, emergency, or unfamiliarity.
II. Components of Stress and Their Consequences
    A. Physical
        1. Increase in heart beat
        2. Increase in respiration
        3. Change in blood pressure
        4. Dry mouth
        5. Wet palms
        6. Body sweats
        7. Pupils dilate
        8. Muscle tremors
        9. Gastrointestinal motility
        10. Bowel and bladder distress
        11. Pilomotor response
        12. Penile and nipple erection
    B. Psychological
        1. Distress
            a. Anxiety
            b. Fear
            c. Panic
            d. Anger
        2. Eustress
            a. Pleasurable anticipation
            b. Joy, happiness, etc.
            c. Elation, ecstacy, "natural high"
    C. Social/Behavioral
        1. Distress
            a. Anxiety
                (1) Avoid the situation
                (2) Delay/procrastinate
                (3) Perform poorly
            b. Fear
                (1) Avoid the situation
                (2) Delay/procrastinate
                (3) Perform poorly
            c. Panic
                (1) Avoid thoughts about the situation in any of its forms
                (2) Avoid the situation in any of its forms
                (3) Avoid people connected with the situation who might get you
                    to perform

continued

Table 6.3 Continued

---

    d. Anger
       (1) Condemn those who got you into this situation
       (2) Condemn self for being in the situation
       (3) Pick fights or behave in other socially inappropriate ways
  2. Eustress
    a. Pleasurable anticipation
       (1) Prepare
          (a) Enjoy the process of preparation
          (b) Anticipate the pleasant outcome
       (2) Procrastinate—NOTE: This undesirable outcome can occur if
          the client's fantasy about doing well or having fun is highly
          rewarding and the effort of actual preparation is perceived as
          too much of a hassle.
    b. Joy, happiness, etc.
       (1) Enjoy the process of performing
       (2) Enjoy the people you are with or the situation you are in
    c. Elation, "natural high"
       (1) Whoops, shouts, cheers
       (2) Impatient for the next time

---

1. Physical Stress is *Normal!* To demand that they not experience it is to demand that they not be alive or fully human.
2. Don't Demand to be Stress Free! Paradoxically, the more they demand that they be totally stress free, the more stress filled they become.
3. Don't Rehearse Symptoms! Rehearsing a speech or other performance behavior usually enhances that behavior, but rehearsing a symptom of anxiety (repeating over and over "I mustn't shake so much" or "I am too fucking scared") only makes that symptom experientially more intense and more unpleasant.

Many clients derive therapeutic benefits from the presentation of this didactic component. They report that knowledge of what to expect physiologically, as well as the changing awareness that these symptoms are normal and not dangerous, is not only reassuring and enhances their coping but also enables them to grasp more readily the B/C connection that disputing requires of them: Changing one's beliefs about the world, one's self, and others leads to changes in one's emotions and behaviors. Many times clients have informed me that once they were willing to see the stress they were experiencing as normal they were also able to experience the situation as nonanxiously stressful and, subsequently, to experience it as eustressful.

Belief Systems

RET conceives of two varieties of belief systems: rational and irrational. A belief is rational if it is factual, that is, empirically verifiable, logical, and life enhancing. A belief is irrational if it is not factual, illogical (a non sequitur), and life diminishing. The consequences of rational thought are emotions and behaviors that are functional, meaning those that encourage creative problem solving, enjoyment of life "as it is," and performing effectively within current limits of ability. The consequences of irrational thought are emotions and behaviors that are dysfunctional, meaning those that discourage the individual from creative problem solving, from enjoyment of life "as it is" by insisting on life "as it should be," and from performing effectively within the limits of current ability by insisting on perfection and comfort.

Common Irrational Beliefs About Performing, Performance Situations, and Performers

Table 6.4 presents a comprehensive (but not exhaustive) list of irrational beliefs that clients have endorsed in private sessions as well as in the performance anxiety workshops held at the IRET in New York City. They have been grouped, for convenience sake, under the four core irrational beliefs described by Albert Ellis (1985, 1977): demandingness, global rating, low frustration tolerance, and catastrophizing/awfulizing.

Many clients, not only those who experience performance anxiety, may tenaciously endorse a series of illogical equations—shown in Table 6.5—that also tend to get them into emotional trouble. The first two are rephrasings of beliefs that lead to ego anxiety and discomfort anxiety, while the third is a belief that assumes, just because the client worried so much, that the client has put in a lot of effort on the problem and is therefore entitled to the supposed benefits that strong effort brings.

Table 6.4 Common Performance-Related Irrational Beliefs

I. Demands
   A. I must perform perfectly.
   B. I must be perfectly prepared.
      1. I'm not ready yet and I must not perform until I am.
   C. I must be seen (heard, etc.) as I perceive myself to be, i.e., perfectly prepared and competent.
      1. I must not be seen/heard as the observer (casting director, critic, audience) prefers to see/hear me.
   D. I must not reveal too much of myself to others via my act, performance, speech, art work, etc.
   E. I must not experience any discomfort in performance.
   F. I must not experience any discomfort in preparation for performance.
   G. I must not experience any discomfort while thinking about preparing or performing.
   H. I must be acclaimed after my performance, audition, etc.
      1. All my hard work in preparation, audition, performance, etc., entitles me to the effortless recognition and acclaim that I must have.
      2. Any delay in acclaim is intolerable.
   I. I must achieve stardom, fame, etc., quicker than at my current rate of progress.
   J. My life must not change in any undesirable way as a consequence of my performance.
II. Low Frustration Tolerance
   A. I can't stand the hassle of . . . .
      1. Preparing.
      2. Practicing.
      3. Auditioning.
      4. Waiting for a reply.
      5. Possibly being rejected.
      6. Possibly being accepted.
      7. Performing.
      8. Having to develop a track record/reputation.
      9. Having to live up to my reputation.
      10. Having to meet the public.
   B. I can't stand the physical discomfort I experience when I . . .
      1. Meet the public.
      2. Have to deal with unpleasant people.
      3. Think about performing.
      4. Prepare.
      5. Practice.
      6. Audition.
      7. Get rejected.
      8. Get accepted.
      9. Perform.

---

continued

Table 6.4 Continued

III. Catastrophizing
    A. It's the end of the world if . . .
        1. I don't do well (perfectly).
        2. I am seen as less than perfectly competent and prepared.
            a. Get a bad rating.
            b. Get negative comments.
            c. Get a bad review.
            d. Reveal my "secret self."
        3. I experience any discomfort.
IV. Global-Rating
    A. The World is utterly shitty because . . .
        1. Its requirements are too hard.
        2. Its requirements are too inconvenient.
        3. It has rules at all.
    B. I am totally worthless when . . .
        1. I believe I have done poorly or not achieved my personal best.
        2. I feel any discomfort.
        3. Others rate me as performing poorly.
    C. Others are completely rotten/stupid when . . .
        1. They rate me negatively and I don't deserve it.
        2. They rate me positively and I don't deserve it.
        3. They don't understand/give me credit for my hard work, preparation, and anxiety.

RET Intervention Strategies

A number of specific interventions can be recommended for use with performance anxious clients, including (a) educating the client as to the causes and effects of stress, (b) disputing irrational beliefs, (c) teaching relaxation and imagery, and (d) using various experiential exercises. All of these possible interventions can be presented in vivo during the session or can be assigned as homework. Table 6.6 provides some brief descriptions of typical interventions.

Table 6.5 Illogical Equations

A.	My work	=	My self
B.	Discomfort	=	Toxicity
C.	Anxiety	=	Effort

Table 6.6 RET Intervention Strategies

I. Disputes
    A. Empirical
        1. What is your evidence that . . .
        2. Where is it written that . . .
            a. You must succeed?
            b. You must not feel discomfort?
            c. People must see you as you wish to be seen?
            d. Things must be quicker/easier than they are?
            e. You are utterly worthless if you do poorly or experience any discomfort?
            f. Situations, people, or affects are toxic?
            g. You would fall apart, disintegrate, or in any way not stand it if you experienced failure, hassle, or discomfort?
    B. Pragmatic
        1. How will thinking . . . enable you to accomplish your goals?
            a. Any of the above
            b. Your own particular brand of mishagoss
        2. How will (doing) . . . enable you to accomplish your goals?
            a. Procrastinating
            b. Not rehearsing/preparing
            c. Not auditioning
            d. Not engaging in the activity
            e. Getting angry
            f. Worrying, getting anxious, panicking
    C. Philosophical
        1. Couldn't you still have (some kind of) a happy, productive life if . . .
            a. The worst happened?
            b. You always experienced discomfort?
II. Relaxation/Imagery
    A. "Quick & Dirty"
        1. Measure subjective units of discomfort (SUD)
        2. Take "good" breath
        3. Hold for slow count of five
        4. Let breath out through pursed lips
        5. Resume normal breathing
            a. Think "Calm" while inhaling
            b. Think "Relaxed" while exhaling
            c. OR visualize your favorite number riding the waves as you inhale and exhale
        6. DO NOT follow any other stray, interesting, or defeating thought during this exercise
        7. Repeat No. 5 and No. 6 for 1-5 minutes
        8. Slowly return to regular activity
        9. Retake SUD

continued

Table 6.6 Continued

     B. Diaphragmatic Breathing
        1. Assessment
           a. Put one hand on upper chest and other on the abdomen
           b. Take a big breath
           c. Which hand moved?
               (1) If lower hand, then teach Rational-Emotive Imagery (REI) or
                   meditative imagery
               (2) If upper hand, then teach diaphragmatic breathing
                   (a) Inhale and expand abdomen
                   (b) Exhale and contract abdomen
                   (c) Lie down on flat surface with a tissue box, paper cup, or
                       light book on your abdomen and "pop the box"
     C. Relaxation Scripts: A variety are available. I have used the ones by
        Arnold Lazarus to good advantage. I have also "tailor-made" tapes
        for specific clients.
     D. REI
        1. Visualize the "dreaded" situation
        2. Strongly experience the negative dysfunctional affect
        3. Try to change the dysfunctional affect into a functional one. Change
           anger to disappointment or frustration; change anxiety to concern.
        4. Examine the change in thinking (iB-rB) that preceded the change
           in affect
III. Experiential Exercises
     A. Stay "in the moment"—Stay *process* oriented, not *product* oriented.
     B. Act *as if*—Remember when Anna met the King of Siam? She pretended
        bravery and convinced herself as well as others.
     C. "Desacredize" the observer
     D. "Who is your audience?"
     E. Self-Acceptance Exercises
        1. "Warts and All"
        2. "Tissue Box Dispute"
     F. Give yourself "permission" to screw up
     G. Symptom rehearsal/symptom permission
IV. Homework
     A. Cognitive
        1. Work on changing your thinking
        2. Do REI
     B. Behavioral
        1. *Try* to practice, prepare, etc.
        2. Do relaxation exercises

The most common RET intervention is disputation. Table 6.6 provides specific examples of the three types of disputes: empirical, pragmatic, and philosophical or "elegant" disputing. All three types of disputing help the client arrive at the B/C connection.

Empirical disputes help clients take a scientific approach to their disturbance by encouraging them to present evidence for their beliefs and helping them to see that maintaining a belief for which there is no factual evidence is usually dysfunctional in that it leads to emotional disturbance.

Pragmatic disputes essentially show clients that tenaciously endorsing irrational beliefs, with their consequent dysfunctional emotions and behaviors, is impractical because it interferes with the attainment of their long-range goals.

The sine qua non of RET disputing is the *philosophical* dispute, which produces what is considered to be the *elegant* solution. This approach encourages clients stoically to accept the fact that even if they had a life filled with challenges, hassles, and discomforts, they could still experience some modicum of pleasure, happiness, and success, although perhaps not as much as they had been demanding. The elegant solution further encourages clients to recognize that it is not awful if they experience less pleasure, happiness, and success than they had been demanding.

A client who was seen at the IRET during one of our Performance Anxiety Workshops reported that she was trained as a singer but that she had never been to an audition because she could not stand the thought of having to perform in front of "all those people." She also felt depressed about her lack of attainment. She was convinced that these defects were proof positive that she could never have a decent life and was a failure as a person. By first attacking the secondary problem (her depression about her anxiety and her conclusion of worthlessness), we got her to see that, while she was arguably a "failure" at going to auditions, this was in no way proof positive that she was or would be a failure in life. We also were able to help her see that experiencing anxiety about performing in front of "all those people," while dysfunctional, was by no means proof of her "shithood." Whereas it would be both frustrating and disappointing if she let her anxiety (stress) prior to auditions stop her from auditioning, this was not proof that she could never accomplish any of her goals or would lead an otherwise worthless life.

The Tissue Box Dispute for Self-Acceptance

Clients who engage in global self-rating typically believe that they will become totally worthless if they do some specific activity poorly. They may believe this about all their activities, or they may *sacredize* (see below) one particular activity or class of activities: "Oh, I know that if I fail math I am not *totally* a worthless shit, BUT if I screw up where it's important to me, then I go right into the crapper." Whether clients' beliefs are specific or general, they can benefit from learning to accept themselves and others as they are and not as they would like them to be, that is, accept themselves and others "warts and all."

The specific client mentioned above was presented with a full tissue box and was asked to list her strengths and weaknesses. As she listed each positive and negative trait, I asked her to pull one tissue from the tissue box. (This occasionally leaves a small number of tissues remaining in the box and a larger number of tissues scattered around the room. The remaining tissues can also be used to remind clients that they can probably never fully know *all* of their positive and negative traits.) When the client was satisfied that we had "seen the worst," I asked her to tell me which tissue *was* the box: that is, which trait is the person. I asked her, "Does the container change value even if the contents are lousy?" Some clients will then remind me of the cliché that "a rotten apple ruins the bunch," but I point out the basket isn't ruined, and the rotten apple can be removed without changing the basket or the rest of the apples. This particular client was able to see that, by globally rating herself based on her lack of accomplishment at either getting to auditions or actually auditioning once she got there, she was trading one problem for two: she was still not auditioning *and* now she was feeling both anxious and guilty. She also saw that, by tenaciously focusing on this one particular negative trait, she was ignoring many of her other valuable traits.

Such a "battle of the metaphors" aids the client in coming to grips with a central value in RET: What people *do* is not what people *are*. It is easier to change rotten behaviors if you realize that the contents are not the container: Behaviors are not the person nor are they the person's soul or essence. This also strikes at the heart of many performers' most basic assumption, "If I lose my craziness, I lose my creativity." Using the tissue box, I can show them that their craziness is but one trait and that their creativity is another. They can lose their craziness and never disturb their creativity.

Desacredization

RET reminds people that it is not religion that gets them into trouble, but religiosity (Ellis, 1983). One technique routinely used to attack a client's religiosity is what I call *desacredization*. Many clients develop an area or person in their life so important to them that the mere thought of possibly losing that person or screwing up in that area is tantamount to breaking one of the Ten Commandments in the Old Testament. They create a Gospel According to Fred (or Phyllis) and act as though they had been told *THOU SHALT NOT APPEAR FOOLISH IN FRONT OF THY BOSS!* or *THOU SHALT NOT FEEL UNCOMFORTABLE!* or *THOU SHALT NOT SCREW UP ON THE AUDITION!* They believe that the situation or the person is *awesome* and then act accordingly. The fear of violating this idiosyncratic commandment looms large on their personal horizons, and they experience a form of moral anxiety or guilt when they believe they might violate their personal precepts.

In the process of desacredization, the client is encouraged to develop mechanisms for putting the person or the event into proper perspective. One actor, who was fearful of his director, was encouraged to remind himself vigorously that his director was human and that, while he might act as if he wanted my client to kiss his ring or some part of his anatomy, not doing so was not a moral fault and would not lead to hellfire. The client was then encouraged to make note of a number of human fallibilities exhibited by his director. Finally, the client was emboldened enough to attempt a shame attack in front of the director. In this case, the client gave himself permission to sing off key during one of the rehearsals. The director merely asked if he needed further help with the song and did not react as my client dreaded he would. The client later acknowledged that his fear of appearing foolish in front of his idol had been so inhibiting that he could not relax during rehearsals or sleep for hours afterward. While it is likely that the director might not appreciate continuously poor performance and might even eventually fire such a performer, it is also true that the client's dread and awe only encouraged poor performance and an unwillingness to take risks, which is the antithesis of creativity.

Students in speech classes as well as public speakers, teachers, and many other "civilians" may experience "speech anxiety" if they likewise tend to sacredize their audience. One young client of mine had so intimidated herself by the thought that her classmates might yawn (or, horror of horrors, laugh) while she spoke in class that she could not speak up in her speech class or any of her other classes. She was convinced it was essential that she be approved of by her teacher, her classmates, and anyone who might even overhear her presentation. When I asked her if she was religious, she remarked that she had been but no longer practiced it. I told her I was surprised by her remark on two counts: (a) she appeared to have turned her listeners into gods whom she had to appease with every word she uttered, and (b) people who practice the Judeo-Christian belief system tend to remember the first commandment and not create other gods.

This client was given the homework of being the idol smasher utilizing the following exercise: She was instructed to visualize herself getting up to speak in class, bowing down to the class, and then kissing their feet. She was then asked to make note of her emotional response. She was further asked to visualize her classmates, teachers, and other potential listeners as little, ugly, stone idols, and again to note her emotional response. Finally, she was asked if she wanted to smash those idols to smithereens. She replied that she not only wanted to but was ahead of me and had already done so.

She willingly accepted the idol smasher assignment and, when she went to class the next day, she practiced in vivo what we had tried in session. During the following weeks, she reported that the homework was a "smashing success." She was able to speak up in class more often than she had in the past, and while she still experienced some discomfort each time she spoke, she was no longer willing to let the discomfort get the best of her. She rightly concluded that by doing so she would have "substituted one false god for another."

Giving Oneself Permission

As was noted earlier, clients who suffer from performance anxiety dread making mistakes, screwing up, or appearing fallible (and therefore human). They also dread (a) the hassles that occur when they make a mistake and (b) the discomfort that occurs when they are in situations where they *might* make a mistake. They diligently attempt to avoid situations in which a mistake or discomfort *might* occur. Giving Oneself Permission is an intervention strategy designed to remind clients that their irrational beliefs act as a Jehovah-like command that they *not* be human. Such beliefs *forbid* them the opportunity to make mistakes, which limits their growth. This strategy helps them discover that when they profoundly believe that they *must not* make a mistake, feel discomfort, or be hassled, they experience more discomfort as a result.

Alternatively, this strategy encourages clients to *give* themselves permission to be uncomfortable or to screw up rather than repeatedly failing in their attempts to live in a perfectly comfortable and hassle-free world. One client suffered from such "uncontrollable" shaking whenever he spoke in public that he was constantly distracted from his speech and rarely got the desired effect. A homework assignment was given to find two different opportunities to speak in public. In the first, he was forcefully to forbid himself the right to shake, in the second he was to say forcefully to himself, "It's OK to shake when I talk; I have *permission*." He was also instructed to note the results. He discovered that, in the first case, the shaking became worse, while in the second, the shaking became not only bearable but was eventually ignored. He got to the point where he accepted that he might continue to shake whenever he spoke but, by giving himself permission to shake, he found he could stand it and get on with his speech, and he more often got the results he desired.

A variant on Giving Oneself Permission is called *Symptom Exaggeration*. Clients are encouraged to make their symptoms worse by shaking harder, making their voice more quivery, and the like. By voluntarily exaggerating the intensity of their symptom, clients give themselves permission to look anxious in public. Once clients realize that they can to some extent control the intensity of the symptom by increasing it, many can also be taught how to reduce the intensity as well.

Staying in the Moment

As was seen in the previous cases, the clients had become so involved with their own *mishagoss*[4] that they could not get on with the activity at hand. When this occurs in the theater, a stage director might instruct an actor to stay in the imaginary moment by focusing on the problem presented in the script itself and to avoid getting bogged down in acting technique or style. Actors are encouraged to ignore what the product will look like and to concentrate on the activity/situation at hand. This emphasis on process over product, on flow rather than result, reminds performers that they can't see themselves act and have no real idea what the audience perceives. As my vocal coach used to remind me, "You can't be an audience and a performer at the same time. If you are trying to hear how you sound, you aren't paying attention to your singing. By the time you hear the note, it's off key."

Performers/clients who stay process oriented are less likely to be anxious about what the observer/audience is thinking and more likely to be involved in enjoying the experience of performing, which is what stress-free performance is all about. People who suffer from performance anxiety tend not to enjoy performing because of all the inordinate concerns that dominate their thoughts while performing. This is doubly regrettable because many who perform anticipate that they "should be" able to perform with joy and, thereby, provide joy for others. In reality such performers end up experiencing distress that in many cases is communicated to the audience during their performance.

In contrast, I once had the privilege of working with a young actor who was partially disabled. He had been hit by a car as a child, which left him with a rolling gait and partially paralyzed left arm. Despite these mechanical problems, which were visible to all in the theater company, he demonstrated unexpected self-acceptance and was not self-handicapping. The only thing anyone paid attention to when he performed was his joy in being on stage. When he stepped out to take his bow, most audiences were shocked to see that he walked with a limp and could not wave back to them. What this young actor seemed to do naturally, accepting himself and giving himself permission to perform imperfectly within his current level of ability, is at the heart of what I attempt to teach all of my performance anxious clients.

Case Study

James D., a 35-year-old fine artist, initially entered therapy in order to work on relationship and career issues. He was anxious and depressed about the possibility that his lover of 10 years might be leaving him. He was also disturbing himself about the possibility that he was in a dead-end job. During our initial session it became obvious that underlying most of his disturbance was his belief that both his job and his relationship were in jeopardy because he had not made more of his professional training and was not the success that he must be. He explained that he had been trained as a fine artist and that all he was doing was pasteups and mechanicals. He found it difficult to believe that anyone, including his lover, could accept him and love him despite his lack of accomplishment. He also believed that, since he was willing to work at a "safe" job, he deserved no success and would never achieve any. James explained that he knew he was capable of producing museum-quality paintings and sculptures but, if he showed his work to dealers and exhibitors, they would see his true self in his work and dire consequences to his worth and self-esteem would result. He further explained that he experienced debilitating stress whenever he: (a) contemplated selecting, let alone actually selected, items for his portfolio; (b) thought about showing his work to others; and (c) looked at a blank canvas that he was planning to work on. As with other performance anxious clients, his anticipation of these dreaded physical symptoms resulted in his unwillingness to do anything that might trigger their occurrence.

As the first session progressed, I asked him about what he hoped would occur if our work together was fruitful: "If our work together is successful, how would you feel and act differently than you do now?" Based on his answer we agreed upon the following therapy goals: (a) to eliminate the secondary problem of depression about the lack of accomplishment and to work on replacing it with self-acceptance about his current level of accomplishment, (b) to work on the irrational beliefs that interfered with his showing his portfolio to dealers and exhibitors, (c) to work on reducing or eliminating his physical distress and to eliminate his awfulizing about its occurrence, and (d) to work on actually getting his work seen by dealers and exhibitors.

As is typical in RET, I used the first session to teach him the B-C connection and gave him a homework assignment to record his self-downing and awfulizing thoughts and to note his emotional reactions when he had them. During the second and third sessions we worked on teaching him to dispute his irrational beliefs concerning his worthlessness due to his lack of accomplishment. I also encouraged him to "rate his behavior and *not* himself."

By teaching how to be more accepting of his current level of accomplishment, with the resultant decrease in self-downing, I hoped to help him establish a set of beliefs that would enable him to cope more effectively with the disappointments and frustrations that he was sure to experience in the weeks ahead. During the weeks that followed, as he began to experience the result of being more accepting of himself, he also began to report experiencing less anxiety on the job and in his relationship with his lover.

Once we were both satisfied that he understood the RET principle of self-acceptance and could dispute his irrational belief that "he *was* his behavior," we moved on to the primary issues: (a) disputing the irrational beliefs that triggered his ego and discomfort anxiety, (b) converting his distress to eustress, and (c) having him actually show his work to dealers and exhibitors.

The first issue was partially addressed during our earlier work on self-acceptance, but the emphasis now shifted to getting him to accept that his self, his worth as a human, was not on the line at *any* time. It was during our work on this issue that his concern about people seeing his "secret self" reemerged.

His secret self was a battered child who could not find love, and he was sure that his neediness and early trauma "bled through the canvas and could be seen by anyone who cared to look." He was also convinced that anyone who saw his secret self would either automatically reject him or feel sorry for him, and that either response would result in damage to his career, reputation, and self-worth. Needless to say, these beliefs acted as a deterrent to his artistic production.

We worked on disputing his irrational beliefs: (a) that it would be awful and terrible if people felt sorry for him, (b) that he *must* only be seen as he prefers to be seen, and (c) that people *must not* think about him as they choose to think. In all cases I chose not to dispute his belief that he had a secret self or that people could see his neediness writ large on the canvas. This is consistent with the RET approach of accepting the client's reality but disputing the client's inferences about that reality.

During these sessions the client began to experience physical symptoms of distress, so I took the opportunity to start teaching him about stress and relaxation. We also started the process of disputing his irrational beliefs about the significance of experiencing stress. I got him to see that stress was normal and that awfulizing about stress only made it worse. He also learned how to control the intensity of his reaction via meditation, imagery, and breathing exercises. By the 15th session he could imagine himself selecting items for his portfolio without experiencing overwhelming anxiety or distress.

In all we had 25 sessions together, at which time we agreed to terminate therapy. By that time James had successfully put together a portfolio and was actually painting pictures of his secret self, which he first showed to friends and then to strangers. (He was mildly shocked and disappointed when most observers failed to see his "naked soul revealed on canvas.") He also was beginning to make the rounds of dealers, exhibitors, and agents to see if he could get his first one-man show.

Conclusions

RET's unique cognitive behavioral approach to emotional disturbance provides mental health practitioners with a rich and varied set of strategic interventions for their clients' presenting problems. This chapter has briefly presented a rational-emotive model of performance anxiety, which characterizes it as an amalgam of both ego and discomfort anxiety. Specific irrational beliefs form the core of a syndrome of beliefs about (a) the familiarity and difficulty of the situation, (b) the level of stress expected within the situation, (c) whether or not clients expect their current level of ability to be adequate to the situation, and (d) whether or not clients expect their self-worth to be on the line.

This chapter also briefly described some of the techniques that I have found most useful in my work with performance anxious clients at the IRET, including (a) normalization of stress, (b) non-rehearsal of symptoms, (c) "pop-the-box" breathing, (d) disputation (empirical, pragmatic, elegant, and tissue box), (e) desacredization, (f) idol smashing, (g) giving oneself permission, (h) symptom exaggeration, and (i) staying within the moment.

Mental health practitioners may use this formulation to create some testable hypotheses about the nature and quality of the performance anxiety that a particular client experiences. Subsequently they may also find that they can provide more sharply focused interventions for the multiplex of problems that such clients experience.

Notes

1. The four core irrational beliefs are (a) demandingness, (b) awfulizing/ catastrophizing, (c) global-rating of self and others, and (d) low frustration tolerance (LFT). Research has shown that people who strongly endorse these beliefs are more likely to suffer emotional and personality disturbances than those who do not (DiGiuseppe, Leaf, Robin, & Exner, 1988; DiGiuseppe, Robin, Leaf, & Gorman, 1989; Robin & DiGiuseppe, 1990).

2. The hypothetical outcomes have *not* been rigorously tested. They are presented as hypotheses to be tested with your clients. It has been my clinical experience that they are reasonable starting points for developing intervention strategies. I would appreciate hearing from you as to your experience with them.

3. Limitations of space prohibit the inclusion of these instruments. Anyone wishing to obtain copies can write to the author at IRET, 45 East 65th Street, New York, NY 10021.

4. *Mishagoss*—a Yiddish term commonly in use—refers to one's own unique brand of "craziness." When I write spoofs for or perform at the Institute's parties, I am known by the pseudonym of Dr. Mitchagoss.

References

Bennett, D. A., Bernard, P. S., Amrick, C. L., & Wilson, D. E. (1989). Behavioral pharmacological profile of CGS 19755, a competitive antagonist at N-methyl-d-aspartate receptors. *Journal of Pharmacology and Experimental Therapeutics, 250*(2), 454-460.

Bryant, J., & Zillmann, D. (1988). Using humor to promote learning in the classroom. *Journal of Children in Contemporary Society, 20*(1-2), 49-78.

Burton, D. (1988). Do anxious swimmers swim slower? Reexamining the elusive anxiety-performance relationship. *Journal of Sport and Exercise Psychology, 10*(I), 45-61.

Chiu, L. (1985). The relation of cognitive style and manifest anxiety to academic performance among Chinese children. *Journal of Social Psychology, 125*(5), 667-669.

Cooper, C. L., & Wills, G. I. (1989). Popular musicians under pressure. Special Issue: Performance and stress. *Psychology of Music, 17*(1) 22-36.

Crocker, P. R. (1989). A follow-up of cognitive-affective stress management training. *Journal of Sport and Exercise Psychology, 11*(2), 236-242.

Dendato, K. M., & Diener, D. (1986). Effectiveness of cognitive/relaxation therapy and study-skills training in reducing self-reported anxiety and improving the academic performance of test-anxious students. *Journal of Counseling Psychology, 33*(2), 131-135.

DiGiuseppe, R., Leaf, R., Robin, M. W., & Exner, T. (1988, September). *The development of a measure of irrational/rational thinking*. Paper presented at the World Congress on Behavior Therapy, Edinburgh, Scotland.

DiGiuseppe, R., Robin, M. W., Leaf, R., & Gorman, A. (1989, June). *A cross-validation and factor analysis of a measure of irrational beliefs*. Paper presented at the World Congress of Cognitive Therapy, Oxford, England.

Ellis, A. (1977). *Reason and emotion in psychotherapy*, Secaucus, NJ: Citadel.

Ellis, A. (1979). Discomfort anxiety: A new cognitive behavioral construct (Part 1). *Rational Living, 14*(2) 3-8.

Ellis, A. (1980). Discomfort anxiety: A new cognitive behavioral construct (Part 2). *Rational Living, 15*(1), 25-30.

Ellis, A. (1983). *The case against religiosity*. New York: Institute for Rational-Emotive Therapy.

Ellis, A. (1985). Expanding the ABCs of rational-emotive therapy. In M. Mahoney & A. Freeman (Eds.), *Cognition and psychotherapy* (pp. 313-323). New York: Plenum.

Emmite, P. L., & Diaz-Guerrero, R. (1983). Cross-cultural differences and similarities in coping style, anxiety, and success-failure on examinations. *Series in Clinical and Community Psychology: Stress and Anxiety, 2*, 191-206.

Fried, R. (1990). *The breath connection: How to reduce psychosomatic and stress-related disorders with easy-to-do breathing exercises*. New York: Plenum.

Gershon, S., & Eison, A. S. (1987). The ideal anxiolytic. *Psychiatric Annals, 17*(3), 156-170.

Kendrick, M. J., Craig, K. D., Lawson, D. M., & Davidson, P. O. (1982). Cognitive and behavioral therapy for musical-performance anxiety. *Journal of Consulting and Clinical Psychology, 50*(3), 353-362.

Matthews, D. B., & Burnett, D. D. (1989). Anxiety: An achievement component. *Journal of Humanistic Education and Development, 27*(3), 122-131.

Nagel, J. J., Himle, D. P., & Papsdorf, J. D. (1989). Cognitive-behavioral treatment of musical performance anxiety. Special Issue: Performance and stress. *Psychology of Music, 17*(1), 12-21.

Neftel, K. A., Adler, R. H., Kappeli, L., Rossi, M., Dolder, M., Kaser, H. E., Bruggesser, H. H., & Vorkauf, H. (1982). Stage fright in musicians: A model illustrating the effect of beta blockers. *Psychosomatic Medicine, 44*(5), 461-469.

Neiss, R. (1988). Reconceptualizing relaxation treatments: Psychobiological states in sports. *Clinical Psychology Review, 8*(2), 139-159.

Robin, M. W., & DiGiuseppe, R. (1990, August). *Irrational beliefs and MCMI-2 personality disorder scores*. A paper presented at the 98th Annual Convention of the American Psychological Association, Boston.

Steptoe, A. (1989). Stress, coping and stage fright in professional musicians. Special Issue: Performance and stress. *Psychology of Music, 17*(1), 3-11.

Warren, R., Deffenbacher, J. L., & Brading, P. (1976). Rational-emotive therapy and the reduction of test anxiety in elementary school students. *Rational Living, 11*(2), 26-29.

Wessler, R. A., & Wessler, R. L. (1980). *The principles and practice of rational-emotive therapy*. San Francisco: Jossey-Bass.

RET and Divorce Adjustment

CHARLES H. HUBER

Almost 90% of the U.S. population chooses to marry at least once. Approximately 50% of these first marriages end in divorce. About 75% of these divorced individuals later remarry; 50% of their remarriages again end in divorce (Glick, 1989). These figures have critical significance when considered with regard to research findings on marital status and mental health. Epidemiologists have consistently demonstrated an association between psychiatric disturbance and marital status (Bebbington, 1987). With remarkably few exceptions, high rates of psychological distress have been reported for separated, divorced, and widowed individuals (Fincham & Bradbury, 1990).

The generally accepted approach to conceptualizing individuals' psychological reaction to the dissolution of their marriage through divorce posits the existence of stages (Kaslow, 1981, 1984; Kressel & Deutsch, 1977). A number of models describing the process of divorce adjustment have been advanced. These models, with differing numbers of stages, range from Kessler's (1975) elaborate seven-stage paradigm to Weiss's (1976) two-stage progression from transition to recovery.

Kaslow (1981), in a review of the professional literature relating to divorce adjustment and the therapeutic positions put forth therein, described the field as encompassing a "broad spectrum."

As a footnote to Kaslow's contention, Gurman and Kniskern (1981) stated:

> In our view, the existence of such a "broad spectrum" of treatment approaches about divorce problems reflects the undeniable fact that there have been developed essentially no intervention strategies or treatment techniques that are *specific* to the emotional, behavioral and interpersonal difficulties caused by separation and divorce. On the other hand, as Kaslow makes clear, there are rather predictable stages in the divorce process, with similarly predictable emotional tasks to be addressed by the patient. (p. 682)

Stage conceptualizations provide a means of recognizing where individuals are and what they may be experiencing as they proceed toward divorce adjustment. Unfortunately, they offer few ideas for accurately assessing the potential intensity and duration of the feelings of loss so commonly experienced in the process of divorce adjustment. Further, and more importantly, they provide equally little information from which to develop specific intervention strategies to help divorcing individuals cope effectively with the circumstances attendant to divorce. Thus interventions formulated from stage conceptualizations of divorce adjustment have tended to be reactive. They provide primarily "supportive" therapy to deal with the symptoms rather than an active plan of intervention designed to facilitate progress toward adjustment by proactively addressing core elements of that process.

The basic tenets of rational-emotive therapy (RET) form the foundation for a model developed by the present author (Huber, 1983) that remedies many of the limitations in the stage approaches. The model was designed to link pivotal antecedents with their consequences so that the potential intensity and duration of any psychological reactions can be assessed. Further, it directly suggests specific strategies for constructive therapeutic intervention.

The Model

Identifying how individuals conceptualize their divorce and/or the circumstances surrounding it forms the basis for the model. The model posits two specific conceptual dimensions emanating from rational-emotive theory: (a) perceived degree of "desirousness/ demandingness" and (b) perceived degree of "disappointment/ devastation." These dimensions provide a means of understanding and accounting for the psychological reaction individuals experience relative to their divorce and/or its accompanying circumstances.

"Adjustment" is considered to be the point at which individuals are coping well with their divorce and/or the circumstances surrounding it; they are making reasonable progress toward the attainment of both specific goals and general life satisfaction. It is not necessarily a point at which they experience *no* negative reactions. Preoccupation with the lost loved one, however, does not dominate nor disrupt normal functioning (Volkan, 1982). With regard to the present model, adjustment is indicated when desires are manifested more often than demands and disappointment is manifested more frequently than devastation in the thoughts of the divorced person.

Disappointment/Devastation

Disappointment is an expected and adaptive cognitive response to loss such as divorce. It realistically relates to a sense of sadness over being frustrated or thwarted in pursuit of certain goals or general life satisfaction. *Devastation,* by contrast, is believing that something is awful, terrible, horrible, and catastrophic. As a consequence of devastation beliefs, individuals experience extremely upsetting emotions. Consider the meaning of being devastated. It does, of course, mean bad. But even more than that, at least for most persons, it means the worst thing that could happen, that is, 100% bad (Wessler & Wessler, 1980). The objective reality of any situation, however, is that a truly devastating event cannot exist. Nothing is 100% bad because something worse could always happen. For example, some persons consider their own divorce to be the worst thing that could happen. This may be 99% bad, but 99.1% might be that they further contracted a seriously debilitating illness immediately following the divorce. The relative badness of an event, therefore, can be judged by determining what could be worse.

The initial response of many divorced persons to the proposition that "nothing is devastating" tends to be one wherein they think it is being suggested that no events should be judged as bad. Most individuals, of course, balk if they arrive at the mistaken conclusion, "It's not bad at all that my spouse and I have divorced." For some persons, such an event can be extremely bad. RET and the present model in no way imply that divorce is never to be considered negative. Badness, as judged by each individual's value system, obviously does exist. The issue, however, is found in the degree of badness.

The clinical basis for making distinctions among gradations of perceived badness, including disappointment and devastation, was long ago pointed out by Beck (1963): "The affective reaction is proportional to the descriptive labeling of the event rather than to the actual intensity of a traumatic situation" (p. 329). Ellis (1971) likewise proposed:

> Just about every time you feel disturbed or upset—instead of merely displeased, frustrated, or disappointed—you are stoutly convincing yourself that something is *awful*, rather than inconvenient or disadvantageous. . . . When you *awfulize* or *catastrophize* about reality, you are setting up an unverifiable, magical, unempirical hypothesis. (p. 168)

When divorced persons experience an extremely negative psychological reaction, they are viewing bad circumstances as much more than *just* bad, (i.e., disappointing). Rather, such circumstances are viewed as "the end of the world" or as "My life will *never* be the same again!" (i.e., devastating). Exaggerated devastation beliefs can often be identified by the presence of such descriptors as *terrible, awful, horrible,* and *unbearable.*

Therapeutic interventions designed to help individuals move toward adjustment will almost always help them to utilize the most encompassing perspective possible in evaluating their circumstances. The thought of devastation allows for only restrictive perspective-taking. While divorce is a reality many persons would consider quite bad, the difference between 100% bad and 95% bad, between devastating and very disappointing or very unfortunate, can impact significantly upon how individuals are able to adjust following their divorce, particularly if the divorce is being misperceived in an excessively negative manner.

Desirousness/Demandingness

Desirousness, like disappointment, is an expected and adaptive cognitive response to the sense of loss that usually accompanies divorce. *Desirousness* is the belief that it is *preferable* for a certain circumstance to have happened or not to have happened. *Demandingness*, however, is the belief that certain things *must* or *must not* happen. Horney (1942) coined the phrase "the tyranny of the should" to describe this type of dysfunctional thinking. Demandingness implies that certain absolute rules or laws must be adhered to and that violation of these standards is unthinkable. Demandingness and devastation tend to go hand in hand: "We *must* not divorce! I'll be utterly devastated if we do." Yet, like devastation beliefs, demandingness beliefs can be objectively viewed for what they are—exaggerated desires. In this regard, Ellis (1971) stated:

> Practically all "emotional disturbance" stems from *demanding* or *whining* instead of from *wanting* or *desiring*. People who feel anxious, depressed, or hostile don't merely *wish* or *prefer* something, but also *command, dictate, insist,* that they achieve this thing. Typically, . . . they *dictate* that life and the world be easy, enjoyable, and unfrustrating; and they *manufacture* overrebelliousness, self-pity, and inertia when conditions are difficult. (p. 168)

Thus, whenever individuals begin to feel and act extremely disturbed or upset, the disturbance usually begins with a wish or desire that gets blocked or thwarted in some way. The desire itself is quite appropriate and usually goal-oriented in the pursuit of greater life satisfaction. Most people desire to have long and happy marriages. Disturbance arises when these desires are taken to extremes and become excessive demands: "My spouse and I divorce—*never!*" If former marital partners retained a more rational belief (desirousness) upon divorcing, such as "I wish that we had gotten along better, but we simply made too many mistakes in trying to work things out," they would subsequently tend to conclude, "I'm very sad that we had to divorce. I'll probably always regret the errors in judgment we made, but I'm better off if I move forward from here and avoid looking back so much."

Longer lasting psychological reactions of a debilitating nature tend to emanate from commanding, demanding beliefs about what "should," "ought," "must," "need" or "have to" happen so that one can "absolutely" and "necessarily" get what he or she desires. When divorced individuals make unrealizable demands upon themselves, their former partners, and/or their circumstances, they only set up magical, impossible, unempirical hypotheses. To demand, for example, that a divorce not have happened when it has already occurred is obviously a dead end that can yield only distress and despair.

As with the disappointment/devastation dimension, many individuals' initial response to the idea of "desiring" or "preferring" instead of demanding is that they take on an "I don't care" attitude. The conclusion "I don't care at all that my spouse and I have divorced" is unrealistic, of course, and suggests a dysfunctional denial. One would likely have some feelings of loss and sadness even if the divorce was anticipated and welcome. But even in the worst of circumstances, a loss is a loss, not an eternal damnation. Just as the functional alternative to devastation is some lesser degree of badness or disappointment, not neutral or good, the more functional alternative to demandingness is a greater degree of desirousness or preferring, not "I don't care." As individuals are able to maintain their desires about their divorce and/or its accompanying circumstances and not escalate them into dire needs and necessities, they progress toward adjustment in a more efficacious manner.

Assessment

The graphic illustration of the model (see Figure 7.1) is a 2 × 2 matrix in which the vertical axis represents the perceived degree of desirousness/demandingness and the horizontal axis represents the perceived degree of disappointment/devastation experienced by the divorced individual. These two dimensions interact to create the potential for four response states that reflect both the intensity and duration of psychological reactions following divorce.

As illustrated in Figure 7.1, assessment can be undertaken by looking at the model as a window through which individuals perceive their divorce and/or its accompanying circumstances. Looking at the four panes of the window in terms of columns and rows, the columns represent the extent to which individuals perceive

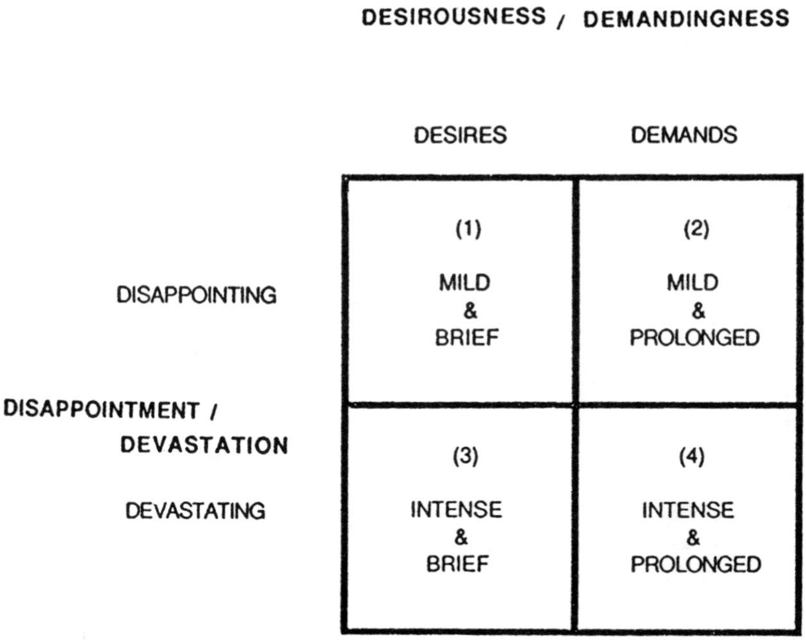

DESIROUSNESS / DEMANDINGNESS

	DESIRES	DEMANDS
DISAPPOINTING	(1) MILD & BRIEF	(2) MILD & PROLONGED
DEVASTATING	(3) INTENSE & BRIEF	(4) INTENSE & PROLONGED

**DISAPPOINTMENT /
DEVASTATION**

Figure 7.1

the various possible degrees of desirousness/demandingness regarding their divorce, and the rows represent how disappointingly/ devastatingly they perceive the divorce affecting them. Column 1 represents individuals' beliefs that they prefer/desire that their divorce or certain circumstances surrounding it would not have occurred or would have occurred differently; column 2 represents individuals' demands that their divorce or its accompanying circumstances absolutely should not have occurred or absolutely should have occurred otherwise.

Desirousness/demandingness beliefs will directly relate to the duration of the psychological reaction experienced. Row 1 represents individuals' beliefs that their divorce or circumstances surrounding it were unfortunate and disappointing; row 2 represents individuals' beliefs that their divorce or its accompanying circumstances were horrible and utterly devastating. Disappointment/

devastation beliefs directly relate to the intensity of the psychological reaction experienced. These beliefs represented in the columns and rows are not static but move from one pane to another as individuals seek to cope with the feelings of loss they experience relative to their divorce. As a consequence of this movement, the size and shape of the panes of the window will vary, as will individuals' responses.

Persons "looking through" the upper left (#1) pane of the window predominantly believe that their divorce is disappointing, and they desire that it not have occurred or have occurred differently. Perceiving their circumstances in this manner, their psychological reaction will be a mild and brief one. In a similar manner, the upper right (#2) pane represents the view that the divorce is disappointing; however, there is a demandingness that the situation should have been different or not have happened at all. Here the consequent psychological reaction will be mild but prolonged in duration. Individuals seeing their divorce through the lower left (#3) pane predominantly believe that the experience of their divorce is a devastating one, and they desire that it would have occurred differently or not at all. Their psychological reaction will tend to be intense but brief in duration. The lower right (#4) pane represents individuals' beliefs that their divorce is devastating, and there is a demandingness in their thinking that it should have occurred otherwise or not at all. In this instance, their psychological reaction will be an intense and prolonged one.

Although each of these four "window panes" potentially describes different individuals' psychological reactions relative to divorce, panes #1 and #4 are the most common. The other two potential reactions are seldom observed because an individual at an extreme on one dimension tends to be at an extreme on the other dimension as well.

Therapeutic Intervention

The goals of therapeutic intervention strategies employing this model are to lessen any potential negative impact that divorce may have upon an individual and to facilitate progress toward adjustment in the most efficacious manner possible. Strategies are designed to lessen the intensity and duration of any feelings of loss experienced and to promote a milder and briefer psychological reaction. These results come about through, first, promotion of adaptive desirousness beliefs and, second, through promotion of adaptive disappointment beliefs. Individuals experience a change in belief from demands to desires regarding the divorce and/or its accompanying circumstances and a change in belief from perceiving the divorce and/or its accompanying circumstance from devastating to disappointing.

When disappointment beliefs predominate, techniques designed to reinforce and strengthen these beliefs constitute the primary interventions. When devastation beliefs predominate, an intensely negative psychological reaction occurs. In order to avoid such intense feelings of loss and to ensure a more mild and manageable psychological response, a shift in belief from perceiving the divorce as devastating to perceiving it as disappointing needs to occur. The primary intervention strategy for facilitating this shift in belief comes from, first, showing the divorced individual how to identify both the devastation and the potential disappointment beliefs and, second, actively and vigorously examining the functional value of each. The emotions and behaviors occurring when the contrasting beliefs are present are also important components to be examined. Does the belief contribute to emotions and behaviors that lead to greater goal attainment and life satisfaction? Disappointment beliefs, as compared to devastation beliefs, will consistently yield "yes" responses.

The second major shift in promoting adjustment via this model requires that desirousness beliefs be reinforced and strengthened when they are already predominant. When demandingness beliefs predominate, the model suggests that the psychological reaction will be a prolonged one. In order to curtail a needlessly prolonged reaction, there needs to be a shift from demands to desires in the individual's belief system. The primary strategy for facilitating this shift comes from, first, showing the divorced individual how to identify both the demandingness and potential desirousness beliefs and, second, actively and vigorously examining the functional value of each. The emotions and behaviors occurring when the contrasting beliefs are present are also important components to be examined. Does the belief contribute to emotions and behaviors that lead to greater goal attainment and life satisfaction? Desirousness beliefs, when contrasted with demandingness beliefs, will consistently yield "yes" responses.

In returning to the illustration of the model as a window, the overall objective in promoting divorce adjustment is to increase the size of the area wherein individuals perceive their divorce and/or its accompanying circumstances as disappointing (although possibly very much so), and desiring (although possibly very much so, as well) that it might not have happened or happened differently. Their consequent psychological reaction will then be of a relatively more mild and brief nature. When persons act upon and manage, rather than being acted upon and controlled by, their psychological reactions in response to divorce, they will proceed with their own lives and their future in more adaptive, satisfying ways. This process is depicted in Figure 7.2.

A Case Session Illustration

The previous sections identified general assessment and intervention strategies emanating from the model. The following case session illustrates how these general strategies were implemented by the author while working with a recently divorced client. Significantly greater specificity in the techniques employed will be obvious. The specific techniques used here reflect only one therapist's selection; selection of techniques is best left to the discretion of the individual therapist. Ellis, Sichel, Yeager, DiMattia, and DiGiuseppe (1989) offer several chapters of recommended assessment and treatment techniques to compliment this model. The critical components for all therapists to remember, however, are those general assessment and intervention conceptualizations discussed throughout the previous sections.

Referral/Background Information

The client, John, is a 35-year-old male referred for therapy by a personal acquaintance of his, a graduate student who was familiar with the present author's research and practice activities regarding individuals' adjustment following a divorce experience. The client reported the referral source as someone whom he had dated several times; she had expressed her concern that he exhibited significant negative affect whenever the topic of his separation and subsequent divorce arose.

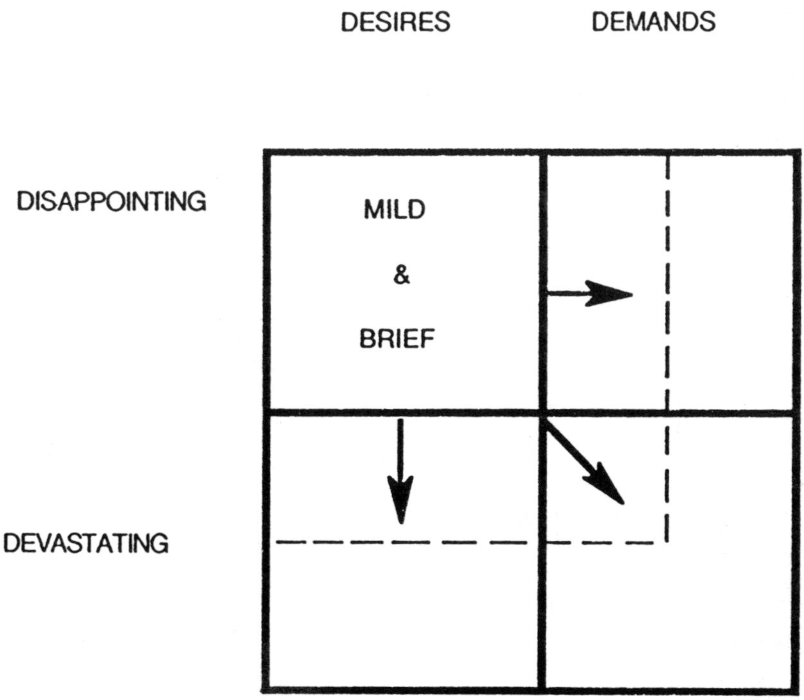

DESIRES   DEMANDS

Figure 7.2

The client and his former wife physically separated seven months ago and were legally divorced approximately a month prior to his initial session. He reported that she had been seeing another man during the last year of their marriage and subsequently left the client and their three daughters, ages 11, 9, and 4, to live with this person. The client was awarded physical custody of the children (his former wife did not seek custody).

The initial session was a "double session" of 2 hours. During that session, background information was taken, an orientation to the therapy provided (including informed consent procedures), a Therapeutic Contract drafted, and formal assessment instruments administered based on the presenting complaint, which was an expressed desire to cope better with the recent divorce experience and the circumstances surrounding it. A homework task concluded the session, that being for the client to compile baseline data relative to the behavioral objectives agreed to in the Therapeutic Contract. The assessment instruments and results of testing are discussed below.

Irrational Beliefs Test (IBT). The IBT (Jones, 1968) is a 100-item inventory with Likert-type response categories measuring the degree of an individual's adherence to 10 basic irrational beliefs (Ellis, 1962). The client's IBT profile showed highest adherence to irrational beliefs in three subscales, High Self-Expectations, Blame Proneness, and Perfectionism. These three subscales have been identified as being most representative of desirousness/ demandingness beliefs, which include, respectively self-desires/ demands, desires/demands of others, and situational desires/ demands. His profile also showed relatively higher scores on two of the three subscales identified as most representative of disappointment/devastation beliefs: Frustration Reactivity and Helplessness (the third being Anxious Overconcern).

Fisher Divorce Adjustment Scale (FDAS). The FDAS (Fisher, 1981) is a 70-item inventory with Likert-type response categories measuring an individual's adjustment to divorce. The client's FDAS profile identified a lower level of divorce adjustment on three of the four subscales: Feelings of Anger, Symptoms of Grief, and Disentanglement of the Love-Relationship. The client's performance on the fourth subscale, Rebuilding Social Relationships, identified him as having a relatively higher level of adjustment in this component of the divorce adjustment process.

The Therapeutic Contract identified a general goal of "coping more adaptively with the consequences of a divorce experience." Specific behavioral objectives were identified by focusing on the three major response systems of human functioning: (a) "To increase the number of adaptive thoughts about my divorce and current circumstances impacted by it" (cognitive), (b) "To increase the frequency of time during the day I am feeling comfortable" (physiological/affective), and (c) "To increase my repertoire of problem-solving skills" (overt-motor). Increases of 30% in each area were identified as target goals. A time frame of eight sessions was established for the therapy, after which an evaluation of progress would occur and, if necessary, recontracting for further sessions. The client was given forms with which to conduct time-sampled frequency counts during the next three days to gather baseline data in each area.

A Selected Session

The following discussion highlights events of the second session with John. While only a second session, the interaction is representative of the author's work with clients using the present model. In lieu of offering a verbatim transcript, a first-person account will be used to convey the thoughts of the author as he worked with this client.

My goals for this session were as follows: (a) Identify a "high frequency" and concrete ABC sequence John is currently experiencing, preferably one wherein degree of desirousness/demandingness is very apparent (the formal assessment indicated this to be a specific area of concern relative to the model); (b) Facilitate his recognition of the relationship between B and C in that sequence by addressing occasions when either demands or desires occur at B and then paying particular attention to accompanying adaptive and maladaptive overt motor and physiological/affective responses at C; (c) Promote cognitive dissonance for John by coupling his predominant demandingness belief with its desirousness belief counterpart and comparing the detrimental effects of the demandingness belief with the beneficial effects of the desirousness belief in terms of his physiological/affective and overt motor responses; (d) Review, question, and confirm how the demandingness belief contributes to distressful physiological/affective responses and poor problem-solving actions while the desirousness belief offers enhanced opportunity for greater physiological/affective comfort (or less discomfort) and more adaptive problem-solving actions; and (e) Negotiate a homework task to facilitate the work of therapy between sessions.

The session began by reviewing the initial session's homework task of gathering baseline data and then requesting information designed to identify a high frequency ABC sequence. John presented two ABC sequences. The first one related to his former wife and had a B of "It was just like total shock. I don't feel like I deserved it." The second related to caring for his children and had a B of "I'm totally frustrated with their behavior. It's just got to be easier than this!." The latter sequence was addressed first because coping with the needs of his three daughters was a daily occurrence that John would be unlikely to disregard through avoidance or distraction. Desirousness/demandingness in his ABC sequence confirmed the IBT profile showing beliefs on this dimension to be more pronounced than desirousness/devastation beliefs.

I then helped John to see the relationship between B and C in that sequence. First, his demandingness beliefs ("It must be easier!") at B promoted nonadaptive physiological/affective (anger) and overt motor responses (screaming at the girls) at C. Second, his desirousness beliefs ("I'd rather have things go more smoothly with the girls") at B would promote more adaptive physiological/affective (calm) and overt motor responses (enjoying being with the girls) at C. As John grasped this relationship, I immediately moved to promote cognitive dissonance for him by coupling his demandingness beliefs and his desirousness beliefs and comparing the detrimental physiological/affective and overt motor consequences of the former with the more beneficial physiological/affective and overt motor consequences of the latter. This strategy was designed to promote an experiential state that would facilitate John's becoming optimally amenable to the cognitive restructuring to follow.

As John began to recognize the potential benefits of desirousness beliefs, the "debate" technique was introduced. He strongly defended the efficacy of his demandingness beliefs ("I don't see how I have any control over that. I mean I'd like to be nicer, but they just don't listen to me unless I yell and scream at them"). Instructing him in debate, I encouraged him to challenge ("How helpful?" "How sensible?") these beliefs and to consider the contrasting arguments presented by his desirousness beliefs and demandingness beliefs. He was helped to increase the frequency of his desirousness beliefs and, thus, his ability to (a) maintain a level of physiological/affective responding that is more compatible with effective problem-solving and (b) exhibit more adaptive overt motor responses.

Given the limited time available in the latter portion of the session, evidence of positive change was quickly reinforced by noting John's increased verbalizations relative to his desirousness/demandingness beliefs ("Yea, I do see more options. Desiring makes a lot more sense"). John still expressed some reluctance ("I guess where I run into trouble is fully believing it until I see it in action"). I would expect such a position at this early point in the therapy and view it as a sign of healthy skepticism. Considering this reluctance in light of the limited time, I moved on to a homework task designed to provide additional data for our next session.

Conclusions

This model offers a well-defined structure for employing basic tenets of rational-emotive therapy to facilitate divorce adjustment. Having its theoretical and therapeutic basis in a major conceptualization of human behavior and psychological functioning (RET), the model is firmly founded in a strong clinical and research base. Since the development of the model in the early 1980s, considerable anecdotal support for its clinical efficacy in facilitating divorce adjustment has been accumulated. In a recent clinical research study designed to evaluate the therapeutic process attendant to this model, Backlund (1991) found consistent outcomes supporting the model's hypotheses when comparing its treatment approach with both a traditional supportive therapy and a waiting list control group.

Given both clinical anecdotal and clinical research support, this model is presented as a practical and productive means of facilitating divorce adjustment. It is a model whose dimensions and components, when understood and applied, tend to generalize to many other aspects of clients' lives. Comprehending the negative psychological reaction engendered by demandingness and devastation beliefs, along with the consequent detrimental impact this has upon one's physiological/affective and overt motor functioning in relation to divorce, provides an opportunity to utilize the same dimensions and components in coping with other life concerns. To desire more than to demand and to view "bad" circumstances more as disappointing than as devastating, can only lead to greater attainment of one's goals and increased life satisfaction.

References

Backlund, B. A. (1991). *The evaluation of a radical model of grief therapy following divorce.* Unpublished doctoral dissertation, New Mexico State University.

Bebbington, P. (1987). Marital status and depression: A study of English national admission statistics. *Acta Psychiatrica Scandinavica, 75,* 640-650.

Beck, A. T. (1963). Thinking and depression. *Archives of General Psychiatry, 9,* 324-333.

Ellis, A. (1962) *Reason and emotion in psychotherapy.* Secaucus, NJ: Citadel.

Ellis, A. (1971). Emotional disturbance and its treatment in a nutshell. *Canadian Counselor, 5,* 168-171.

Ellis, A., Sichel, J. L., Yeager, R. J., DiMattia, D. J., & DiGiuseppe, R. (1989). *Rational-emotive couples therapy.* Elmsford, NY: Pergamon.

Fincham F. D., & Bradbury, T. N. (1990). *The psychology of marriage: Basic issues and applications.* New York: Guilford.

Fisher, B. (1981). *Rebuilding: When your relationship ends.* San Luis Obispo, CA: Impact Publishers.

Glick, P. C. (1989). Remarried families, stepfamilies, and stepchildren: A brief demographic profile. *Family Relations, 38,* 123-129.

Gurman, A. S., & Kniskern, D. P. (Eds). (1981). *Handbook of family therapy.* New York: Brunner/Mazel.

Horney, K. (1942). *Self-analysis.* New York: Norton.

Huber, C. H. (1983). Feelings of loss in response to divorce: Assessment and intervention. *Personnel and Guidance Journal, 61,* 357-361.

Jones, R. (1968). *A factored measure of Ellis' irrational belief system, with personality and maladjustment correlates.* Unpublished doctoral dissertation, Texas Technological College.

Kaslow, F. W. (1981). Divorce and divorce therapy. In A. S. Gurman & D. P. Kniskern (Eds.), *Handbook of family therapy* (pp. 662-696). New York: Brunner/Mazel.

Kaslow, F. W. (1984). Divorce: An evolutionary process of change in the family system. *Journal of Divorce, 7*(3), 21-39.

Kessler, S. (1975). *The American way of divorce: Prescription for change.* Chicago: Nelson-Hall.

Kressel, K., & Deutsch, M. (1977). Divorce therapy: An in-depth survey of therapists' views. *Family Process, 16,* 413-444.

Volkan, V. (1982). Complicated mourning. *Annual of Psychoanalysis, 12-13,* 323-348.

Weiss, R. (1976). *Marital separation.* New York: Basic Books.

Wessler, R. A., & Wessler, R. L. (1980). *The principles and practice of rational-emotive therapy.* San Francisco: Jossey-Bass.

8

A Rational-Emotive Education Program to Help Disruptive Mentally Retarded Clients Develop Self-Control

WILLIAM J. KNAUS
NANCY HABERSTROH

In this chapter, we describe a rational-emotive education (REE) treatment/research approach to help higher functioning but disruptive mentally retarded persons develop coping skills and gain use of more of their functional potential. We introduce rational-emotive education, describe its structure, present research findings, illustrate its application through case example, define mechanisms for change, and identify research/treatment applications.

Rational-emotive education (REE) is an offshoot of rational-emotive therapy that differs from the main system in the structure and form of delivery of mental health concepts.

The crux of rational-emotive theory is that we feel the way we think (Ellis, 1957a, 1957b, 1958, 1962, 1979, 1988; Ellis & Dryden, 1987; Ellis & Knaus, 1979; Knaus, 1982; Knaus & Hendricks, 1986; Maultsby, 1986; Wessler & Wessler, 1980). Substantive literature reviews support the rational-emotive system with no meaningful disconfirming results (Ellis & Grieger, 1980; Ellis & Whiteley, 1979; Engles & Diekstra, 1986; DiGiuseppe & Miller, 1977; DiGiuseppe,

Miller, & Trexler, 1979; McGovern & Silverman, 1984; M. Smith & Glass, 1977; T. Smith, 1989).

Rational-emotive education (Bernard & Joyce, 1984; DiNublie & Wessler, 1974; Eyman & Gerald, 1981; Hooper & Layne, 1985; Knaus, 1974, 1983, 1985; Knaus & Eyman, 1975; Vernon, 1980, 1984) is a structured, research-tested psychological education program. Although originally designed to help normal children in regular classrooms develop effective problem-solving skills, mental health and educational specialists have also applied the method with children and adults with special disabilities and problems. It is a positive mental health system practitioners can use to help mentally retarded people with disruptive patterns prepare for community living.

The REE System

Rational-emotive education (REE) involves teaching children to develop perspective, build healthier self-concepts, increase frustration tolerance, and establish a realistic locus of control. It consists of a structured series of lessons designed to help students or clients build psychological skills they can use to meet a wide range of everyday challenges.

The REE system follows the pattern below.

1. REE concepts are taught through structured lessons.
2. The concepts are integrated into the educational curricula. For example, rational critical thinking skills are used for separating fiction from fact when children and youth review current events.
3. Instructors assure the students know the concepts through content acquisition measures.
4. Teachers and counselors use problem-solving simulations to enable clients to apply and test the validity of the ideas.
5. Practitioners observe and reinforce taught strategies the students use to solve problems in spontaneous situations.

The REE Lessons

The structured REE lessons and games include:

1. What are feelings and where do they come from?

2. An expression-guessing game to show there is no one right way to express feelings; different people sometimes express their feelings in different ways
3. Strategies for building healthy self-concepts
4. Strategies for developing perspective
5. Strategies for developing a fact-based belief system
6. Strategies for developing frustration tolerance

Each REE lesson builds upon the preceding one. However, once beyond the basics, you can use a wide range of supplemental lessons for special circumstances. For example, a counselor who wants to teach children how to resist drugs can follow the model and develop a series of REE drug resistance lessons that draws upon previously taught REE concepts. A teacher can help procrastinating students with REE lessons on this timeless topic.

The Efficacy of the REE System

We're better off when we think clearly, maintain a realistic self-concept, manage frustrating events, and accept responsibility for our behavior. How well does REE help achieve these results?

Researchers tested the model with children in the regular classroom and with special populations. The following summarizes the results.

REE With Regular Classroom Children

REE research with children in the regular classroom has been consistently encouraging with no meaningful divergences. Several outcome studies have shown positive results (Ayers & Theodore, 1987; Brody, 1974; Casper, 1981; DiGiuseppe & Kassinove, 1976; Grassi, 1984; Greenwald, 1984; Harris, 1976a, 1976b; Katz, 1974; Knaus & Bokor, 1975; Leibowitz, 1979; Miller, 1977; Zionts, 1983).

REE With Special Populations

The research points to a consistent pattern of efficacy for the REE approach with special populations.

Although it was developed for use with sixth-grade inner-city school children, researchers have used the REE method with special needs populations including the learning disabled (Knaus, 1985; Knaus & McKeever, 1977; Lo Fuang-luan, 1985; Omizo, Cubberly, & Omizo, 1985; Omizo, Lo Fuang-luan, & Roberts, 1986; Omizo, Lo Fuang-luan, & Williams, 1986); disruptive adolescents (Block, 1977; Knaus & Block, 1976); withdrawn and acting out adolescents in residential treatment (Dye, 1980; Voelm, 1983); court committed adolescents (Matuozzi, 1986); adolescents in the regular class (Handleman, 1981); special education students (Eluto, 1980); the hearing impaired (Gerzhols, 1980); older adults (Keller, Croake, & Brooking, 1975; Krenitsky, 1978); seriously disturbed children (Leopold, 1984); hidden children of alcoholics (Triperinas, 1988); children with severe physical disability (Sweetland, 1979); teacher burnout (Russell, 1987); student burnout (Knaus, 1985); selective mutes (Knaus, 1970); test anxious children (Albert, 1970; Baither & Godsey, 1979; Knaus & Bokor, 1975); and parent study groups (Bruner, 1984).

The Content Acquisition Measure

REE studies normally include content acquisition measures. The evidence is compelling that REE groups show significant increases in the acquisition of rational-emotive concepts. The content acquisition tests normally are paper-and-pencil inventories for children and adolescents with adequate written test taking skills. However, there are other methods.

Knaus and McKeever (1977), working with 5- and 6-year-old learning disabled children, found they could test this group for content acquisition by using oral and picture recognition tests. Indeed, Miller (1977), Krenitsky (1978), and Wasserman and Vogrin (1979) independently found that outside of the extremes, a person need not be intellectually bright to acquire the REE concepts.

REE and Developmental Levels

We find the data on the acquisition of rational concepts by diverse populations very encouraging. Nevertheless, we need to be sensitive to developmental issues. For example, Lang (1980) notes that we would wisely assure that REE applications follow the ontogenetic development of theories of causality as described by Piaget (1952, 1972, 1981; Piaget & Inhelder, 1958). She correctly points out that the practitioner must be knowledgeable about both the REE framework and developmental theory. Landesman and Ramey (1989) share the spirit of Lang's views when they discuss integrating scientific rules and developmental psychology with treatment practices for the mentally retarded.

Rational-emotive strategies are teachable and learnable using experiential learning methods as advocated by Dewey (1900). This educator and psychologist has taught us to test analogue experiences "by gradual reapproximation to conditions of life."

REE With Mentally Retarded Populations

Can a cognitive and behavior therapy method prove helpful to disruptive, mildly retarded populations? Our literature review shows a dearth of data on the application of rational-emotive therapy, rational-emotive education, or cognitive-behavior strategies with higher functioning mentally retarded persons.

Except for Eluto's (1980) study of "special education" students, there is a lack of work on the efficacy of REE with the mentally retarded. This is unfortunate because the system would seem especially well suited as an intervention strategy for those capable mentally retarded persons who can profit from problem-solving skill development.

To describe the application of the system with the mentally retarded, we present a case study. The results are suggestive. There are many known pitfalls to quasi-experimental single-subject treatment designs (Campbell & Stanley, 1963). Nevertheless, Lazarus and Davison (1971) wisely advise us to apply scientific principles in our work to help clients develop self-knowledge and coping skills. We offer the following as a start.

Case Study

REE was originally designed for use in the classroom. However, a counselor can readily adapt the system for use with individual students or clients (Knaus, 1977a, 1977b, 1983, 1985).

The following is an example of using REE with George, a disruptive 37-year-old man who has been institutionalized since age 13.

Background Factors

Before admission, school personnel and authorities and his family found George disruptive and difficult to manage. This pattern was exacerbated by a serious life crisis that resulted in commitment.

After admission, George's behavior problems escalated. He became increasingly assaultive. Besides assault, George's acting out behaviors included verbal abuse and threats with dangerous weapons. This pattern led to a charge of assault with a deadly weapon and a 40-day transfer to a maximum security facility. Upon his return, a repeated assault resulted in a second incarceration.

In the early years of his tenure, the administration moved George from residence to residence within the facility. They hoped to control his behavior by finding a corrective environment. The pattern persisted.

George was treated using anxiolytic medication with limited effect.

Our Assessment

George's negative assaultive behavior patterns, while understandably worrisome, reflected poor self-control and feelings of deep hurt. George lashed out against a world he believed responsible for so much of the pain and anguish he experienced.

George's behavior was also related to other conditions. A conceptual and behavioral diagnosis showed a pattern of low frustration tolerance, poor impulse control, a highly negative self-concept, an external locus of control, and limited coping resources. He lacked a realistic sense of perspective. It was this conceptual-emotive-behavior pattern, along with neurological vulnerability, that correlated with George's pattern of disruptive behavior.

Despite his troubled history, George periodically showed charm, a good sense of humor, social interests, and some ability to reflect. Moreover, in his unguarded moments, he expressed a desire to make his life better.

Unfortunately, George developed a very negative reputation. Just the sound of his name figuratively sent shivers down the spines of many staff persons, who pretyped him as being a dangerous troublemaker. The mention of his name caused immediate reaction from most members of the staff. Staff therefore often treated him as though he were a "bad actor." When staff dwelled on his less desirable behaviors, this attention seemed to reinforce rather than extinguish the pattern. On those occasions when George showed socially appropriate responses, these initiatives normally went unrecognized or rewarded.

The majority of staff gave up on George so he did what he wanted. He stayed up as late as he pleased, then slept until 3:00 p.m. or later. When he awoke, he stumbled into the day hall in his pajamas or underwear in an unpleasant and abrasive mood.

George received negative attention for his troubled behaviors that further disadvantaged him. The prevocational workshop group, for example, claimed his behavior was too volatile. They excluded him from vocational help.

The majority of staff and administration frequently overlooked George's likeable qualities. His loud verbalizations and assaultive episodes dominated the perceptions of most. A few staff members, who could see George's potential through his rough facade, lobbied to have him placed at a facility with an outdoor logging program. George's reputation and history were the deciding factors against the placement.

The REE Intervention

Because traditional treatment approaches and behavior modification interventions proved ineffective, one of us (Nancy Haberstroh) began work with George using REE.

Following a prescription suggested by Knaus (1977), she defined the method as "mental karate." She explained to George that this approach was different from karate because it helped people build self-control inside themselves. A mental karate student could earn different colored wrist bands that showed what he or she had learned.

George liked the idea that he could learn mental karate and that he could earn different colored wrist bands depending upon his level of accomplishment. He understood that the idea behind the system was to learn new ways to cope with recurring problems. Thus the mental karate system immediately appealed to him. He also liked attention. The new treatment program provided him with this opportunity.

In the beginning stage of the program, George learned REE skills 20 minutes per day, three times per week. The sessions followed the structured mental health lessons outlined in *Rational-Emotive Education: A Manual For Elementary School Teachers* (Knaus, 1974).

George first learned to recognize irrational beliefs in other people. He initially found it amusing to recognize irrationalities, especially those of the staff. However, he intensely disliked making mistakes himself. Thus he found it difficult to identify and deal with the disturbing belief that he too made mistakes.

At first he found it notably uncomfortable facing his human tendencies to err and to have human flaws. Nevertheless, he slowly came to realize that he could never achieve perfection. Even the President of the United States can make a significant mistake.

Around the end of 6 months of intensive REE training, George showed clear signs he was sometimes able to use the REE model to recognize some of his irrational thinking patterns. Nearing the end of 18 months of treatment, he made a series of important breakthroughs. He could verbalize and apply the idea that people who seek perfection often do so because they think poorly of themselves. You make real progress in mental karate when you accept yourself even when you make a mistake. That way you don't fall into the perfectionism trap. Most important, you can more wisely change what you don't like about yourself when you admit you have something to change!

He progressed steadily through the REE system with the help of many repetitions. This practice was important to reinforce and stabilize the basic rational ideas. As he struggled to build a more fact-based belief system, George slowly changed his pattern of disruptive behaviors to more socially appropriate behaviors.

The second author employed and faded the REE program over an eight-year period. This opportunity to work with an institutionalized person for such a long time is unusual. Under most conditions, staff turnover may cause a program to be discontinued, or motivation may wane. Fortunately, the major therapeutic gains took place for George within a 3- to 4-year time frame.

Longer term programs may prove viable providing interested parties remain committed. If a long-term program is effective, the potential benefits in the reduction of a residential person's emotional pain and anguish and the potential increase of opportunity and "pursuit of happiness" is worth the price.

The Outcome

Analogue study changes are often limited because they may not generalize to real-life situations. They include changes in test scores, reductions in recorded anxiety levels, and sometimes evidence for actual behavior change. Generally, researchers prefer these studies to case reports. Case studies, for example, may be supported by ex cathedra statements based on proclamation.

A single subject case process may not be adequately controlled, so replication may not be possible. In George's case, the second author followed a defined REE program. The changes were positive, significant, and documentable. They took place in real life circumstances. The following describes some of George's accomplishments.

1. He learned about CPR and asked to learn how to help resuscitate his fellow residents after an accident. George did eventually complete a special course on how to take action in emergency situations. He now routinely acts to identify fellow residents with medical problems, reporting them to nursing staff.

2. George's sense of humor became well developed. For example, one day he came running into Nancy's office and asked if, by any chance, she had lost anything. The author looked around and said, "No," and proceeded to take a walk to get her mail with George. George again asked if she had lost anything and she said she hadn't. Then George produced a whole set of her keys, saying, "So you didn't lose anything, huh?" George still remembers and laughs about that incident.

3. George has now gone three years without assaulting anyone. His rate of seriously threatening people is down to about once every 6 months.

4. He is no longer required to take anxiolytic medication.

5. His WAIS performance and verbal I.Q. test scores have significantly improved. His most recent verbal I.Q. score increased one standard deviation over baseline measures. The program did not raise his I.Q. We believe REE and other supports helped increase George's test motivation and helped him improve his ability to attend and concentrate.

6. His retardation is now marginal. He no longer suffers from a severe emotional disturbance that contaminates his real intellectual skills.

7. He now works in the community and has the distinction of earning more money per hour than any other resident at the institution.

8. George actively sought an opportunity to serve as an assistant coach for a peewee league soccer team. He initiated and followed through with his coaching responsibilities totally on his own. He had seen the children playing and went to see if he could help out. The coach appointed him to this role. In this capacity, he has proven himself to be reliable and seems well regarded by the youngsters he seeks to help. He received recognition from the press for this accomplishment. He has now spent five years with the team.

9. In contrast to the days when staff feared him, George won a community citizenship award for his ongoing help and sportsmanship. The group of coaches, parents, friends, and peewee soccer players applauded him for his unswerving devotion to the team. It was an important tribute that the peewee players and other community members recognized him for his contribution.

10. George's quarters have historically been disorderly. Staff now routinely complain to George that he must keep his room neater in appearance. We find this outcome significant. Staff now see him as approachable and they don't fear him. Some staff actively argue this point with him. Sometimes the second author receives calls at home regarding complaints about George's room. These complaints tell us that staff treats George like an emotionally stable person. They want to help him in what they see as one of the final hurdles before his community placement.

Once beyond his assaultive defenses, we find George to be a sensitive, concerned, social person. He continues to develop his rational coping resources. He now awaits an opportunity to live in the community, having received strong endorsement for this move.

Alternative Explanations

We can explain the change mechanisms in George's case:

1. The REE intervention provided concrete REE coping skills that he could apply and that often worked.

2. Program repetition—continuing opportunities to learn and apply REE principles.

3. The availability of a therapist who acted as an advocate.
4. Acknowledgments for progress, as in wristbands.
5. Acknowledgments for progress, as in positive staff attention and external accomplishments.
6. Growing self-confidence in the use of the system. This accompanied the development of a healthy fact-based self-concept.
7. Developing skills in reflecting before reacting that led to observable increases in frustration tolerance.
8. Increasing ability to take advantage of his mental resources, especially ability to attend and concentrate, which led to a sense of perspective.
9. Client maturation.
10. The elimination of medication.
11. George's discovery that people did care about him if he made the effort to reach out.

Perhaps these and other mechanisms combined like a slowly brewed spaghetti sauce where all ingredients count.

There are many explanations why some therapeutic work proves productive. In this case, we cannot know the precise degree to which REE was the salient feature. We do know, however, that there was no basic change in George's behavior from the date of institutionalization to when he participated in the REE program. There was evidence for deterioration in his behavior during his tenure at the institution. We know that when a facility administrator terminated George's treatment against the advice of the second author, his behavior deteriorated until the REE program was reinstated. At the time, George was involved in several major changes including a job and residence change. Presently, George's REE program is at a maintenance level.

George's case points to the importance of rigorously researching the REE method to determine its efficacy in influencing the therapeutic outcome among disruptive mentally retarded clients. It also shows reason for optimism that even the more disruptive have significant positive resources to develop.

George Teaches Us the Importance of Patience

Our work with George teaches us to be patient with those who seem, at times, the most difficult to reach. He shows us the importance of taking time to teach the basics before we ask that they be tested. He shows us we must expect to spend many hours going over the same principles and of looking for new ways to say the same thing when the idea seemed elusive. He teaches us that we would wisely tie taught coping skills to real life experience before they become a useful and permanent part of a person's coping repertory. He reinforces our work to make REE a truly useful system.

Mentally retarded residents with limited psychological coping skills may lack the opportunity to contribute to their communities and to live normal lives. Fortunately, we may be able to teach rational problem-solving approaches that help higher functioning dually diagnosed mentally retarded men and women, with serious emotional overlays, lead more normal lives. Our experience with George demonstrates we can offer more hope that some retarded residents, including those who behave disruptively and impulsively, may find a way to overcome this pattern and have new opportunities to live less restricted lives in community environments.

When we position the program between the institution and community living, we help the person develop coping skills that are relevant to both dimensions.

Research/Treatment Applications

We encourage the use of the highly structured REE format with disruptive mentally retarded clients who have the potential to profit from the REE system. We suggest the following treatment/research format.

1. Identify environmental determinants: what sets off the reaction?
2. Make a conceptual diagnosis: What does the person believe or tell him- or herself that provokes a disruptive emotional behavioral response?
3. Present REE lessons, taking special care to reinforce thinking and behaving that run counter to the disruptive pattern.
4. Create special scenarios to enable the client to rehearse positive coping strategies that run counter to the disruptive pattern.
5. In support of the above, use varied approaches to teach the same idea.
6. Assure that the client understands pivotal ideas and their application before progressing to the next level.

7. Repeatedly show the client how rational thinking applies to the management of a wide range of related environmental conditions.

8. Where possible, intervene in disruptive practices by showing the client how to apply what he or she has already learned and practiced.

9. Reinforce progress verbally and, when part of the program, through mental karate wristbands.

The key variables in these REE programs include: a consistently positive and encouraging counselor attitude; a deliberate time frame; a consistent REE structure; appropriate but slight content variations to help develop rational principles; the use of "rational games" to make the ideas appealing to learn; reinforcement for accomplishment through Skinner's (1953) differential reinforcement through successive approximations; behavioral rehearsal (Gittleman, 1965; Lazarus, 1966, 1971; Wolpe & Lazarus, 1966); and practice, practice, practice.

References

Albert, S. (1972). *A study to determine the effectiveness of affective education with fifth grade students*. Unpublished master's thesis, Queens College, New York.

Ayers, J., & Theodore, S. (1987). Visualization, systematic desensitization, and rational-emotive therapy: A comparative evaluation. *Communication Education, 36*(3), 236-240.

Baither, R. C., & Godsey, R. (1979). Rational-emotive education and relaxation training in large group treatment of test anxiety. *Psychological Reports, 45*(1), 326.

Bernard, M. E., & Joyce, M. R. (1984). *Rational-emotive therapy with children and adolescents: Theory, treatment strategies, preventative methods*. New York: John Wiley.

Block, J. (1978). Effects of a rational-emotive mental health program on poorly achieving, disruptive high school students. *Journal of Counseling Psychology, 25*(1), 61-65.

Brody, M. (1974). *The effects of a rational-emotive affective approach in anxiety, frustration tolerance, and self-esteem with fifth grade students*. Unpublished doctoral dissertation, Temple University, Philadelphia.

Bruner, G. (1984). Rational-emotive education for parent study groups. *Individual Psychology: Journal of Adlerian Theory, Research, and Practice, 40*(2), 228-231.

Campbell, D. T., & Stanley, J. C. (1963). Experimental and quasi-experimental designs for research on teaching. In N. L. Gage (Ed.), *Handbook on research on teaching* (pp. 171-246). Chicago: Rand McNally.

Casper, E. (1981). *A study to determine the effectiveness of rational-emotive education on sixth grade children*. Unpublished doctoral dissertation, University of Virginia, Charlottesville.

Dewey, J. (1900). Psychology and social practice. *Psychological Review, 7*, 105-124.

DiGiuseppe, R., & Kassinove, H. (1976). Effects of a rational-emotive school mental health program on children's emotional adjustment. *Journal of Community Psychology, 4*(4), 382-387.

DiGiuseppe, R. A., & Miller, N. J. (1977). A review of outcome studies on rational-emotive therapy. In A. Ellis & R. Grieger, (Eds.), *Handbook of rational-emotive therapy* (pp. 72-95). New York: Springer.

DiGiuseppe, R. A., Miller, N. J., & Trexler, L. D. (1979). A review of rational-emotive outcome studies. In A. Ellis & J. M. Whiteley (Eds.), *Theoretical and empirical foundations of rational-emotive therapy* (pp. 218-235). Monterey, CA: Brooks/Cole.

DiNublie, L., Wessler, R. (1974). Lessons from the Living School. *Rational Living, 9*, 29-32.

Dye, S. O. (1980). *The influence of rational-emotive education on the self-concepts of adolescents living in a residential group home.* Unpublished doctoral dissertation, University of Virginia, Charlottesville.

Ellis, A. (1957a). *How to live with a neurotic.* New York: Crown.

Ellis, A. (1957b). Outcome of employing three techniques of psychotherapy. *Journal of Clinical Psychology, 13*, 344-350.

Ellis, A. (1958). Rational psychotherapy. *Journal of General Psychology, 59*, 35-49.

Ellis, A. (1962). *Reason and emotion in psychotherapy.* Secaucus, NJ: Lyle Stuart.

Ellis, A. (1979b). Rational-emotive therapy: Research data that support the clinical and personality hypothesis of RET and other modes of cognitive-behavior therapy. In A. Ellis & J. M. Whiteley (Eds.), *Theoretical and empirical foundations of rational-emotive therapy* (pp. 101-173). Monterey, CA: Brooks/Cole.

Ellis, A. (1988). *How to stubbornly refuse to make yourself miserable about anything—Yes, anything!* Secaucus, NJ: Lyle Stuart.

Ellis, A., & Dryden, W. (1987). *The practice of rational-emotive therapy.* New York: Springer.

Ellis, A., & Grieger, R. (Eds.)(1977). *Handbook of rational-emotive therapy.* New York: Springer.

Ellis, A., Knaus, W. J. (1979). *Overcoming procrastination.* New York: New American Library.

Eluto, M. (1980). *The effects of rational-emotive education and problem solving therapy on the adjustment of intermediate special education students.* Unpublished doctoral dissertation, Hofstra University, Hempstead, NY.

Engles, G., & Diekstra, R. F. W. (1986). Meta analysis of rational-emotive therapy outcome studies. In P. Eelen & O. Fontaine (Eds.), *Behavior therapy: Beyond the conditioning framework* (pp. 121-140). Hillsdale, NJ: Lawrence Erlbaum.

Gerald, M., & Eyman, W. (1980). *Thinking straight and talking sense: An emotional education program.* New York: Institute for Rational Living.

Gerzhols, J. S. (1980). *The effects of rational-emotive education on a hearing impaired high school population.* Unpublished doctoral dissertation, Hofstra University, Hempstead, NY.

Gittleman, M. (1965). Behavior rehearsal as a technique in child treatment. *Journal of Child Psychology and Psychiatry, 6*, 251-255.

Grassi, R. (1984). *Effects of self-instruction training and rational-emotive education on adjustment in elementary school children.* Unpublished doctoral dissertation, Hofstra University, Hempstead, NY.

Greenwald, E. (1984). *Effects of rational-emotive education and bibliotherapy on self-concept, individual achievement, and anxiety in 6th grade children.* Unpublished doctoral dissertation, Hofstra University, Hempstead, NY.

Handleman, D. (1981). *The effects of rational-emotive education courses on the rational beliefs, frustration tolerance, and self-acceptance of high school students.* Unpublished doctoral dissertation, Temple University, Philadelphia.

Harris, S. (1976). *Rational-emotive education and the human development program: A comparative outcome study.* Unpublished doctoral dissertation, University of Oregon, Eugene.

Harris, S. (1976). Rational-emotive education and the human development program: A guidance study. *Elementary School Guidance and Counseling, 11*(2), 113-122.

Hooper, S. R., & Layne, C. C. (1985). Rational-emotive education as a short-term primary prevention technique. *Techniques, 1*(4), 264-269.

Katz, S. (1974). *The effects of locus of control and self-concept.* Unpublished doctoral dissertation, Hofstra University, Hempstead, NY.

Keller, J. F., Croake, J. W., & Brooking, J. Y. (1975). Effects of a program of rational thinking in older adults. *Journal of Counseling Psychology, 22*(1), 54-57.

Knaus, W. J. (1970, January). *Innovative uses of parents and teachers as behavior modifiers.* Paper presented at the Seventh Annual School Psychologists Conference, Queens College, New York.

Knaus, W. J. (1974). *Rational-emotive education: A manual for elementary school teachers.* New York: Institute for Rational-Emotive Therapy.

Knaus, W. J. (1977a). Rational-emotive education. In A. Ellis & R. Grieger (Eds.), *Handbook of rational-emotive therapy* (pp. 398-408). New York: Springer.

Knaus, W. J. (1977b). Rational-emotive education. *Theory Into Practice, 14*(4), 251-255.

Knaus, W. J. (1982). *How to get out of a rut.* Englewood Cliffs, NJ: Prentice-Hall.

Knaus, W. J. (1983a). Children and low frustration tolerance. In A. Ellis & M. Bernard (Eds.), *Rational-emotive approaches to the problems of childhood* (pp. 139-158). New York: Plenum.

Knaus, W. J. (1983b). *How to conquer your frustrations.* Englewood Cliffs. NJ: Prentice-Hall.

Knaus, W. J. (1985). Student burnout: A rational-emotive education treatment approach. In A. Ellis & M. Bernard (Eds.), *Clinical applications of rational-emotive therapy* (pp. 257-276). New York: Plenum.

Knaus, W. J., & Block, J. (1976). *Rational-emotive education with economically disadvantaged inner city high school students: A demonstration study.* Unpublished manuscript.

Knaus, W. J., & Bokor, S. (1975). The effects of rational-emotive emotional education lessons on anxiety and self-concept in sixth grade students. *Rational Living, 11*(2), 25-28.

Knaus, W. J., & Hendricks, C. (1986). *The illusion trap: How to achieve a happier life.* NY: World Almanac Publications.

Knaus, W. J., & McKeever, C. (1977). Rational-emotive education with learning disabled children. *Journal of Learning Disabilities, 10*(1), 10-14.

Krenitsky, D. L. (1978). *The relationship of age and verbal intelligence to the efficacy of rational-emotive education with older adults.* Unpublished doctoral dissertation, Hofstra University, Hempstead, NY.

Landesman, S., & Ramey, C. (1989). Developmental psychology and mental retardation: Integrating scientific principles with treatment practices. *American Psychologist, 44*(2), 409-415.

Lang, J. (1980, June). *Rational-emotive education and the developmental stages of Jean Piaget.* Paper presented at the National Conference on Rational-Emotive Therapy, New York.

Lazarus, A. A. (1966). Behavior rehearsal vs. non-directive therapy vs. advice in effecting behavior change. *Behavior Research and Therapy, 4*, 209-212.

Lazarus, A. A. (1971). *Behavior therapy and beyond.* New York: McGraw-Hill.

Lazarus, A. A., & Davison, G. C. (1971). Clinical innovation in research and practice. In A. E. Bergin & S. L. Garfield (Eds.), *Handbook of psychotherapy and behavior change* (pp. 196-213). New York: John Wiley.

Leibowitz, A. (1979). *Effects of ABC homework sheets, initial level of adjustment, and duration of treatment on the efficacy of rational-emotive education in elementary school children.* Unpublished doctoral dissertation, Hofstra University, Hempstead, NY.

Leopold, H. (1984). *Cognitive training with seriously disturbed children: Effects of cognitive level, cognitive strategy, and additional time in training.* Unpublished doctoral dissertation, Hofstra University, Hempstead, NY.

Lo Fuang-luan, G. (1986). *The effects of a rational-emotive education program on self-concept and locus of control among learning disabled adolescents.* Unpublished doctoral dissertation, University of Houston.

Matuozzi, R. T. (1986). *Predictors of content acquisition in rational-emotive education.* Unpublished doctoral dissertation, Hofstra University, Hempstead, NY.

Maultsby, M. C., Jr. (1986). *Coping better . . . anytime, anywhere: The handbook of rational self-counseling.* Englewood Cliffs, NJ: Prentice-Hall.

McGovern, T. E., & Silverman, M. S. (1984). A review of outcome studies of rational-emotive therapy from 1977 to 1982. *Journal of Rational-Emotive Therapy, 21*, 7-18.

Miller, N. (1977). *Effects of behavior rehearsal, written homework assignments, and level of education on the efficacy of rational-emotive education in elementary school children.* Unpublished doctoral dissertation, Hofstra University, Hempstead, NY.

Omizo, M. M., Cubberly, W. E., & Omizo, S. A. (1985). The effects of rational-emotive education groups on self-concept and locus of control among learning disabled children. *Exceptional Child, 32*(1), 13-19.

Omizo, M. M., Lo Fuang-luan, & Williams, E. (1986). Rational-emotive education, self concept, and locus of control among learning disabled students. *Journal of Humanistic Education and Development, 25*(2), 58-69.

Piaget, J. (1952). *The origins of intellect.* New York: Norton.

Piaget, J. (1972). Intellectual evolution from adolescence to adulthood. *Human Development, 15*, 1-12.

Piaget, J. (1981). Intelligence and affectivity: Their relationship during child development. In M. R. Rosenzweig & L. W. Porter (Eds.), *Annual Review of Psychology* (Vol. 33). Palo Alto, CA: Annual Reviews.

Piaget, J., & Inhelder, B. (1958). *The growth of logical thinking.* New York: Basic Books.

Russell, T. T. (1987). *The effectiveness of a rational-emotive education program for the prevention and treatment of teacher burnout.* Unpublished doctoral dissertation, University of Oregon, Eugene.

Skinner, B. F. (1953). *Science and human behavior.* New York: Macmillan.

Smith, M. L., & Glass, C. V. (1977). Meta analysis of psychotherapy outcome studies. *American Psychologist, 32,* 752-760.

Smith, T. W. (1989). Assessment in rational-emotive therapy. In M. E. Bernard & R. A. DiGiuseppe (Eds.), *Inside rational-emotive therapy* (pp. 135-153). Orlando FL: Academic Press.

Sweetland, J. (1979). *Effects of teacher disability and grade level on the efficacy of rational-emotive education program for severely physically disabled children.* Unpublished doctoral dissertation, Hofstra University, Hempstead, NY.

Triperinas, M. (1988). *Rational-emotive education: Its effects on locus of control and school behavior of hidden children of alcoholics.* Unpublished doctoral dissertation, University of Oregon, Eugene.

Vernon, A. (1980). *Help yourself to a happier you: Emotional education exercises for children.* Lanham, MD: University Press of America.

Vernon, A. (1983) Rational-emotive education. In A. Ellis & M. Bernard (Eds.), *Rational-emotive approaches to the problems of childhhod* (pp. 467-484). New York: Plenum.

Voelm, C. E. (1983). *The efficacy of teaching rational-emotive education to acting out and socially withdrawn adolescents.* Unpublished doctoral dissertation, California School of Professional Psychology.

Wasserman, T. H., & Vogrin, D. J. (1979). Relationship of endorsement of rational beliefs, age, months treatment and intelligence to overt behavior of emotionally disturbed children. *Psychological Reports, 44,* 911-917.

Wessler, R. A., Wessler, R. L. (1980). *The principles and practices of rational-emotive therapy.* San Francisco: Jossey-Bass.

Wolpe, J., & Lazarus, A. A. (1966). *Behavior therapy techniques.* Elmsford, NY: Pergamon.

Zionts, P. (1983). A strategy for understanding and correcting irrational beliefs in pupils: The rational-emotive approach. *Pointer, 27*(3), 13-17.

RET and Sudden Infant Death Syndrome

RICHARD S. SCHNEIMAN

Sudden Infant Death Syndrome

Mental health specialists who are involved professionally in the treatment of death and dying issues with their patients are very aware of the challenge that these events bring to a successful therapeutic outcome. A plethora of professional articles and books have been written to guide mental health professionals in their work with this particular population (Willinger, 1989). This chapter presents methods of treating a group of individuals who share a unique type of loss—sudden infant death syndrome (SIDS)—using rational-emotive therapy strategies and techniques in combination with other therapeutic modalities. This patient population presents unique features that call for special knowledge prior to initiating treatment.

SIDS is defined as the "sudden death of an infant or young child which is unexpected by history, and in which a thorough postmortem examination fails to demonstrate an adequate cause for death" (Beckwith, 1970, p. 1). Approximately 7,000 infants will die annually in the United States with a diagnosis of SIDS as the cause of death (Willinger, 1989). The resulting trauma to the parents and family members can lead to severe emotional and physiological reactions. It is important that caregivers to this population have a good knowledge of SIDS as a means of helping the victims through their bereavement.

Sources of clinical information regarding SIDS are abundant (Berger, Booth, & Snyder, 1988). The National SIDS Foundation provides booklets regarding SIDS and keeps a current record of research being conducted in the area. The National Institute of Health, through the National Institute of Child Health and Human Development, provides a governmental responsibility for conducting SIDS research and also has created federal and state programs to provide information for those interested in this field. Most states in the continental United States have SIDS chapters that are certified members of the National SIDS Foundation. These chapters are essentially self-help organizations, which for the most part are created and supported by parents who have experienced the SIDS tragedy. The Utah Chapter is supported by a state agency as well. The Utah Department of Health, through the Division of Family Health Services, supports the efforts of a SIDS advisory council, which brings together concerned individuals from a variety of fields to discuss issues pertinent to the SIDS phenomenon. There is also involvement on the part of specially trained health service nurses who work through the County Health Services programs in Utah.

The author's professional involvement in SIDS issues has occurred through (a) membership on the Board of Trustees of the Utah SIDS Foundation and (b) membership on the SIDS Advisory Council sponsored by the Utah Department of Health. In addition, professional services have been provided on a pro bono consultancy basis to the organization in terms of clinical assistance, training individuals who are outreach parents to new-loss patients, providing therapeutic input through large group workshops and monthly support group meetings, and creating small group meetings specifically for new-loss parents.

It is useful to be aware of how professionals can be effectively involved with self-help groups, and especially to understand that "professional assistance is appreciated when it is understood that the decision making authority lies within the group itself" (Chutis, 1983, p. 2). Professional assistance is valued when the professional serves as an intermediary between the group and the professional community, assists in articulating the group's ideology for the group itself, acts as a resource person in planning, facilitates group process as an organization, and assists in research (Klass & Shinners, 1982-1983). Professionals can also be helpful in dealing with grief-related psychotic-like behavior expressed within the group (Klass & Shinners, 1982-1983).

Some important statistical data useful to mental health professionals who work with this population are as follows: (a) a SIDS event will occur in approximately 2 out of every 1,000 live births in the United States (Kinney & Filano, 1988; Wegman, 1988; Willinger, 1989); (b) approximately 90% of all SIDS deaths occur before the age of 6 months, with a preponderance of deaths peaking between 2 and 4 months (Hoffman, Damus, Hillman, & Krongrad, 1988; Naeye, Ladis, & Drage, 1976); (c) there is a higher incidence of death in the winter months in North America; (d) SIDS occurs at a slightly greater rate to male infants; (e) SIDS deaths seem to occur during a sleep period, although no specific observation exists that the infant was asleep at the time of death (Hoffman et al., 1988; Naeye et al., 1976); (f) black infants have a three times greater risk of dying from SIDS than Caucasians (Hoffman et al., 1988; Naeye et al., 1976).

There currently is no scientifically verified cause of SIDS. Major areas of research are being conducted in cardiorespiratory control and sleep, the developing immune system of the infant, brain stem dysfunction, and inherited metabolic diseases (Hunt, 1990). Despite rigorous research, no findings have been presented that scientifically explain the SIDS phenomenon.

Behavioral and Psychological Effects of SIDS

There is no doubt that a SIDS episode represents one of the most catastrophic and tragic losses that humans can experience. The impact on parents, siblings, extended family, neighbors, and friends is often devastating. The SIDS phenomenon is composed of events that meet the American Psychiatric Association's (1987) criteria for Post-Traumatic Stress Disorder (PTSD). Understanding SIDS through a PTSD model has been most helpful in developing methods of intervention.

Despite the common features of SIDS and PTSD in both the acute and chronic stages, there are still certain features of a SIDS loss that make the treatment for this population unique. The special circumstances of this population can be better understood by considering the following features:

1. Hypersensitivity to the Death of the Infant. Most parents are psychologically, emotionally, behaviorally, and to some degree hormonally directed to care, nurture, and protect their infant. The sudden death, without any warning of imminent harm, leaves these people in a state of profound trauma and frustration. The insult to their role as a parent is so great that their initial grief reactions can best be described as anguish beyond the comprehension of those who have never gone through such a tragic event.

2. Vulnerability to Guilt and Blame. Because of the ambiguity regarding a SIDS death, parents try to find an explanation for the death through obsessing over actions that they had or had not taken. The notion of the responsibility for the child's death is quite common (Bergman, Pomeroy, & Beckwith, 1969; Culbertson & Willis, 1988) and constitutes one of the major challenges in treating this population. This pattern of blaming self or others can lead to a pattern of pathological bereavement unless it is addressed quickly.

3. Limited Knowledge of SIDS. Most parents have some degree of awareness of SIDS but have no understanding of its unique nature. This ignorance further leads SIDS parents toward assuming responsibility for the death of their child despite all evidence to the contrary.

4. Vulnerability to Social Criticism. If the parents are exposed to comments from members of the community that are also based on an ignorance of SIDS, these comments can further reinforce the parents' irrational sense of guilt and responsibility for the death of their child (Meier, 1973).

5. Social Rejection and Isolation. Within a few months after the death of the child, many SIDS parents begin to feel a sense of isolation from members of their community or their work force. They often report that other individuals have a difficult time knowing either what to say or how to relate to them and tend to deal with their loss by avoiding them completely. SIDS parents whose bereavement process involves a desire to talk about their child and the SIDS circumstances frequently find others unwilling to participate in such a discussion. Such avoidance is perceived as pressure from others to have SIDS parents "move on with their life" and "get back to normal." This pressure often confounds the process of a healthy bereavement (Mandell & Belk, 1977; Markusen, Owen, Fulton, & Bendiksen, 1977-1978).

6. Therapist Challenges. Because SIDS affects all members of society, issues regarding age, socioeconomic status, race, religion, educational experience, intellectual capacity, and emotional stability are all variables that test the skills of the helping professional. Also, individuals involved in SIDS support groups may have experienced loss at varying periods of time so that there is likely to be a mixing of individuals in acute stages of grief with those who are in chronic stages of pathological bereavement. Additionally, such factors as single mothers versus married, marital conflicts that existed prior to the SIDS death, and communication problems can impact the capacity of the therapist to be of assistance (Culbertson & Willis, 1988). Because the degree of anguish and emotional distress in this group is so profound, it is important that therapists have direct experience with the nature of personal loss. This shared history often lends credibility to therapists who are working with this highly distressed and agitated population.

7. Public Agency Involvement. Additional situational stress may impact SIDS families as a result of their experiences with personnel investigating the SIDS death. Many families have experienced accusations from police, suspicion of wrongdoing from medical personnel, or callous insensitivity by other individuals involved in the investigation surrounding the death of the infant. It is not uncommon for SIDS parents to be angry at paramedics, police, emergency room personnel, individuals involved with the autopsy of the child, and others who are viewed as being insensitive and uncaring (Cain, 1979; DeFrain & Ernst, 1978; Stitt, 1971).

8. Discovery of the Deceased. An issue of importance in terms of assessing the severity of the PTSD reaction and its implications for future treatment has to do with (a) whether the parents found the child, (b) the condition the body was in at the time of discovery, and/or (c) whether the baby died while in the care of others. Reports of SIDS events reveal infants dying in their parents' arms, infants dying a few seconds after being placed in their crib, and parents finding their children hours after their death. Typically, death leads to dramatic physical changes that can be horrifying to persons who discover SIDS victims. These transformations involve a soaking of the sheets and blankets around the infant from released body fluids, a pinkish foam or froth around the infant's mouth, and varying stages of rigor mortis. These changes add a grotesqueness to the trauma that has significant implications for the severity of the PTSD response and increases the risk of lifelong emotional problems (Figley, 1985).

The SIDS event frequently victimizes family members who witness the trauma or who are vicariously exposed to the trauma, in the most severe manner (Rosenthal, Sadler, & Edwards, 1987). Consequently, individuals at risk in the SIDS tragedy include baby-sitters, siblings, other relatives, and friends. Research on PTSD indicates the high risk of an "infection" of family members from the trauma (Figley, 1985). All affected family members are vulnerable and carry the psychic pain of the survivor with them (Figley, 1985; Green, Wilson, & Lindy, 1985).

Rational-Emotive Approaches to the Problems of SIDS

Therapist Characteristics

RET therapists have traditionally been trained to devote clinical energy to offering RET insights and strategies to their clients without spending too much time developing a therapeutic alliance with their client (Ellis, 1962; Walen, DiGuiseppe, & Wessler, 1980). Clear exceptions exist in the RET literature in regard to creating therapeutic alliance between therapist and client when treating children and adolescents (Bernard & Joyce, 1984; Ellis, 1962; Ellis & Bernard, 1983; Walen et al., 1980; Young, 1983). Regardless of the therapy approach selected, PTSD research indicates that the therapist must focus on joining with the client (Minuchin & Fishman, 1981). Therapists who have the capacity to demonstrate support, regard, empathy, and caring for their clients create an opportunity to be far more valuable and effective in terms of offering RET insights that will be of assistance to the SIDS victims. As mentioned earlier in this chapter, there may be a distinct benefit in forming a therapeutic alliance with SIDS victims if the therapist has experienced a SIDS loss or has gone through some sort of catastrophic loss that may in some way provide a sense of mutual understanding of the intensity of grief and bereavement that affects those who have experienced the death of loved ones. Although this level of homogeneity between therapist and client is not essential, it may be useful for those who are inclined to assist this particular population. Additionally, it is important that therapists be able to demonstrate compassion and concern without being overwhelmed by the profound aspects of the SIDS loss. Marmar (1989) and his investigators on PTSD suggest that therapists balance their practices thoughtfully so that they are not inundated with PTSD patients, a caveat also appropriate to any practice involving SIDS treatment.

The manner in which cognitive therapy is often applied may exacerbate PTSD patients' feelings of being alienated and misunderstood (Walker & Nash, 1981). This can be prevented by working hard to form relationships of trust, whether working in an individual or a group setting.

Certain issues related to SIDS victims and their functioning can be treated best in a group setting. The group itself provides relationships that can be supportive and that help individuals to realize that they are not alone in their anguish nor in their experience. Individuals also can benefit from observing the work of others on shared issues without exacerbating problems or being hurt by the process (Yalom, 1970).

RET Psycho-Educational Methods

Psycho-educational methods of treatment, combined with other forms of therapy, may help entire families to cope with PTSD situations (Anderson, 1986). The model presented here has been used with parent support meetings and with therapy groups sponsored by the Utah Chapter of the National SIDS Foundation. The goals of the sessions are to offer information, insights, and skills to individuals affected by the SIDS tragedy that will enable them to develop individualized patterns of healthy bereavement (Balter, 1990).

Alliance With Participants. The sessions start out with a traditional introduction of each participant. They give their name and involvement in a SIDS loss, including the name and age of their child and the date of the child's death. The therapist is introduced last and has an opportunity to divulge any personal involvement with SIDS, including loss if that is the case. It is useful to reveal modest goals to the participants in terms of the therapist's capacity to help them with their grief. The sharing of concern for the severity of their problem does not so much reinforce their irrational beliefs of the "awfulness" of their tragedy but rather reveals the presenter as sensitive and caring to their particular plight.

The Rational Analysis. The therapist encourages group participation and then responds to the issues and needs of the participants. In order to assist in conceptualizing and organizing the issues that many of the participants are struggling with, the use of the RET rational analysis model has been found to be most beneficial.

Typically, the therapist will describe rational analysis as a system useful in helping to understand what is happening to those who are involved in the SIDS tragedy. Using a blackboard, the presenter will describe A—the activating event—as being the SIDS death. Next, the focus of the Rational Analysis will go directly to C—the consequences. C is described as focusing on feelings and behavior. The participants are then encouraged to express how they felt when they found out that their child had died.

Identifying the Cs. Typical C responses, as might be expected, include the most frequently experienced responses to catastrophic loss: shock, uncontrolled crying, confusion, panic, despair, anger, rage, guilt, and blame (American Psychiatric Association, 1987).

It is not uncommon for individuals who are in an acute PTSD phase to believe that they are going "crazy" (Walen et al., 1980). The physiological responses related to PTSD include the typical General Adaptation Syndrome responses described by Selye (1956). Dizziness, hyperventilation, high heart rate, and feelings of shock, nausea, and vertigo are commonly experienced. Survivors of SIDS often report vivid dreams involving the death of their child, nightmares, startle responses, acting or feeling as if the traumatic event is recurring, distressing memories of the death of others, hypervigilance, avoidance of thought, symptom increase when presented with similar stimuli to that of the tragedy, difficulty feeling close, and fear of losing control (Keane & Penk, 1986).

Behaviors participants engaged in after hearing of their child's death are commonly described as "going through the motions," "being in a fog," "functioning like a zombie," being irritable and hostile in response to others, behaving in thoughtless and irresponsible ways, loss of appetite, binge eating, avoiding others, dreading to be alone, having to be in the company of others, and inability to do the most basic and simple tasks around the house or at work. Although this list is far from inclusive, it demonstrates the commonality of responses this particular population experiences. The process of describing the Cs generally provides the participants with a sense of relief. Most participants believe that their emotional reactions are unique to them (Yalom, 1970), and it is reassuring for them to discover that almost everyone who has been involved in the SIDS experience has similar feelings.

There are symptoms unique to SIDS groups that are presented in these support sessions. Mothers describe their "arms aching to hold their baby," along with feelings of emptiness, isolation, frustration, and futility associated with a thwarted readiness to nurture or protect their child. These feelings of frustration are reported as being so profound that they are almost unbearable.

Periodically, participants will openly acknowledge excessive use or abuse of alcohol and drugs or thoughts of suicide. Marital conflicts are described as being so severe that the couple is considering divorce. These extreme symptoms are usually brought to the attention of the therapist after the session or in phone calls a few days later. The severe signs of pathological bereavement are often shared with the author in his capacity as a mental health consultant by concerned family members or by SIDS outreach staff.

The process of encouraging the participants to express their feelings and behaviors is valuable in terms of gaining a kinship with other SIDS parents. It is also particularly useful in setting up opportunities for the therapist to begin to separate healthy bereavement responses from unhealthy ones.

Getting at the Bs. After the participants have exhausted their expression of feelings and behaviors related to their SIDS experience, the therapist identifies and supports the commonalities of their responses and the severity of the distress that the group experiences. At this point, the therapist starts to home in on the connection between thoughts and feelings. The therapist describes physiological responses that are natural to catastrophic loss (Ochberg, 1991; Selye, 1956) to begin the distinction between rational and irrational evaluations. Symptoms related to physiological changes are then labeled as being appropriate to the nature of the loss. The therapist introduces the cognitive concept that the degree of distress that an individual experiences is partially related to the perception of the tragedy. This is usually in response to questions regarding the duration and the intensity of the emotional anguish and the physiological discomfort that these traumatized individuals are experiencing. Members of the SIDS support group who experienced their SIDS loss 3 or 4 years prior will state that the anguish that they experienced does lessen over time. They also support the presenter's ideas as being very helpful in terms of coping with the SIDS tragedy.

Disputing the Irrational Beliefs

This subject predictably leads us into assessing the beliefs that people hold about the SIDS experience and the effect those beliefs will have on the creation and maintenance of many of their feelings and behaviors.

Awfulizing. Probably the most important cognitive concept in terms of healthy versus unhealthy bereavement has to do with the RET concept of "awfulizing" (Ellis, 1962, 1977). Not only is awfulizing a crucial concept, it is also one of the most difficult concepts to present to this population in a way that does not come across as offensive (Walker & Nash, 1981).

A valuable strategy for the introduction of the concept of awfulizing to the SIDS population has been to combine it with Wolpe's (1969) Subjective Units of Discomfort Scale (SUDS). The SUDS is used as a mechanism to quantify the severity of the individual's life problems from zero to 100%. It is also used to generate discriminations over a continuum of emotional reactions. Clients are instructed to consider the 100% end of the scale as constituting "the worst events that could ever befall you or your loved ones." Most people will identify the death of loved ones, particularly children, as being the worst thing that could ever happen to them. Here is the major sticking point in presenting awfulizing to a SIDS population. In their minds the very worst event *has* happened to them. If the presenter is viewed as attempting to argue with them regarding this perception, whatever hope there was for a therapeutic alliance will be destroyed.

RET itself has acknowledged this conflict and has made changes in its descriptors and synonyms for "awfulizing." Ellis (1971) addressed this very issue when "catastrophizing" was removed as a synonym for awfulizing. This refinement was based on the awareness that catastrophic events do occur to human beings and that tragedies of a profound nature are a part of our human condition. Therefore, these events are not considered as an exaggeration. Indeed, SIDS is perceived and described as being a catastrophic event. Now the framework for helping SIDS families understand that SIDS is not "awful" can be more effectively addressed.

Once the analysis of the beliefs about the SIDS experience is underway, the SUDS is drawn on the board with 99+% representing the most extreme end of the scale. Clients sometimes are perplexed by the 99+ and will ask why the scale does not stop at 100. If this question is not raised, the therapist will identify this aspect of the scale to the group. Then the therapist, as is typically done with the SUDS, will reveal that *nothing* is 100% bad. As tragic and as unfortunate and catastrophic as an event is, it could always be worse. So, what does that do to the severity of the SIDS loss? For most of us who have worked with this population or have personally experienced this tragedy, we perceive it as being 99.99999% bad. The concession is "it doesn't get much worse than this." This acknowledgment, as weak as it may seem, still provides an opportunity for those who survive misfortune to reduce their anguish through a healthy bereavement process. The therapist may say, "Over time, the emotional intensity related to loss may slide down the SUDS scale; 80 to 70 to 50, to a point that enables us to function adequately in life although knowing that our life will be different as a result of our personal loss." A hopeful and encouraging prediction of lessening of symptoms and an increased capacity to function adaptively is also made at this time.

Self-Blame. Guilt is commonly found in this population, not only because of the irrational sense of failed parental responsibility, but also because of the ambiguous circumstances surrounding the SIDS experience. Guilt and self-blame feed off of the ambiguity and the suddenness of the death. Parents often express beliefs that maintain feelings of depression and self-loathing based on the belief that they should have done something to stop SIDS from happening and, because they didn't, they are at fault. The dispute for this irrational belief has to be solely based on scientific evidence. The evidence is that there is no known cause of SIDS, nor are there any warning signals that could lead to any sort of intervention that would stop this death from occurring. While parents are in their acute PTSD phase, they often express some sort of correlational or superstitious ideation regarding their responsibility for the death of the child; "I put too many blankets on the baby," "I didn't have enough blankets on the baby," "I should not have put the baby down when the baby was crying," "The baby had sniffles and I should have taken him to the doctor," and the like. These irrational beliefs are best addressed in a kind yet vigorous manner. Otherwise, the maintenance of pathological bereavement is likely.

The therapist, in addressing superstitious ideation, is encouraged to help clients make a distinction between correlational data and causal data. The therapist, in attempting to identify correlational data, might say to the group in a semiserious way, "Did you know that in all households where a SIDS death occurred there was milk in the refrigerator . . . or diapers in the house . . . ?" From such exaggeration of illogical associations, the logical arguments against the superstitious beliefs can be better understood and accepted. Another example might be, "all children get colds and have the sniffles and only 2 out of 1,000 of those children actually die of SIDS. All children are covered or uncovered with blankets for a substantial period of their developmental life without harm befalling them. All infants cry, as we know too well, and that has nothing to do with a SIDS result." In order to overcome guilt, persistent disputation is necessary. Clients are encouraged to argue vigorously against any self-incriminating notions.

Blame. Typically, individuals who engage in this type of irrational thinking direct their blame toward the individual who was responsible for the infant at the time of its death. This could involve spouse blaming spouse or parents blaming baby-sitters, friends, or members of the extended family. This irrational belief is also based on the notion that if "something this awful has happened, someone must have done something wrong and must be punished!" Again, disputes based on scientific evidence, logic, and good judgment are required to help the blamer modify this pattern of distorted thinking. If blame is not modified, it can lead to dramatic life changes such as divorce and alienation among family members.

Blaming can also be observed through the client's religious beliefs. Individuals may believe that some form of divine intervention caused the death of their child, and that belief is totally inconsistent with their perceptions of God. "God must be punishing me for my sins," or "How could my God do such a thing?" Religious beliefs, which may be found in other-blame as well as in self-blame, need to be addressed as most religious issues are by RET therapists (Walen et al., 1980). If the individual's religious belief is supportive and enhancing of a healthy bereavement, then that belief system is viewed as being therapeutic. RET therapists are to encourage that line of thinking. For example: "God has special plans for my child," or "the Lord called my baby back because it was so perfect."

If religious concepts are maintaining irrational feelings of anger, hatred, guilt, or depression, and there is a risk of harm to self and others, it is recommended that the individual seek some guidance from their religious leaders surrounding this issue as well as entering psychotherapy.

Encourage clients to grieve and mourn the loss of a child as a normal part of their bereavement process. It is understood that there is no one way to mourn. Each person mourns differently and that is OK. Since many participants have never experienced the death of a loved one, they are confused as to how they should feel and benefit from hearing that the intensity of their emotions during the acute PTSD phase is appropriate to the severity of the loss. Separating rational beliefs from irrational beliefs is done by sorting through the interpretations, judgments, and evaluations of the death that are elicited from the group. This process usually leads to acceptance rather than blame.

Demandingness. Within the many irrational ideations that are found in SIDS-related cognitions is the question of fairness. Almost all SIDS parents will state or agree that they have thought at least once that what has happened to them is "not fair" and have followed that thought with the question of "Why me?" These individuals are somehow expecting or demanding special privileges, namely to be protected and immune from harm or tragedy in their lives. This issue is best approached with delicacy and tact. The therapist is well advised to maintain a scientific and pragmatic perspective regarding the reasons for these particular families having experienced a SIDS death. Present the client with the scientific evidence that 2 out of every 1,000 live births ends in a SIDS incident. The research surrounding the demographics of SIDS, the universality of SIDS, and the history of SIDS dating back to Biblical times can be presented. The ultimate conclusion strived for is that "all human beings who exist on this planet are exposed to varying degrees of risk regarding accidental death and catastrophic loss due to illness and disease. It was for no more reason than the sake of probability that you had the misfortune of having SIDS occur to your child."

The issue of fairness may be addressed as follows; "As RET points out, fairness is not a law of nature. It is a preferred and desired way for individuals to experience life, but there are no guarantees that fairness will happen in any sort of predictable manner. Life is certainly not fair. Life is neither fair nor unfair . . . life just is." Clients also learn to answer the question "Why me?" with a more realistic response, which is "Why not me?" We are not immune to the tragic aspects of life. But when tragedy does befall us, we can survive and move on.

Despite SIDS parents accepting the loss of their child from a rational perspective, they are still left with a great deal of frustration surrounding this tragedy. RET has taken the position that it may be better for people to channel their frustration into some constructive direction instead of dwelling on the "awfulness" of the event, to wit: "Until modern science discovers causes and cures for SIDS, what can we do to help? If we take our frustration and experience and channel it into constructive outlets such as fund-raising, lobbying for research, community education, and parent contact, we may derive some degree of satisfaction that we are helping in ways that make a difference."

Case Examples

Examples of integrating RET into helping a client deal with issues related to a SIDS loss are presented.

Supporting Healthy Bereavement

The client is a 22-year-old Caucasian female, married. Her male child died at the age of 2½ months. It has now been 3 months since the death of her child.

Therapist: What would you like to talk about today?

Client: Well, I was referred to you by the Parents Chapter of the SIDS group. I lost my son, Jerome, 3 months ago. (Patient tears up and begins to sob.)

T: I'm very sorry to hear that. How old was your son when he died?

C: He was just 2½ months old . . . he was perfectly healthy other than having a few sniffles. We were going to take him to the doctor some time that week but never had a chance. (Client begins to cry again.) I'm sorry for making such a fool of myself, but I can't seem to stop crying. That's one of the reasons why people suggested I come and talk to you.

T: It's all right. It's perfectly understandable that you would be upset. It's okay for you to cry here or anywhere else.

C: Well, my husband doesn't think so.

T: Why? What are his thoughts about your reaction to your son's death?

C: Well, he thinks I talk too much about the baby and spend too much time looking at his pictures and going through his things. He thinks that makes it worse for me. I don't think so, do you?

T: I think you need to be encouraged to do whatever is going to make you feel better about the loss of your child. It's not uncommon for a husband and wife to mourn and grieve in different ways. By the way, how is your husband handling the death of his son?

C: In the beginning he was teary but supportive of me. Lately he's just kind of closed off from me. He doesn't want to talk about the baby. As a matter of fact, he doesn't want to talk about anything. He just goes to work, comes home, eats, and stares at the TV all night. I'm really bothered by that.

T: It sounds like there is some conflict developing between the two of you surrounding the loss of your son.

C: For sure! [He] was so excited to have a boy. This is our first child, you know? Bob had already started thinking about doing things with the baby. He would tell me about planning to take him fishing and to have catches with him in the backyard when he came home from school. (Client breaks down.)

T: There are major disappointments that all people who are affected by SIDS have to deal with. As you're noticing, some men deal with powerful emotions differently than women. Oftentimes they hold them in and try to deny the pain that they are feeling. Although this is a common reaction, I'm not convinced that it's a particularly good one. My hope is that your husband will be able to join us in future visits. Do you think that's possible?

C: Well, he was going to come to this one but at the last minute backed out. He said to me, "How can he help me? He can't bring my baby back to life." So I'm not sure if he'll become involved.

T: Sometimes if you are patient and demonstrate that you're learning things about your dealing with the death of your son that's helpful to you, your husband might be inclined to participate. Let's hope that that happens.

Dealing With Self-Blame

T: You mention that your husband gets upset when he thinks about things that he had hoped to do with your son, but now will not be able to do. What kinds of thoughts seem to upset you the most?

C: Well, I guess I just miss the whole experience of having Jerome with me. I miss hearing him cry. I miss being able to go into his nursery and look at him sleeping so peacefully. I think that what upsets me the most is the thought that I did something that caused his death. (Client cries.)

T: What do you think you might have done that could have contributed to his death?

C: (through her tears) I'm not sure. Maybe I put too many blankets on the baby. When I found him, his sheets were soaked. I can't help but think that if I had gone in to check on him a few minutes sooner, maybe he would have been alive. (Client continues to cry.)

T: Do you know very much about SIDS? I mean, why it happens or what causes it?

C: No, not really.

T: Has anybody ever talked to you about SIDS?

C: Well, some nurse came to my house a few days after the baby died, and I remember her talking to me, but I don't remember much about what she had to say. Some parents from the SIDS group came and visited me, and they were real nice, but I don't think I remember much about what they said, either.

T: Well, it's really important for you to know as much about SIDS as possible so you will not be making the death of your son worse for yourself by blaming yourself for something you didn't do.

C: Well, I can't help but blame myself. After all, I'm his mother. I should have been able to do something.

T: Almost all parents feel exactly that same way. That's what makes the sudden death of our babies so difficult to bear. But the fact is that there is nothing you could have done to stop SIDS from happening to your baby, as the 7,000 parents in this country who are going to lose their babies to SIDS will not be able to stop SIDS from happening either!

C: How do you mean?

T: Despite all the research that has been going on for many years now, there is no known cause for SIDS. There are no warning signs, nor are there any indications that certain babies are more likely to die from SIDS than others. All we know is that in North America 2 out of 1,000 babies die of SIDS. Most of them die between the 2nd and 6th month of life and slightly more male babies die than female babies. Most of the deaths also occur during the winter months. This leads us to suspect that there is some sort of vulnerability, some sort of weakness the infant carries that breaks down during their development. But what's most important for you to realize is that you did nothing, absolutely nothing, to cause your child's death. (Client sits quietly, under more emotional control and listening intently to the therapist.)

    Your worrying about having too many blankets on the baby is a very common worry that SIDS parents have. They also worry that they didn't have enough blankets on the baby or that they carried the baby too much, or that they didn't carry the baby enough or that they didn't look in on the baby soon enough. All of these worries are based on the belief that the parents could have done something to have prevented SIDS from happening. That belief, as we now know, is not true. There is absolutely nothing that we can do to stop this tragedy from occurring. So it's very important that you begin to work to accept the fact that your baby died for reasons that you had no control over whatsoever and work hard not to blame yourself for something you had no control over.

C: Well, what about what other people think?

T: How do you mean?

C: Well, I've had people ask me if we have a cat in the house, like a cat could smother the baby. One lady said to me that she raised six children and she never had anything like this happen. How do you think that makes me feel?

T: I can see that would make you feel really upset . . . until you begin to realize how ignorant those people are to be making such comments to you. There's a lot of ignorance in our culture about SIDS, and our organization works very hard to try to educate people to become more aware of SIDS so that they will not be feeding into the superstitions about SIDS. Unfortunately, because SIDS does not have a precise cause of death, people begin to speculate about all sorts of nonsense that might explain SIDS to them. These unfounded and unproven notions can cause a lot of pain to our vulnerable and uninformed parents. Once you really understand SIDS, you still might be bothered by statements of the type you described, but you won't be devastated by them.

Conclusion

Examples of how RET strategies have helped SIDS survivors cope with their loss have been presented. RET in combination with support groups, therapy groups, and time have helped many people experience a healthy bereavement process. Many individuals report personal growth as a result of this tragedy. They view themselves as being more compassionate toward others, able to cope with life's problems more effectively, not taking life for granted, and striving to enjoy the here-and-now. RET has clearly been of great value in helping this underserved population cope with their unique and tragic loss.

References

American Psychiatric Association. (1987). *Diagnostic and statistical manual of mental disorders* (3rd ed., rev.). Washington, DC: Author.

Anderson, C. M. (1986). A comparative study of the impact of education vs. process groups. *Family Process, 25*(2), 185-206.

Balter, R. (1990, June). *Bereavement lecture.* Presented at World Congress on Mental Health Counseling, Keystone, CO.

Beckwith, J. B. (1970). The sudden infant death syndrome. In A. B. Bergman, J. B. Beckwith, & C. G. Ray (Eds.), *Proceedings of the Second International Conference on the Causes of Sudden Infant Deaths in Infants* (pp. 14-22). Seattle: University of Washington Press.

Berger, J. M., Booth, S. G., & Snyder, B. N. (1988). *Sudden infant death syndrome and other losses among adolescent parents.* McLean, VA: National Sudden Infant Death Syndrome Clearinghouse.

Bergman, A. B., Pomeroy, M. A., & Beckwith, J. B. (1969). Psychiatric toll of the sudden infant death syndrome. *GP, 40*(6), 99-105.

Bernard, M. E., & Joyce, M. R. (1984). *Rational-emotive therapy with children and adolescents.* New York: John Wiley.

Cain, A. C. (1979). Impact of sudden infant death syndrome on families: Some lessons from our recent past. In S. E. Weinstein (Ed.), *Mental health issues in grief counseling* (pp. 65-78). Washington, DC: Bureau of Community Health Services.

Chutis, L. (1983). *Special roles of mental health professionals in self-help group development*. Chicago: Hamorth Press.

Culbertson, J. L., & Willis, D. J. (1988). Acute loss and grieving reactions: Treatment issues. In J. L. Culbertson, H. F. Krous, & R. D. Bendell (Eds.), *Sudden infant death syndrome: Medical aspects and psychological management* (pp. 157-181). Baltimore, MD: Johns Hopkins University Press.

DeFrain, J. D., & Ernst, L. (1978). Psychological effects of sudden infant death syndrome on surviving family members. *Journal of Family Practice, 6*(5), 985-989.

Ellis, A. (1962). *Reason and emotion in psychotherapy*. New York: Lyle Stuart.

Ellis, A. (1971). *Growth through reason*. North Hollywood, CA: Wilshire.

Ellis, A. (1977). *Anger: How to live with it and without it*. Secaucus, NJ: Citadel.

Ellis, A., & Bernard, M. E. (1983). *Rational-emotive approaches to the problems of childhood*. New York: Plenum.

Figley, C. F. (1985). *Trauma and its wake: The study and treatment of post-traumatic stress disorder*. New York: Brunner/Mazel.

Green, B. L., Wilson, J. P., & Lindy, J. D. (1985). Conceptualizing post-traumatic stress disorder: A psychosocial framework. In C. R. Figley (Ed.), *Trauma and its wake: The study and treatment of post-traumatic stress disorder* (pp. 53-72). New York: Brunner/Mazel.

Hoffman, H. J., Damus, K., Hillman, L., & Krongrad, E. (1988). The sudden infant death syndrome. In P. J. Schwartz, D. P. Southall, & M. Valdes-Dapena (Eds.), *The sudden infant death syndrome: Cardiac and respiratory mechanisms and interventions* (Vol. 533, pp. 13-30). New York: New York Academy of Sciences.

Hunt, C. E. (1990). Sudden infant death syndrome and apnea of infancy. *Seminars in Respiratory Medicine, 11*(2), 15-25.

Keane, T. M., & Penk, W. E. (1986). *Systematic internal review: PTSD*. Washington, DC: Veterans Administration Memorandum.

Kinney, H. C., & Filano, J. J. (1988). Sudden infant death syndrome. *Pediatrician, 15*, 240-250.

Klass, D., & Shinners, B. (1982-1983). Professional roles in a self-help group for the bereaved. *Omega, 13*(4), 361-375.

Mandell, F., & Belk, B. (1977). Sudden infant death syndrome: The disease and its survivors. *Postgraduate Medicine, 62*(4), 193-197.

Markusen, E., Owen, G., Fulton, R., & Bendiksen, R. (1977-1978). SIDS: The survivor as victim. *Omega, 8*(4), 277-284.

Marmar, C. R. (1989). Time-limited dynamic psychotherapy. In H. H. Holdman (Ed.), *Review of general psychiatry* (2nd ed.). Los Altos, CA: Lange Medical Publications.

Meier, C. A. (1973). Sudden infant death syndrome: Death without apparent cause. *Life-Threatening Behavior, 3*(4), 298-304.

Minuchin, S., & Fishman, H. C. (1981). *Family therapy techniques*. Cambridge, MA: Harvard University Press.

Naeye, R. L., Ladis, B., & Drage, J. S. (1976). Sudden infant death syndrome. A prospective study. *American Journal of Diseases of Children, 130*, 1207-1210.

Ochberg, F. M. (1991). Post-traumatic therapy. *Psychotherapy, 28*(1), 5-15.

Rosenthal, D., Sadler, A., & Edwards, W. (1987). *Families and post-traumatic stress disorder*. Rockville, MD: Aspen Publishers.

Selye, H. (1956). *The stress of life*. New York: McGraw-Hill.

Stitt, A. (1971). Emergency after death. *Emergency Medicine, 3,* 233.

Walen, S., DiGuiseppe, R., & Wessler, R. (1980). *A practitioner's guide to rational-emotive therapy.* New York: Oxford University Press.

Walker, J. I., & Nash, J. L. (1981). Group therapy in the treatment of Vietnam combat veterans. *International Journal of Group Psychotherapy, 31*(3), 379-389.

Wegman, M. E. (1988). SIDS research complications. *Pediatrics, 82,* 817.

Willinger, M. (1989). SIDS, a challenge. *Journal of NIH Research, 1,* 73-78.

Wolpe, J. (1969). *The practice of behavior therapy.* Elmsford, NY: Pergamon.

Yalom, I. D. (1970). *The theory and practice of group psychotherapy.* New York: Basic Books.

Young, H. S. (1983). Principles of assessment and methods of treatment with adolescents: Special considerations in rational-emotive approaches to the problems of childhood. In A. Ellis & M. Bernard (Eds.), *Rational-emotive approaches to the problems of childhood* (pp. 89-107). New York: Plenum.

Overcoming the Fear of Flying

ROBERT F. HELLER

Introduction

> Getting off the ground, for one thing, I would be very apprehensive as the plane taxied to its starting point on the runway. I would look and listen anxiously as we waited to take off behind several other planes. I would hope, almost aloud, for those other damned planes ahead of us to get out of the way as soon as possible, mainly to put a halt to my agony of suspense. Finally, when we were racing down the runway, I would clutch the arms of my seat almost frantically, practically pray (though I am not a religious man) for the wheels to get safely off the ground, and breathe a sign of relief when we were definitely rising and it seemed that we were going to clear the nearby rooftops and wing safely on.

These are the words and personal experiences of none other than the founder of rational-emotive therapy, Dr. Albert Ellis (1972, p. 1). Let me assure you that Dr. Ellis's description is by no means extreme nor exceptional among fearful flyers. During a group program I helped conduct for fearful flyers, which was sponsored by Pan American Airlines, one of the participants described his level of distress like this: "I love my mother very dearly, but if a hijacker held a gun to her head and demanded that I either get on the plane or say goodbye to my mother, I really think I would rather say goodbye than to board that plane." On a note closer to home, my own aunt has never flown and absolutely refuses to do so. Although she loves traveling and regularly makes the trek from New York to Florida by train, she would much rather endure the inconvenience of train and bus travel than tolerate her discomfort associated with flying.

Should you believe these are isolated cases, consider that the fear of flying is a major problem affecting millions of adults. In 1980, the Boeing Company published the results of a National Survey on the Fear of Flying (Dean & Whitaker, 1980). Based on a sample of 5,000 American adults, they found that 1 in 6 were afraid to fly. Of those passengers who do fly, 24% were considered to be afraid or anxious about flying. Overall, 25 million adult Americans are estimated to be afraid of flying. The estimated loss in revenue to the air travel industry was extrapolated to be more than $1.5 billion a year in domestic travel alone.

Motivated by concern for the consumer, desire to create good public relations, and pressure to sustain profit, some airlines began sponsoring free and low-cost seminars to help people overcome their fears. Despite their apparent clinical success (Forgione & Bauer, 1980), the marketing gurus within some airlines, apparently believing that having such a program was drawing attention to a problem and creating negative publicity for the airlines, dropped official sponsorship.

What Is the Fear of Flying?

Actually, I don't know a single person who is afraid of flying. In reality, people are afraid of a variety of underlying and associated fears. In 1980, I developed a belief survey to help identify the core irrational beliefs of fearful flyers (Heller, 1980). The self-administered 50-item questionnaire includes such topics as fear of losing control, embarrassment, dying, getting sick, and discomfort anxiety. For first-time flyers, novelty anxiety, or the tension caused by any new experience, and separation anxiety, or the tension caused by being far away from the normal emotional supports of home and family, may also contribute to fear (Forgione & Bauer, 1980). More complex explanations have been suggested, including (a) deep-seated guilt feelings relating fear of crashing to punishment, and (b) secondary gain, such as in getting sympathy and attention from others for not flying or in avoiding visiting relatives one may not like (Ellis, 1972).

Fears of flying appear to be learned in ways similar to the development of other phobias. Modeling, for example, involves observing significant others avoid, act fearfully, or talk anxiously about flying. The flyer may have developed a sensitivity to dramatic accounts of plane crashes in the media, or may have experienced a traumatic event either related to flying or associated in time with flying.

One client clearly related his flying phobia to a negative experience in which the plane dropped several thousand feet in a matter of seconds and narrowly avoided crashing. Another client related the onset of his fear to being on board a Navy ship when it came under attack by enemy aircraft. Some patterns are more difficult to trace, like a stewardess who had flown comfortably for many years but began to develop increasing fear and discomfort while flying. Fortunately, we can treat many of these individuals successfully even without knowing the original cause of their fears.

Characteristics of the Fearful Flyer

The most common characteristic I have observed among fearful fliers is a strong need to control their surroundings. One client believed if he knew he could get the pilot to land the plane on his say-so, he would be alright. Another believed that just sitting closer to the pilot made him feel more comfortable. Other fearful fliers have taken flying lessons and actually fly their own planes as a way of mastering control.

Although I have made no statistical study, both males and females seem to seek out treatment in equal numbers. Some have never flown, but the desire to travel or to improve their career position has motivated them to seek treatment. Motivation for others who fly uncomfortably include the desire to fly with less anticipatory anxiety and to have more pleasant and enjoyable trips. For the majority, the fear has come on gradually and gotten progressively worse rather than being the result of any sudden trauma. While many flying phobics appear generally well adjusted, others indicate that their flying fear is just one of many fears and problems they have. Most appear less bothered by things like the fear of heights, of the plane crashing, or even dying in a plane crash. Rather, they seem more concerned about experiencing negative feelings, their perceived loss of control, and what others may think of them. There may be important differences between those who fly uncomfortably and those who refuse to fly at all, but I am not aware of any studies in this area as yet.

Survey of Treatment Programs

Given the apparently large numbers of people afflicted with flying phobia, what is being done to help them? My experience with many clients who have sought me out after sometimes years of psychoanalytic therapy have convinced me that insight alone just doesn't work, at least for most people. In behavior therapy, systematic desensitization has been the traditional treatment of choice for phobias. To discover the state of the art with respect to the treatment of the fear of flying, I decided to do a brief survey on who was doing what in the field.

In 1990, I sent letters to many of those programs whose listing in the *National Treatment Directory for Anxiety Disorders* (Phobia Society of America, 1989) indicated specifically that they worked with flying phobics. I requested whatever information and research they had about their programs. I received a total of two responses, both coming from former airline pilots who traveled around the country running group treatment programs. One program was described as desensitization of fear of flying and related fears. It began with audiocassette tapes and a booklet, continued with guidance and other opportunities found in group meetings, and concluded with a graduation flight. The other program was described as a one-day total immersion group seminar conducted by an airline captain and clinical psychologist team. A review of the other brief program descriptions listed in the treatment directory revealed the main treatment components to be relaxation training and systematic desensitization.

In a phone interview with one of the respondents, I asked him about his criteria for claiming a 99% success rate. He told me it was based on his screening techniques of excluding skeptical and unmotivated participants. He further assumed that, since he offered a money back guarantee and none of the "graduates" had asked for their money back, they were all successful.

A very complete group program description is provided by Forgione and Bauer (1980). This 10-week program may be thought of as "holistic" in nature. The main components include group discussion, lectures about the body's response to fear, the aerodynamics of flying, success stories from former phobics who completed the program, the role of nutrition and diet on stress and fear responses, and the technique of thought stopping. There is a graduate flight, followed by a graduation party complete with a diploma and flight pin.

Individual Treatment Approaches

Lazarus (1977) describes the treatment of an airplane phobic using imagery therapy. Through interview and a word association test, he determined that she was afraid of the plane malfunctioning and crashing. Whenever she thought about flying, she would create all sorts of catastrophic images in her head. Lazarus discussed with the client the idea of low probability catastrophes (LPCs) and high probability catastrophes (HPCs), that is, the likelihood that the client's fears would come true. His main treatment consisted of creating a very pleasant image of the client enjoying herself on board the plane by eating, watching a movie, and meeting interesting people. Gradually, images of the sound of the landing gear, hitting some turbulence, and other feared events are added to the image. Treatment covered eight sessions over a two-month period. The client, reportedly, is flying comfortably at a four-year follow-up.

In the treatment as described, there does not appear to be any direct work or instruction on disputing the core irrational beliefs, so it remains unclear how well the client would cope if irrational ideas began to dominate her thinking later on. Another limitation of this technique might be that certain individuals may well lack the capacity to form clear, vivid images.

Sanders (1991) describes the use of behaviorally oriented hypnosis in treating a female airplane phobic who had a panic attack on the plane following a "crash course in accounting." The approach combined self-hypnosis and hypnosis desensitization during four individual treatment sessions.

> In hypnotherapy, she recognized the need to expose herself in a gradual progressive manner to airplanes. With self-hypnosis practice she recognized she could counteract any anxiety she experienced. Finally, she was able to develop a number of positive attention distracters to occupy herself in the airplane. She pictured herself in a safe, comfortable place where she felt warm and relaxed. She described her home. Then she stated she liked to ride on buses. I asked her to imagine she was on a wide bus, with me, feeling very comfortable and relaxed. After she nodded, I asked her to imagine she had a cassette tape player and a number of tapes of music. . . . The second week, she spontaneously transformed the big bus to a comfortable airplane that remained at the gate. . . . The third week she transformed the plane so that it was no longer stationary . . . she continued to experience getting involved with her distraction materials. . . . The fourth week, she experienced the airplane moving down the runway and taking off. Rather she was amazed to find herself at the Charlotte airport (her destination). (p. 76)

While this traditional technique is sound for mild phobics, I have not found four sessions of relaxation and desensitization, along with suggestions to distract oneself, to be particularly effective or enduring for most of the phobics I have seen. In terms of RET, there again is no focus on disputing the basic ideas that were probably maintaining the fears in the first place such as "I can't stand the anxiety," "It will be awful if the plane crashes," and the like.

The RET Way

The orthodox approach to overcoming the fear of flying is beautifully laid out by Ellis (1972). First, identify the negative, self-defeating thoughts, such as, "I'll be very anxious and I couldn't stand that." Then, using Socratic methods, help the client see that they probably wouldn't have to be anxious in the first place and that they could stand it even if they did get anxious. Next, using rational-emotive imagery, have the client imagine (a) being on the airplane feeling uncomfortable and thinking negative thoughts, (b) challenging the negative thoughts with such coping thoughts as, "It would be highly unfortunate if I were killed in a crash on this plane, but that's all it would be—unfortunate," and (c) enjoying the flight while experiencing less anxiety. Continued practice in disputing negative thoughts and using coping imagery helps the client gain mastery over both thoughts and feelings. Ellis recommends daily practice of between 10 and 30 minutes.

My own experience is that most flying phobics will not be very receptive to adopting the philosophy, "If I die in a plane crash, I die, and that's only unfortunate." It may work for Ellis, given his clinical skills, verbal persuasiveness, and international reputation. I have found it better to dispute irrational beliefs using a hierarchical approach. Begin by challenging those beliefs that are least strongly defended, and then facilitate acceptance of new beliefs that are most likely to be accepted and acted upon.

In comparing behavioral, hypnotic, and rational-emotive techniques, the behavioral approach relies heavily on relaxation as a coping or distraction technique, hypnosis uses imagery to distract oneself away from uncomfortable feelings and thoughts, and rational-emotive therapy aims at getting clients to change their dysfunctional thoughts through active disputation. Relaxation and other distraction techniques are used by RET therapists but are more often used as secondary techniques to help clients change their underlying philosophy.

Having been trained as a behavioral psychologist and subsequently experiencing some initial success using systematic desensitization with phobias, I was puzzled as to why, when things had gone so well in the office, one of my flying phobic clients didn't do so well on her "graduation" flight. She was able to relax well and to clearly imagine all the situations outlined to her on the anxiety hierarchy. We considered that she was properly prepared for her flight. Utilizing an electromyographic machine (EMG), I had her again imagine scenes on the anxiety hierarchy. As I presented the scene, "You are putting on your seat belt," the EMG picked up a marked increase in muscle tension. I immediately asked her to verbalize to me what she had just pictured or thought about. It was a picture of the door of the airplane being secured and the thought, "Now I can't get out." That idea was very upsetting to her. As I shifted the desensitization to the hierarchy of not being able to leave the plane, she was eventually able to fly with greater comfort and ease.

It wasn't until several years later that I became aware of rational-emotive therapy. An RET analysis of the above case would have revealed that the consequence (C) was fear, while the activating event (A) was putting on the seat belt. What was actually causing and maintaining the anxiety was the belief (B) that "Now I can't get out," along with the implied evaluative thought, "That's awful." The problem with traditional systematic desensitization is that it usually attempts to desensitize to the situation and not the real culprit, the irrational belief.

Assessment and Treatment Strategies

My assessment usually consists of (a) conducting a general clinical interview, (b) conducting a cognitive-behavioral problem-focused interview, and (c) asking clients to complete the Flying Belief survey (Heller, 1981) and the Fear of Flying survey (Forgione & Bauer, 1980). I want to determine the severity, frequency, and duration of the problem, and how it affects job, personal life, and self-esteem. I want to know if there are other fears, as well as if there are personal and/or medical problems that may affect the problem and its treatment. For example, an inner ear problem could affect a person's balance and sense of control, thereby allowing changes in cabin pressure to trigger an anxiety response. My questions get more direct during the interview and serve to give me a clearer picture of the client's problem and how it relates to his or her life. I believe it also conveys a thoroughness to the fearful flyer that builds confidence in his or her perception of my ability to be effective in helping. The questions also serve to elicit possible irrational beliefs that could interfere with treatment later on.

I use the Flying Belief survey (Heller, 1981), which was designed to help systematically identify underlying attitudes contributing to and maintaining anxiety and avoidant behavior in flying phobics. The survey contains 50 questions and identifies many of the irrational beliefs first formulated by Ellis (1962). The survey can be used with either individuals or groups and provides a baseline from which to compare attitude changes during the course of treatment. Careful discussion of the survey results with the client can facilitate understanding, rapport, and later compliance with homework assignments. Statements include, "I would feel ashamed if other passengers noticed my nervousness," "I can't stand the thought of being anxious while flying," and "I worry that the plane will crash upon take-off."

Clinical experience has shown that the survey is helpful in selecting treatment strategies. For example, "worrying that the plane will crash upon take-off" might be dealt with by educating the client on the odds against this happening, as part of a disputing tactic. "Feeling ashamed if others noticed my discomfort" might suggest utilizing a shame attack exercise.

To help identify the specific situational triggers associated with flying fear, I administer the Fear of Flying survey (Forgione & Bauer, 1980). This form contains 46 items on which individuals rate their level of fear in response to specific situations. The survey takes the form of an anxiety hierarchy. Typical situations include:

> You are in the lobby waiting for your flight, and as you sit and wait you are aware of the activity of other people coming and going on other flights.
> You feel the first lurch as the plane begins to move toward the runway.
> As the plane climbs, you are thrust back in your seat, and you feel the small changes in air pressure and the vibrations as the plane cuts through the air.

The detailed survey provides a structure to help identify any additional irrational beliefs not picked up in the clinical interview and, occasionally, on the Flying Belief survey.

The treatment phase starts with providing the client with a clear explanation of the treatment rationale. The greater the clarity and logic with which it is presented, the greater the likelihood of compliance. The treatment rationale I present to the fearful flyer might sound something like this:

> Regardless of how you first learned to be fearful, what is maintaining your current fear is the thoughts that you keep repeating to yourself over and over again in your head. These thoughts give rise to increasingly uncomfortable feelings, which tend to trigger additional negative and worrisome thoughts. What we need to do is to figure out exactly what you tell yourself when you fly or think about flying and to examine more closely how you may be unnecessarily upsetting yourself with negative, exaggerated, and distorted think-

ing. Then I will show you different ways either to modify these upsetting thoughts or to replace them with healthier ways of thinking, so that eventually you will be able to fly more comfortably. It's important for you to realize that your feelings are going to be the last thing to change in the process. First, you will change the way you think; second, you will change what you do; and third, you will notice your feelings changing. It's necessary that you learn not to give in immediately to your feelings of anxiety by avoiding or running away from them, since this will only prolong things for you. The feelings of anxiety need to become a signal for you to cope, not escape, and I will show you several different ways to do this as we go along.

At this point, I would ask what the client thought of what I had just explained. This allows me to ascertain their degree of understanding and agreement with the approach so far. It also allows for further clarification or explanation if needed.

Another approach is to present a formulation of a related problem and then ask the client to relate their problem to the formulation presented. I might say, for example:

When someone comes in with a phobia about public speaking, they are frequently terrified that they will look and feel uncomfortable, that they will not perform well, and that others will think less of them because of their poor performance. As they think about these things, they get more and more anxious and distracted. By the day of their talk, they have worked themselves into a state of panic. What do you think you tend to tell yourself when you feel uncomfortable about flying?

I have found that the above approaches can create for the client a tremendous amount of confidence in the therapist's knowledge and expertise, which will likely enhance trust, motivation, and compliance.

Most flying phobics tend to believe that because of their problems, they are less adequate and, therefore, feel ashamed and have a low opinion of themselves. RET therapists are especially attuned to these clients who have a problem about having the original problem and work to get such clients fully to accept themselves— with the problem. In such cases, I talk to my clients along the following lines:

It's human to have problems. As long as you are alive, you are going to have them, so you might as well accept them and stop putting yourself down for having them. This self-downing is a waste of time and energy and actually keeps you from moving ahead to overcome your original problem. So accept yourself as one of the 25 million or so American adults who suffer from the fear of flying, and let's get on with helping you to overcome it.

I also utilize "thought stopping" to help control self-downing tendencies. The client is instructed to picture a big red stop sign in front of their face and hear the word, STOP, go off very loudly in the back of their mind. Then, they are instructed to take a long, slow, deep relaxed breath in and gently begin to exhale. I suggest that they feel a sense of calmness and control come over them and notice that negative thoughts have disappeared. I have the client practice thought stopping several times in the office and suggest continued practice at home.

Relaxation training is often a second step in treatment since it helps calm the body and focus the mind to facilitate using cognitive techniques more effectively. I usually combine diaphragmatic breathing with Jacobsonian muscle relaxation and a positive visualization. I have found that this combination gives these clients a sense of control and a feeling that they don't have to be helpless in the face of negative thoughts or uncomfortable feelings. I emphasize that our primary goal is to challenge and eliminate the irrational attitudes they hold about themselves and about the flying experience itself and show them how relaxation can help them focus more easily on that goal. While personally training the client in the office, I make a tape of the relaxation procedure to help the client continue to practice at home.

The third treatment step involves helping clients create an ideal picture of how they would like to think, feel, and behave with respect to their flying. As homework, I have them write a description of this picture and go over it with them in detail at their next visit. I explain that they have long held a negative image of themselves in connection with flying and that this image tends to perpetuate the fear. By creating the thoughts and images of how they want to think, feel, and act, they can facilitate the treatment process. I usually do some editing of their version of the story and, after they relax, I present a picture to them of this idealized experience. The procedure is taped, and they are asked to listen to the tape daily until the next visit.

During the fourth step, clients learn to use coping self-statements, which are particularly useful when they need to think of something quickly before negative thoughts take over and anxiety develops. Rational-emotive imagery may also be used and can be combined with coping self-statements. Below are several examples of coping self-statements for anxiety:

1. I can handle this.
2. Stay focused; don't worry.
3. I can use the anxiety as a cue to cope.
4. The fear will soon be over. Let it pass.
5. This is what I expected; no need to panic.

Clients are taught the use of affirmations in the fifth treatment step. These are positive statements repeated to oneself as if they are already true. They help steer the client's thinking and behavior in the desired direction and help break the conditioned pattern of negative thinking associated with their fear. I often recommend that they write down their affirmations on 3 × 5 cards and repeat them frequently throughout the day. Some typical affirmations are:

1. I am comfortable and relaxed when I fly.
2. For me, flying is a natural experience.
3. When I fly, I enjoy all aspects of my trip.
4. My mind is calm and clear.
5. I am in control of my thoughts, feelings, and behaviors.

I encourage clients to try to associate an image along with each affirmation. I remind them that these are idealized goals that they can work toward, but that they are not necessary to achieve in order to be able to fly with reasonable comfort. For example, even if they don't like the feelings in their body when the plane takes off, they can still tolerate them and basically enjoy their flying experience.

The sixth treatment step focuses on formally training clients to dispute their core beliefs in an active, vigorous, and relentless manner. They are taught five new beliefs. First, their self-worth is never determined by whether or not they ever fly comfortably. Second, they can learn to tolerate, although perhaps never like, the feelings of anxiety they may experience from time to time. Third, they are unlikely to die in a plane crash. If they do, however, it probably would not be that bad a way to go, since it would be over quickly and with very little time to experience panic or pain. Fourth, people rarely lose control or act strangely on planes even when they feel very anxious. Fifth, even if their worst fear is realized—if they yell, scream, cry, and bang on the seat in front of them—and other passengers notice this and think less of them because of it, SO WHAT? In the end, it really doesn't matter what the other passengers think. They are unlikely ever to be encountered again and much less likely to have any meaningful personal influence over the client. Lastly, no one has the right or ability to rate any human being's self-worth.

I use a variety of strategies to transform clients' old ways of thinking into newer healthier philosophies. In rational-emotive imagery, clients imagine becoming anxious in the feared situation. They then imagine making themselves more comfortable in that situation. This is followed by an examination of how they brought about the change, which usually involves challenging the negative thoughts underlying the anxiety.

Another strategy involves clients writing their negative beliefs on one side of a sheet of paper and their more appropriate rational responses on the other side. A variation of this is to have them tape-record negative thoughts first and then record appropriate disputations. The therapist can use this material to fine-tune and reinforce the client's efforts.

The above "steps" and sequencing of strategies are guidelines. Clinical judgment in each case will have to be used to determine what to use and when.

A critical part of the treatment process is to get clients to stop avoiding and start facing their fears. At the earliest opportunity, I encourage them to visit the airport. My goal is to begin associating the airport with positive experiences, so I might suggest that they (a) have lunch or dinner there, (b) begin doing relaxation exercises at the terminal while planes are landing and taking off, and (c) imagine actually buying a ticket, going to the gate, boarding the plane, and taking off. Occasionally, I am able to arrange for a client to board an empty plane, receive a tour of the cockpit, and do a brief relaxation and positive imagery exercise while seated in the plane on the ground. At other times, I have actually accompanied clients on brief flights as a prelude to a longer flight they may be taking.

Case Study

One of my current clients, a 28-year-old white male, described his feelings about flying this way:

> The feelings I have are strongly related to plane travel. I have feelings of anxiety long before I get on the plane. In fact, from time to time I make plans to travel. I have feelings of anxiety and fear on a daily basis. The feelings at this time are basically that I will not be able to get on the plane or that, once I am on the plane, I will freak out in some way. I also have trouble sleeping during these times. Once I get to the day of the flight, I start to feel sick to my stomach and become more nervous as the day goes on. When I actually get on the plane, I start to shake and my heart starts to beat much faster. I feel very enclosed. The smaller the plane or space, the stronger the feelings. I am in a situation that I am not in control of. I have a strong desire to get off the plane, but I think I try and quell this for fear of embarrassing myself. This tends to make me more anxious and sometimes emotional because I feel annoyed that I can't show my true feelings without being too obvious. I sometimes cry or kick the back of the chair in front of me to release some of my frustration. Although I do not want to show my feelings for fear of embarrassment, I also feel it would be much easier to deal with my fear if everyone knew what I was going through. I try to come to terms with the situation by trying to convince myself that I am in control of the situation and that if I wanted to, I could have the plane stopped at any time.

At the time of this writing, this client is preparing himself for a trip to Europe. He appears confident that the relaxation exercises he has practiced will take the edge off of any panicky feelings that he may have and that he could tolerate the anxiety if he needed to. He expects he will be less anxious during the flight. He is less concerned about the likelihood of his losing control and far less concerned about what others might think about him. He is still perfectionistic and self-critical and worries that, if he isn't as successful as he thinks he should be, he will perceive himself as a failure. We are working on this by encouraging him to do things "less perfectly" and accepting this as alright. I am also encouraging him to take shorter airplane trips in the meantime to bolster his confidence in his newfound cognitive and behavioral skills. Perhaps on his departure, I will present him with a T-shirt with the inscription, "No one's perfect."

References

Dean, R. D., & Whitaker, R. M. (1980). *Fear of flying: Impact on the U.S. air travel industry* (Document No. BCS-00009- RD/DM). Seattle, WA: Boeing Computer Service Company.

Ellis, A. (1962). *Reason and emotion in psychotherapy.* New York: Lyle Stuart.

Ellis, A. (1972). *How to master your fear of flying.* New York: Curtis.

Forgione, A. G., & Bauer, F. M. (1980). *Fearless flying.* Boston: Houghton Mifflin.

Heller, R. F. (1981). *Flying belief survey.* Unpublished manuscript.

Lazarus, A. (1977). *In the mind's eye.* New York: Guilford.

Phobia Society of America. (1989). *National treatment directory for phobias and related anxiety disorders* (4th ed.). Rockville, MD: Phobia Society of America.

Sanders, S. (1991). *Clinical self-hypnosis.* New York: Guilford.

Rational Recovery From Addictions

JACK TRIMPEY
EMMETT VELTEN
ROBERT DAIN

Background

Rational Recovery Systems[1] is a not-for-profit organization head-quartered in Lotus, California. It manages an international network of self-help groups—Rational Recovery (RR)—that use principles of self-reliance contained in rational-emotive therapy (RET) (Ellis, 1988; Ellis, McInerney, DiGiuseppe, & Yeager, 1988). Rational Recovery is an extrapolation of RET into the self-help sector to deal with problems of substance abuse. RR's main text is the third edition of *Rational Recovery From Alcoholism: The Small Book* (J. Trimpey, 1991), and unless participants have a basic understanding of RET as described in it they are unlikely to make the best use of meetings. About 190 new RR groups formed in the first nine months of 1991, bringing the total to 250. In addition, several Rational Recovery hospital and brief residential treatment settings now offer people the opportunity to work on their chemical addictions with ideas of self-mastery rather than self-surrender. The therapeutic purpose of RR is to offer people in need a method using RET for achieving and maintaining sobriety while affirming positive human values. RR espouses the RET values and criteria of mental health, including self-interest, self-direction, flexibility, acceptance of uncertainty, scientific thinking, nonutopianism, self-responsibility for one's own emotional disturbances, long-range hedonism, and skepticism.

Twelve-step approaches—from which RR differs dramatically— dominate the addiction care industry in America, and RR aims to establish a strong alternative. Such an alternative is important for people who are not suited to the 12-step approach. Therefore, in addition to its aim to provide self-help tools, RR has a political purpose. While the availability of RR groups has been strongly opposed by some within the chemical dependency treatment industry, RR has already brought another option to many consumers and practitioners. This exciting change will affect every agency and practitioner in some way.

When first established, RR was intended only for people who were chemically dependent. However, people with eating disorders, problems with gambling, love or sex addictions, and other addictions and compulsions sought out RR. Most RR groups now are comprised of a mixture of alcoholics and other substance abusers and addicts. The first major exception to mixed groups was specialty RR groups of people with eating disorders. These "RR-Fatness" groups, which are also proliferating, use *Rational Recovery From Fatness: The Small Book* (Trimpey & Trimpey, 1990) as their central guide. In addition, RR "SoDA" groups have formed in several American cities. They provide a rational alternative to Codependents Anonymous (CoDA). The acronym, *SoDA*, stands for "Sodependents Anonymous" and is meant to highlight the RR belief that dependence is the problem rather than "the disease of codependency." The term *SoDA* also satirizes the codependency movement, which RR considers quite excessive in scope and claims. Moreover, RR holds that the lengthy group attendance encouraged by CoDA *promotes* dependency and thereby helps make participants "so dependent."

RR meetings are free of charge. In some meetings, participants pass the hat to collect money to pay the rent for the meeting room or to purchase RET and RR literature or refreshments. All meetings are self-supporting. RR meetings typically last an hour to an hour and a half. The only requirement for participation is desire to work on one's addictions, and most RR meetings are "closed": All participants actively use the RR method to work on addictions. People who simply want to learn more about Rational Recovery or to discuss how it compares with other approaches may be invited to "open" meetings that may take place after the closed meeting finishes. In addition, Rational Recovery meetings welcome people who themselves are not working on personal substance abuse problems, but who know rational-emotive therapy or other cognitive-behavioral therapies and who want to commit themselves to becoming a Coordinator or Advisor of an RR meeting.

The Coordinator secures a meeting room, opens and closes the room, stocks flyers and literature, handles the room rent and other expenses, maintains a record of donations and expenses, does publicity for RR, learns basic RET, and is first among equals in RR meetings. The Advisor is usually a mental health professional whose chief purpose in attending meetings is to teach RET, to provide occasional rational input to the group, and to survey the group members for unusual problems that may indicate the need for a higher level of care. Like Coordinators, Advisors are volunteers. They do not act as therapists or counselors to the RR group and do not make referrals to their practices (if any), but they are free to introduce information that is relevant to the group discussion. They can participate in any way they wish in meetings. Sometimes, Advisors may suggest readings, teach cognitive-behavioral self-help techniques not included in the basic RR writings, and encourage participants to help each other (and themselves) using those techniques.

The chief activity at RR meetings is discussion. "Cross-talk," the interrupting of or responding to others that is forbidden in traditional 12-step meetings, predominates in RR meetings. Group members refer to rational literature, challenge and dispute each other's "stinking thinking," and learn to think rationally. The goal is for each participant to become a rational counselor to her- or himself as well as for others. Those attending RR meetings are not "clients" of anyone, but simply participants in an open discussion meeting. Although rational-emotive therapy places strong emphasis on feelings, therapeutic change in RR self-help is based on the human intellect. RR's saying, "Bring your mind and your body will follow," modifies AA's famous saying, "Take your feet to a meeting, and your mind will follow."

The Rational Mode of Recovery

RR accepts DSM-III-R descriptive definitions of drug and alcohol dependence as disorders marked by chronic use, intoxication, and psychosocial impairment. There are many points of difference between RR and AA. RR, for example, puts little emphasis on the etiology of alcoholism and other addictions. Instead, it focuses on helping participants identify and change factors that maintain their addictions. Rational Recovery Systems views addiction as a set of dependency-creating irrational beliefs. This dependency includes both psychosocial and physical dependence on specific mood- and mind-altering substances. Whether there is some inherited or constitutional basis for the emergence of these dependencies is largely irrelevant in RR. The solution to the resulting problems is the same either way: The individual will begin to suffer less from the use and abuse of certain substances when he or she chooses to stop using them. The issue is how best to achieve that solution.

The emphasis on abstinence is a point of agreement between AA and RR. In RR, however, the decision to abstain will preferably be based on rational assessment of consequences in the light of self-interest rather than upon belief that a "disease" causes powerlessness over voluntary actions. In addition, without abstinence, many substance abusers fail to learn to recognize and combat their irrational beliefs and may not learn new coping skills (Ellis & Velten, 1992).

RR recognizes that most of the people who recover from chemical dependencies do so without any form of treatment and without attendance at meetings of any sort, rational or otherwise. Thus, RR's purpose is to help people augment and make more efficient their natural self-directed growth processes. It is when self-guided bibliotherapy at home is insufficient that attendance at local Rational Recovery meetings can accelerate the learning process and support the individual's sincere efforts.

Competence Versus Powerlessness

The traditional disease theory as espoused by AA holds that people are powerless over their alcohol and drug cravings and, therefore, not responsible for what they put in their mouths, noses, and veins. The RR view is that people have considerable voluntary control over their hands and facial muscles. RR also disbelieves the idea that people have little control over their feelings and actions. Instead, RR believes that people feel the way they think and thus have considerable control over their emotions, actions, and disturbances. RR holds that people cannot really "be" alcoholics but just people who believe some of the central ideas of the alcoholism philosophy.

RR also disagrees with the traditional belief in the chemical dependency field that if one "is" an alcoholic or drug addict, then one needs something or someone stronger or greater than oneself upon which to rely. Instead, RR holds that dependency is such a person's original problem, and it is better to start now to take the risks of thinking and acting independently.

RR states in clear terms that each of us had better learn to control our own moods and behaviors because, as individuals, we are ultimately alone in our struggle against alcohol or drug dependence. In RR, spiritual/religious matters are considered private and separate from recovery. Rational Recovery relies on no Higher Powers in teaching people to become and remain sober. In RR, such dependencies are discouraged in favor of personal responsibility.

Instead of presenting abstinence as an extremely difficult task, one that cannot be achieved without outside, divine help, RR presents abstinence as a relatively easy goal to reach. The ability to abstain from intoxicants is regarded as within the sphere of human competence, and ideas of powerlessness, therefore, are considered self-defeating. RR participants try to discover and dispute residual ideas of powerlessness. This is especially so in connection with the future use of drugs or alcohol. It also applies to negative emotions that may lead to an intensified desire to use intoxicants or that otherwise interfere with personal happiness.

The Motivation to Abstain

Many people seek help with alcohol and drug dependence in order to feel better about themselves. They have feelings of guilt and shame that stem from a litany of disapproval and failure, and they view sobriety as a way to build self-esteem: "If I were sober and doing better, I could earn some self-respect." While such an idea may motivate a person to start a plan of recovery, RR challenges such newcomers with the question, "Do you believe that sober people are more worthwhile than intoxicated people?"

RR disagrees with the idea that in order to feel like a worthwhile person, one must stop drinking. Instead, RR holds that it is because one holds oneself as worthwhile to oneself that one had better decide to stop drinking and build a better life. RR also disputes the common irrational belief that in order to feel like a worthwhile person, one must be competent, intelligent, talented, and achieving in all possible respects, and to fail in any significant way, such as having an alcoholic relapse, constitutes proof of what one probably has always suspected and feared—that one is defective, inferior, and worthless as a person. RR holds to the RET view that doing is more important that doing well, trying is the first step toward succeeding, and accepting oneself unconditionally as a fallible human being is entirely possible and highly desirable.

Thus, a major purpose in RR groups is to help participants develop unconditional self-acceptance. This is done by directly teaching RET ideas about self-rating and self-blaming and how to stop those processes and develop self-acceptance. RET readings are suggested and pamphlets may be available in meetings. Discussion in the RR group, or just reading *The Small Book*, may help the newcomer to comprehend that feelings of guilt or shame and feelings of worthlessness are caused by irrational beliefs that one's worth depends on doing well and gaining approval. RR teaches the rational-emotive therapy ideas that succeeding does not make one into a success, and failing does not make one into a failure. In RR, slips, lapses, and relapses are looked at as feedback and learning experiences.

The conscious value in RR on enlightened self-interest and on influencing one's own destiny is a major distinction between RR and AA. In the latter, putting oneself first and believing that one is captain of one's own ship is considered pathological. Self-control, however, is a matter of degree, and it is different from control over others. In RR, the self-centered motivation to abstain is based on reverence for human life starting with "Number One." The purpose of stopping using or drinking is the same one that may have originally inspired the addiction: To obtain pleasure, fun, and satisfaction with life.

One Day at a Time

The most revered saying in chemical dependency treatment—"One day at a time"—has only limited usefulness in RR, where the interest is in closing the chapter on chemical dependency. The RR idea of graduating from addiction and from being "in recovery" and getting on with life is quite different from the traditional approach in which being a victim of a "disease" and attendance at meetings is drawn out indefinitely. A further difference is that RR encourages people to think of themselves as ongoing processes, rather than as "having" an immutable identity ("I am an alcoholic"). The RR view is that when sobriety is undertaken for only one day at a time, there is always some room for negotiation: The addictive voice checks back tomorrow and tomorrow and tomorrow.

The observation in RR is that humans beings have a remarkable capacity for self-correction and that there is much more to life than a continuous, one-day-at-a-time struggle to remain sober. Therefore, in order to gain mastery over the relentless addictive voice, RR members are encouraged, during the first few months of sobriety, to develop a *Big Plan:* "No more ever!" Making a covenant with oneself is usually a formidable undertaking, but, once accomplished, it can be exhilarating and well worth the effort. Once in place, a Big Plan knocks the wind out of the addictive voice so that it loses its commanding strength. By practicing rational self-forgiveness, the prospect of relapse is not viewed in catastrophic terms, so that should one lapse the abstinence violation effect is mitigated. Because the appetite for alcohol or drugs requires refreshment to maintain its strength, the desire for intoxication is usually further weakened with time.

The Illusion of Denial

RR avoids giving people things to deny, because it does not use certain 12-step/disease theory musts and other ideas that large numbers of people have difficulty believing. For example, RR does not assume that there is a specifiable entity called "an alcoholic" that heavy drinkers must admit they "are." Nor does it say one must admit powerlessness and character defects or that one must believe in Higher Powers to get better. RR does not extend "denial" to partners, relatives, and friends of the substance abuser by stating or implying that they, too, "have a disease." On the other hand, RR does assume that persons who appear at meetings accept that they have a significant problem. It teaches them that they are responsible for their own choices and that they are not forced to drink or use drugs by their beloveds or by having been treated shabbily years before.

Substance abusers do face a vexing choice. On one hand, they genuinely enjoy and desire the altered states of consciousness that the intoxicant brings. On the other hand, they also wish that they did not have to suffer consequences of their drinking and drugging behavior. Soon after they have suffered poor results from substance abuse, addicts typically "see the light" and may get on the wagon. As time passes and the distance from the poor results increases, many addicts easily refocus on the substance's positive result. They then invent that they can have the positive results "this time" without getting negative results. Then they resume drinking or using drugs.

Thus one way that RR looks at people "in denial" is that they are in a state of ambivalence. They have two distinct, opposite values on the same behavior. They see and want the positives of drinking and drugging, but they see and don't want the negatives. In the consciousness of each chemically dependent person, there is a conflict about the dependency. Sometimes the wish to be sober is a faint one, but rarely will anyone attend RR meetings who does not recognize that there is a better life than intoxication can provide.

Issues of Maturity

Because each person is directed toward emotional independence, RR does not diagnose or otherwise indict a substance abuser's immediate family or family of origin. There is simply no expectation that family members will bear a burden of change because another has become addicted. The recovering addict's chief responsibility is to come to accept others *as they are* instead of expecting them to participate reluctantly in treatment.

Instead of calling the substance abuser's overly dependent significant others "codependent," RR regards them as showing the morbid dependency that some family members have on the love and approval of others in the family system. For those who are so dependent that they expose themselves to long-term abuse by an addicted person, we recommend *The Small Book* or other literature from the Institute for Rational-Emotive Therapy,[2] consultation with an RET or other cognitively oriented therapist, or Sodependents Anonymous (SoDA) groups where they exist. People who are unhappy with such self-labels as "adult child" or "codependent" as well as those who want to separate confidently from a co-dependency group may also find rational readings helpful.

What Are Rational Recovery Meetings Like?

RR meetings are structured more loosely than are traditional AA-type meetings. As already mentioned, professionals interested in volunteering their services may attend meetings and participate. Group Coordinators and Advisors need not have a history of substance abuse. When they facilitate or lead a meeting, different ones of them do it differently. The RR dogma is that there are no dogmas. This idea is consistent with RET as well as with the current status of knowledge about substance abuse and relapse prevention. One way in which RR works against dependency is to see it as helpful for group leaders not to come across as know-it-alls with a direct line to the Higher Power.

RR meetings are discussions that focus on the problems of chemical dependence and staying sober. Participants refer to *The Small Book* as a guide to rational relapse prevention methods and no-higher-power sobriety. Everyone in the group, and especially the Advisor and the Coordinator, is supposed to know the contents of *The Small Book* well enough to mention specific sections that deal with certain problems. Other material from the Institute for Rational-Emotive Therapy is usually available at Rational Recovery meetings.

RR Coordinators post meeting schedules and advertise the availability of meetings. The meeting may be held in a community room, a private home, library, or even a church. The Coordinator arrives early, opens the room, arranges chairs in a circle, and sets out literature. Participants arrive, and the meetings start on time. The Coordinator, the Advisor (if present), or a designated group member will give a brief introduction to RR for newcomers, explaining its ground rules, such as confidentiality, and some of its distinctions from AA meetings.

An RR group is neither a fellowship nor a support group. Instead, it is a task-oriented self-help discussion group in which members engage in open discussion of the common difficulties they have in staying clean and sober. The agenda involves learning and practicing RET concepts, discussion of self-defeating thoughts and actions, identification of ABCs, and members helping each other dispute irrational beliefs (iBs) and formulate more self-helping ways to think. Members are expected to become rational counselors both for others and themselves. The goal is to become one's own therapist.

RR actively discourages dependency whenever possible. RR founder Jack Trimpey recommends that people attend no more than two meetings a week. Meeting participants sometimes ask for a list of meetings so they can attend RR around the clock, as they may have done with AA meetings in the past. In that case, the RR Coordinator and group members encourage the person to make an active plan for alternate activities. The person may say, "But if I don't have meetings to go to, I'll drink." Typically, group members point out that the person actually attended only one or two meetings a day in the past, but kept himself or herself from drinking 24 hours a day. "What did you tell yourself in your head to keep yourself from drinking?" they may ask. Or, "OK, so you went to 90 meetings in 90 days, but you did go back to drinking. What did you tell yourself to go back to drinking?"

The RR view is that people are capable of learning to act in their own interest and had better not lean on the group prolongedly. An RR Coordinator is not a sponsor or a therapist, a leaning post, or a spiritual, financial, marriage, or sex counselor. Coordinators do not make decisions for others and are not responsible for how others behave. What others do with their lives is their own choice; in RR, no one is the other's keeper.

One way to get the feel for RR group process is by listening to RR audiocassettes such as "Take It From Here," a series of short statements totaling about 10 to 15 minutes in length, that can be played at the beginning of a meeting. The statements are brief, sometimes informative, and always provocative, for the purpose of stimulating group discussion. They contain rational ideas that can help with integrating one's philosophy along rational lines.

One of the Coordinator's roles during meetings is simply to point out that certain ideas that are being expressed in the discussion are irrational, to explain why, and then to offer a rational concept as a better alternative. The best way to do this is by asking questions of a person who holds an irrational idea.

Meetings typically begin when the Coordinator or Advisor asks the question, "Who's been thinking of drinking or using drugs this week?" and lively discussion ensues. If that question produces no input, then the second question, "Then who has a trouble to talk about?" may be asked. Here a spectrum of issues may come out, and whatever problem is identified can very likely be traced to one of the common irrational beliefs—or "central ideas of alcoholism," as they are called in *The Small Book*.

If an RR meeting participant reports she or he was clean and sober for a while, but then resumed drinking or drugging, a common question in RR meetings is, "How did you decide to start up again?" This questions focuses the discussion on the heart of lapses, relapses, and continued substance use, namely the fact that the person makes a decision to use or continue to use the substance. From the rational-emotive therapy viewpoint, the question focuses on the belief system, or the B in RET. The question implies that the person could decide not to use, which of course is the object of the RR meetings.

Sarah, for example, attended her first RR meeting recently. She reported that she'd stopped drinking for several months two years earlier and had little trouble staying sober. However, she slipped and resumed drinking, as she had in the past. "That shows I wasn't really motivated," she said. "I hadn't hit bottom. I'll always go back to drinking until I hit bottom."

Group participants offered support, but they asked Sarah how she had decided to go back to drinking. She indicated that she didn't decide anything, and maybe it had something to do with her "issues" with her mother. The RR Coordinator offered the opinion that the alcohol couldn't get into her body by itself, that Sarah must have decided something. "I was depressed," Sarah said. "It (drinking) seemed like the answer." The next several questions from group members boiled down to, "Was drinking the answer?" Sarah said, "No, it's worse now." Group members then asked her what she could tell herself in the future when she got depressed.

The above example raises many questions about other or more elegant interventions. While the self-help setting allows the teaching and use of simple, practical interventions, it is not suitable for sophisticated therapy.

Addictive Voice Recognition

The object of discussion in RR is to bolster the decision not to use, to label the thinking in the decision to use as self-defeating, and to link the using thoughts to the nonusing rebuttal thoughts. RR writings often refer to the self-defeating "addictive voice" (irrational beliefs, automatic disturbing thoughts, rationalizations) as "the Beast." Many RR participants find it useful to dramatize the irrational belief system by calling it "the Beast," "the inner alcoholic," or "it": "I have to have what I want when I want it and suffer no ill effects." Such a belief is primitive and appetitive. The Beast personifies people's self-defeating tendencies, and the RR hypothesis is that this tool helps many people by clearly labeling "the enemy."

Once the RR group has brought out a participant's self-defeating thinking, a follow-up question is, "What could you say back to the Beast?" The group Coordinator or other group members ideally then encourage the person to practice these rebuttals vigorously, rather than relying on "intellectual insight."

Usually the addictive Beast voice does not boldly say, "I want what I want when I want it, and the consequences be damned," but it spins off more subtle thoughts and rationalizations. The newcomer to RR frequently is unable to rebut rationalizations. Some typical rationalizations heard at RR meetings are, "One won't hurt," "I can afford it," "I deserve this one," "I'll stop tomorrow," "I've got to work through my issues before I can stop," "to hell with it," and numerous others. Almost always the person's track record has established these statements quite well as rationalizations that are contradicted by the accrued evidence. However, the person believes them again and again. Why? Because underneath the rationalizations probably lies the belief, "I should be able to have what I want when I want it without any ill effects." People want to believe this, and then they decide to follow this belief even though they know at another level that it is a poor decision.

The central task in the rational mode of recovery is to help participants strengthen their skills in pursuing their rational goals of survival and personal happiness. The rational voice can then dominate the commanding addictive voice that argues endlessly for short-range hedonism and intoxication. Instead of beseeching the addict to surrender to a Higher Power, RR teaches group participants to dispute the "musturbatory" addictive voice.

A key insight for RR participants is that they do in fact think or decide something before they drink or use drugs. However, they usually have practiced their thoughts and decisions so much that they need not go to much trouble to repeat those decisions and thoughts. A transition in RR occurs when the individual stops saying, "I really wanted a drink," and says instead, "I decided I wanted to drink, but then I told myself that I wanted *more* not to because drinking causes me so much trouble." Or (in reference to the mythical Beast), "It told me to have a drink, but I said back to it, 'No way!' "

When participants minimize the extent of their problem with intoxicants, RR hypothesizes that their addictive voices are telling them to shade the truth so as to protect the supply. When the cognitions themselves are finally recognized as a personal enemy, then the rational self may choose to refuse to act on the urgings of the so-called Beast. Addictive voice recognition (AVR) is simple: It is any thinking that supports any use of drugs or alcohol in any amount, in any form, ever. AVR plays the same vital role in RR as the Higher Power does in AA.

Participants in RR groups are taught the three main RET insights: They decide to drink or use drugs; wherever the original tendency to make such decisions came from, they themselves are responsible for such decisions now; and it takes work and practice to change one's habits. Emphasis in RR groups is on the "work and practice" insight, since most participants want the first two insights to change their lives.

A typical example is Tony. He had tired of AA and had tried SOS,[3] and reported at his first RR meeting that AA and SOS did not "work" for him. He said he came to RR looking for "the answer." As he explained, "When I do well at work, or get a date with a new woman, or win some money in the lottery, I figure that I deserve a reward. So, I go to the store and get two six-packs of beer and drink it. The next morning I feel awful and then I absolutely promise myself never ever to do that again!"

Tony then went on to ask what RR would say about *why* he drank the two six-packs, since he'd previously promised himself not to do so again. He was looking for an insight, but not just any insight. He wanted, understandably, an insight that would stop his self-defeating behavior.

To Tony's surprise, the participants focused on *how* he decided to undo his promise to himself not to drink. Tony, of course, replied he didn't decide anything—it just happened! The group then pointed out that he'd really already said *how* he changed his decision, by saying something to himself like, "I deserve a reward." "That's it?" he asked, disappointed.

When the group Advisor, the RR Coordinator, and various participants went on to suggest he could label the "I deserve a reward" thinking as "the Beast" and that he had better practice very energetically talking back to the Beast, Tony did not understand. Members asked, "Was it a reward to have the beer?" When Tony replied that it was not, group members suggested that he say so back to the Beastly thought. Tony, however, immediately went back to asking those present what they thought made him keep repeating his self-defeating behavior although he knew it was self-defeating. He wanted an *idea* to stop him rather than to have to stop himself. He expected there to be a deep, dark, dramatic insight that would stop him. The group did not see Tony again. A better outcome came about in the case of Sherry.

Sherry attended her first RR meeting several months ago. Though she was in her late thirties, she reported that she'd never used heroin until about a year earlier and that she used it then to help her deal with the pain of the deaths of several friends. In time she addicted herself to the heroin, spent all her money, lost her house, went on welfare, and even lost her welfare check. Sherry said she knew she had to stop using and wanted to, but, "I can't stand withdrawal because I have three children to take care of. I can't be sick as a dog for 5 days." She described the vomiting, cramps, diarrhea, and other symptoms in vivid terms. The group Coordinator pointed out that "I can't stand it" was the addictive voice, the Beast speaking. Sherry heatedly asked, "Have you ever had to go through heroin withdrawal?" The Coordinator hadn't, and Sherry went on to complain bitterly and lengthily about people who have the gall to offer advice without having "been there."

Other group members, however, chipped in and asked Sherry if she had ever stood withdrawal before. The answer was no. Group members suggested various A (Activating event) solutions, such as getting child care during the five days of withdrawal, but none of these ideas would work, according to Sherry. Group members pointed out that her children surely knew that she had a problem, so perhaps her oldest daughter, a teenager, could take care of the younger ones. Sherry admitted that she simply could not endure withdrawal, regardless. The Coordinator then did an ABC on a white board, with the B identified as "I can't stand it." Group members who had withstood heroin withdrawal before began suggesting disputes of the Beastly belief. Sherry finally developed the idea, "I have to stand it for my children. There is no easy way out of this mess."

Some newcomers to Rational Recovery get hung up on the word "rational." For instance, at his first meeting Billy said, "I'm good at rationalizing," and that therefore he knew that Rational Recovery was not the thing for him. For example, he said that he would tell himself that he would just use drugs on the weekend, and that therefore it would be OK. But then, he said, "I keep using after the weekend!" Group members pointed out that rationalizations were irrational, because they led him into trouble. They encouraged him to devise and practice a strong rebuttal when he heard the Beast rationalizing.

The Course of Recovery and Graduation

Two of the most important ingredients of Rational Recovery are (a) lack of dogma, creed, or articles of faith to follow, and (b) the meetings are relatively unstructured and freewheeling. In these ways, RR meetings reflect real life, because there seem to be no absolute or perfect truths and because life seldom provides a structure to keep people out of trouble or on the best course. In RR, participants are encouraged to learn to give structure to their own thinking and then live an unpredictable life without resorting to drugs or alcohol.

Because RR perceives that recovery is about as difficult as one makes it out to be, it is not expected or considered desirable that people attend recovery meetings forever. Each person is the final judge of when recovery is complete, and one Rational Recovery Systems ground rule is that there will be no predictions that any group member will have future problems with relapse or with other personal difficulties. When a member announces her or his intention to leave the group, the group's most useful response is sincere well-wishing. It is acknowledged in RR that more people recover from chemical dependency in the privacy of their own homes than get better in recovery programs.

An example of a graduate from RR was Marvin, a crack cocaine addict who attended RR meetings weekly for about 3 months. During that time he first developed a list of alternative behaviors, such as working out in the gym, that would keep him from thinking about and searching for crack cocaine. As he got more clean time, he began to fantasize about smoking crack. The group Coordinator suggested that Marvin construct, and review often, a "shitlist" to remind himself of all the gruesome results he had suffered from smoking crack. Marvin also developed a list of the rationalizations and irrational beliefs that he had used habitually to get himself back into smoking crack after he'd stopped on previous occasions. The group Coordinator wrote these on separate pieces of paper, and held them up one by one for Marvin to dispute in front of the group. This exercise led to much enjoyment and laughter in the group and to Marvin's devising and practicing forceful disputes. When, after 3 months of meetings and 2½ months of clean time, Marvin announced that he wanted to do it on his own, the group wished him well. The Advisor suggested that Marvin continue to practice his relapse prevention methods, to treat any slips as useful information, and to return to RR if and when he chose to do so.

Implications for the Future

There is a growing awareness that 12-step approaches may have become victims of success. Because of their virtual monopoly in America's agencies and hospitals, as well as in the self-help community, a strong tendency has arisen for many people to say that there is only one way. "Resistance to the 12 steps" is often treated as another "disease" symptom. As a result, many seeking help with their addictions have been left out in the cold or else are compelled to undergo treatment methods they disapprove. RR's emergence into the mainstream of addiction care offers another option to consumers and is an antidote to the widespread notion that the 12 steps are good for all comers. With RR groups available, Higher Power-resistant people need not be told that "anything can be your Higher Power" and then taught to depend on other humans or inanimate entities as Higher Powers.

Many people who seek out RR feel refreshed to find other people like themselves, who do not wish to be humble, who want to learn to depend on themselves, and who are skeptical that Higher Powers exist and must be contacted with prayer. Usually such people tried the traditional approach and were told that there was something wrong with them that they were unable to get traction on their chemical dependencies. They often felt as though they had failed to "work a good program," but they were probably in the wrong program all along.

Some such people contact Rational Recovery Systems, saying elatedly, "This means I'm not crazy!" Others are angry that no one has talked sense to them before and are frustrated that the spiritual teachings have not been helpful. Others have incorporated the concept of powerlessness in a way that aggravates their addictions, and still others are intellectually disoriented as a result of endless exhortations to adopt the central concepts of spiritual healing.

There has been increasing concern about the "addiction to recovery meetings" phenomenon in which people acquire compulsive moods and attitudes and believe they must attend meetings forever. RR provides affirmation and vindication to all of these people. It offers them an avenue to kick the recovery habit and get on with life (Katz & Liu, 1991; Peele, 1989; Peele & Brodsky, 1991).

Differential Diagnosis

The scientific literature recognizes that there are subtypes of alcohol and drug dependent people. Due to many factors, including cognitive style, some individuals will respond better when "matched" to a corresponding recovery program. Receptiveness to rational versus spiritual concepts is a most important determinant of treatment outcome. However, mental health and other professionals routinely refer—and courts routinely mandate—clients to AA and at best tell them to overcome any objections they may have to such components as "the God part," group prayer, and permanent attendance at meetings. At worst, they consider objections to religious and dependency concepts to be "the disease talking" and tell the client so.

This lack of sensitivity to clients on the part of professionals is partly because of the relative lack of availability of self-help alternatives. There is also the widespread but mistaken notion that it has been proven that "AA is the only thing that works." In fact, this notion is supported by little more than testimonials. These inequities are being addressed now by the activist stance of RR, which provides advocacy for people who want to seek legal recourse for ill-advised referrals and mandated attendance at spiritual healing meetings.

Selecting the correct recovery program is just as important as choosing the correct blood type before administering a transfusion. Treatment is based on taking a sample first. Often, the client has a good idea of which recovery approach is going to be most relevant, so one method of assessment is to ask questions about past attempts to stop drinking or using. Questions about what the client does or does not like about the 12-step approach are highly appropriate. The client's preferences for nonspiritual healing programs are signs of individuality, not psychopathology. It is far more likely that these comments are indicators for referral to Rational Recovery or other nonspiritual programs. A single past failure in the spiritual healing approaches is sufficient to suggest that a rational mode of recovery may be indicated.

Treating clients and patients with methods from which they have failed to profit time and again raises uncomfortable clinical and ethical questions. When clients are also stating that they do not want to undergo such an approach, there may also be legal problems, as pointed out by William Olcott (1991), co-chair of the National Ethics and Standards Committee for the National Alcohol and Drug Abuse Council.

Repeated exposure to any treatment modality without success can expose the client to unacceptable risks, including death. Appropriate differential diagnosis and referral will be facilitated by the results of a study now being conducted at Harvard University Medical School, a study that will describe the population that responds positively to the concepts of Rational Recovery.

Summary

Rational Recovery Systems is a fast-growing self-help alternative that extrapolates RET into the self-help sector. RR espouses all the RET humanistic values and criteria of good mental health. Professionals who know RET or other cognitive-behavioral therapies volunteer their time as Advisors to RR meetings. Participants at RR meetings learn and practice rational relapse prevention methods. The core of these methods is learning to recognize and dispute self-defeating thinking that RR frequently labels "the Beast" or "the addictive voice." In addition to its treatment purposes, RR has a political purpose in advocating for people who are mandated to attend spiritual healing groups but who find that approach useless or offensive. Furthermore, RR attempts to educate professionals about available options and sensitize them to the ethical and possible legal issues involved in overriding clients' objections to spiritual healing approaches.

Notes

1. For information, contact Rational Recovery Systems, P.O. Box 800, Lotus, CA 95651, or phone (916) 621-4374.
2. Institute for Rational-Emotive Therapy, 45 E. 65th Street, New York, NY 10021.
3. SOS stands for Secular Organization for Sobriety.

References

Ellis, A. (1988). *How to stubbornly refuse to make yourself miserable about anything: Yes, anything!* Secaucus, NJ: Lyle Stuart.

Ellis, A., McInerney, J., DiGiuseppe, R., & Yeager, R. (1988). *Rational-emotive therapy with alcoholics and substance abusers.* Elmsford, NY: Pergamon.

Ellis, A., & Velten, E. (1992). *When AA doesn't work for you.* New York: Barricade Books.

Katz, S., & Liu, A. E. (1991). *The codependency conspiracy: How to break the recovery habit and take charge of your life.* New York: Warner Books.

Olcott, W. (1991). Are you doing the right thing? *Addiction Program Management: American Health Consultants, 5,* 5.

Peele, S. (1989). *The diseasing of America.* Lexington, MA: Lexington.

Peele, S., & Brodsky, A. (1991). *The truth about addiction and recovery.* New York: Simon & Schuster.

Trimpey, J. (1991). *Rational recovery from alcoholism: The small book* (3rd ed.). Lotus, CA: Lotus Press. (P.O. Box 800, Lotus, CA 95651)

Trimpey, L., & Trimpey, J. (1990). *Rational recovery from fatness: The small book.* Lotus, CA: Lotus Press. (P.O. Box 800, Lotus, CA 95651)

Managing Change in the Workplace

ALFRED R. MILLER

We live in a world that is constantly changing. Political, social, technological, and economic developments have a severe impact on the way people think, live, and work. One characteristic of today's worldwide marketplace is the unrelenting drive for a competitive advantage. Spurred by popular publications by authors such as Kanter (1983), Mackay (1988), Naisbitt (1982), Ouchi (1981), Peters (1987), and Peters and Austin (1985), many managers have turned to human resource management as the key to unlocking a company's capacity to perform. The success of a company in today's competitive marketplace depends greatly on how effectively management can bring together the creativity, skill, and productivity of their employees in providing a better and/or cheaper product or service. Maintaining a high degree of job satisfaction, low employee turnover, and a highly skilled work force all contribute to reduced operating costs and a competitive edge in the marketplace. To meet the ever-increasing demands for improved and cost-effective products and services, it is critical for managers to learn how to change existing work environments to support new behaviors and productivity standards.

AUTHOR'S NOTE: Requests for information concerning this article should be addressed to the author, Institute for Cognitive Development, 2171 Jericho Turnpike, Suite 235, Commack, NY 11725.

Typical organizational change strategies designed to successfully meet the demands and challenges of a competitive marketplace include:

1. Initiating major reorganizations that create new lines of authority, new roles, and new reporting relationships.
2. Switching from manual to more automated and computerized work systems.
3. Implementing new work procedures and production quotas.
4. Training managers and supervisors to deal more effectively with the greater range of skills, values, and ethnic makeup of today's work force.

These kinds of changes are often quite complex and require different change strategies to accommodate individual readiness and receptivity for change. The effects of change can be addressed in terms of: (a) organizational factors, including structure, technology, and production, and (b) human factors, including personal welfare and adjustment, receptivity, commitment, readiness, and individual psychological and emotional well-being.

For many people, the uncertainty associated with change represents threat, which consequently generates feelings of apprehension and fear, along with general psychological distress. This chapter will primarily address strategies for managing the human factors associated with change and will suggest ways of minimizing those dysfunctional emotional characteristics that often develop as a consequence of the attempts to change an organizational culture.

Resistance To Change

Employee resistance to change is frequently cited as a major obstacle to organizational effectiveness (Lawler, 1986). Employee concerns over future employment, salary, and career opportunities negatively affect their support of change efforts. These concerns often contribute to high employee stress, anxiety, increased sick leave, and increased alcohol and drug abuse (Yeager & Miller, 1991) and are frequently overlooked or ignored when anticipating the impact of organizational change. Employees are often expected to adjust to the initiated change with little or no psychological difficulty. Failure to implement organizational change effectively with employee receptivity can cause unnecessary confusion, misinformation, and resistance to the change initiative.

Research shows that employee participation in decisions regarding a change strategy can significantly reduce their resistance to change (Lawler, 1986). Lawler asserts that employee participation in the design of the change strategy fosters a psychological commitment to its successful implementation. Having employees participate in developing change strategies that will correct what they view as important work-related problems has also been demonstrated as an effective strategy for building understanding and support for organizational change efforts (DelBalzo & Miller, 1989; Miller & DelBalzo, 1989).

Participation in decision strategies also promotes greater understanding and less opportunity to misperceive the consequences of the change. Misperception and misunderstanding often occur when the language used to define the need or the strategy for the change is unclear. Taylor and Fiske (1981) demonstrated that language and communication are key elements that effect how people think. Similarly, Argyris and Schön (1978) suggest that when people attempt to solve problems with vague and unclear information they will create conditions that reinforce and compound cognitive errors and create additional vagueness, lack of clarity, and inconsistency. However, when information is communicated in a clear and concrete manner, decision making and collaboration are improved. If employees are not involved in both planning and implementing change efforts, they will often perceive them as threats. This tendency to expect a negative outcome exists despite the fact that the changes may improve their jobs (Lawler, 1986).

The way employees think about the change determines the way they will react both emotionally and behaviorally. If a new idea diverges from a presently held view or idea, it may be rejected because it does not agree with previous information (Mahoney, 1991). Popper (1969) suggests that reasoning is at the core of how individuals construe reality. People draw conclusions and act based on the premises they assume to be valid. Thus resistance to change can best be understood as a normal outgrowth or consequence of an individual's thinking and not as some kind of psychological aberration. In undertaking programs to change the way employees think or behave, their resistance to the change should be anticipated and made part of the planned change effort.

Stages of Change

Prochaska and DiClemente (1982, 1986) developed a model that is helpful in conceptualizing and planning for individual change. Based on their research, change occurs in six stages or steps.

Stage 1. Precontemplation. The person is not considering change. Told that he or she has a problem, the precontemplator may be surprised or defensive, because of being unaware that a problem exists.

Stage 2. Contemplation. The person is aware of but ambivalent toward the change. Often the characteristic style of the contemplator is "yes but," or a kind of oscillation between wanting to change and staying the same. This ambivalence reflects the acknowledgment that they might want to change but are not ready to commit to initiating a change.

Stage 3. Determination. The person ceases to oscillate between wanting to change and staying the same and makes a decision in favor of a change.

Stage 4. Action. The person actively engages him- or herself in initiating the actual change.

Stage 5. Maintenance. The person's main task is to maintain the progress or gain made in the Action stage and to avoid falling back into the original or prechange habit pattern.

Stage 6. Relapse. The person does fall back into the prechange habit pattern. If this occurs, the goal of this stage is to help the person restart the change process starting with Contemplation (Stage 2) and working through Determination (Stage 3) to Action (Stage 4).

In adapting the Prochaska and DiClemente (1982, 1986) model for an organizational change effort, some important activities that can be included in each of the stages are:

Stage 1. Precontemplation. Gather data to assess accurately and measure objectively the extent of the problem. For example, administer an employee attitude survey to measure the importance of and satisfaction with specific work issues (Miller, 1988).

Stage 2. Contemplation. Present and discuss the results of the assessment in Stage 1. Analyze the pros, cons, risks, and costs versus benefits of correcting the problem with those individuals responsible for managing the change initiative.

Stage 3. Determination. Assess the extent to which there is support for the change effort with those having managerial responsibility for its success. Assure that there is agreement in favor of proceeding with the change.

Stage 4. Action. Develop a plan for the change strategy. Develop objective measures that can be used to measure the progress from the current to the future state.

Stage 5. Maintenance. Encourage all those individuals involved in the change effort (e.g., managers, supervisors, employee work groups) to discuss the progress and problems associated with the change. Frank and open discussion will promote greater understanding, generate new ideas and learning, and promote a team spirit. It also gives employees the message that their opinions and ideas are valued.

Stage 6. Relapse. In Webster's (1983) dictionary *relapse* (second definition) is defined as "the act or instance of backsliding, worsening or subsiding." It is important to anticipate the occurrence of mistakes and setbacks. Be careful not to assess the progress of the change using a failure versus success dichotomy. Assessing the change effort in terms of a continuum ranging from failure to success is more realistic. Mistakes and relapses will occur. However, not every relapse is a total failure. A study of the kinds of mistakes and setbacks that occur will often contribute to additional learning and can provide valuable information about what will and will not work in the organization.

If you are managing a change effort it is important to keep in mind that employee resistance to change is to be expected, to some extent, and that resistance to change is a normal consequence of the way people think. To optimize understanding, the language used to communicate the change should be clear and concrete. If the change is described in terms of what, where, and when things will happen, the less opportunity there will be for misunderstanding and unnecessary confusion. It is helpful to plan a change process in terms of the employee's receptivity, understanding, and commitment for the change. Using a change model such as that developed by Prochaska and DiClemente (1982, 1986) will afford the opportunity to address any emotional consequences that may develop as a consequence of the change effort. Finally, people in charge of introducing change in the workplace (e.g., change agents and management consultants) often unwittingly create additional problems that sabotage the success of a change effort by engaging in rigid and self-defeating thinking. Rigidly believing that there is only one way to introduce change and that management and the employees should be more receptive to the change will almost certainly minimize the success of a change initiative (DiGiuseppe & Miller, in press).

Case Example

Consider the case of Company X, a large multinational company that acquired a previously owned American manufacturing company that was on the verge of bankruptcy. Over a period of 3 years, Company X replaced all of the original managerial staff with new managers. New quality control programs were put into place, and state-of-the-art manufacturing equipment was installed. Despite the new management and manufacturing equipment, however, the company failed to achieve a competitive manufacturing position. Employee productivity was low, and there was a high turnover of employees.

According to the company's president, changes had been in progress for the past 3 years, and he believed that they were only partially successful. He believed that something might be inhibiting the success of the change effort but was unsure what the problem was. He indicated that his opinion was not shared by his senior staff and wanted help in determining if his perceptions were accurate. The senior executive staff indicated that they believed the change strategy was working as expected but needed more time to achieve the target productivity and profit objectives. They were confident in their managerial and supervisory staff and believed they were working effectively with their employees and were doing everything possible to achieve maximum productivity.

Developing a Change Strategy

In developing a strategy for working with the management team, an adaptation of the change model described by Prochaska and DiClemente (1982, 1986) was used. An interview with the company's president revealed that he was in the Contemplative stage. He was aware that there was a problem but was unsure about what to do. Interviews held with the senior executive staff revealed that they were in the Precontemplative stage. They were not aware of any problems employees might be having in getting their work accomplished and were somewhat defensive about any possible criticism of their managerial and supervisory staff.

To create an awareness of the extent to which a problem may or may not exist, a decision was made to administer an employee attitude survey. Large organizations, such as Bank of America, General Electric, General Motors, Honeywell, IBM, Kodak, and the United States Federal Aviation Administration routinely survey employees for this kind of information (DelBalzo & Miller, 1989; Lawler, 1986), and the executive staff agreed that a survey would provide important information regarding the possible existence of any problems.

Employee Attitude Survey

The Managerial Effectiveness Questionnaire and the Supervisory Effectiveness Questionnaire (Miller, 1988) were administered to the company's 1,400 employees. In each of the surveys, employees were asked to rate both the importance and satisfaction for each item. Employees rated the relative importance of the nine performance areas from 1 (Most Important) to 9 (Least Important). Adapting the concepts of rational-emotive therapy (RET), developed by Ellis (1977, 1978) and Ellis and Harper (1961, 1975), the importance dimension serves as a hierarchy of employee expectations about specific activating events. The items, or activating events, employees believe are most important are viewed as having the greatest potential for affecting their satisfaction and dissatisfaction. According to RET theory, the beliefs (rational or irrational) that individuals have about activating events determine their emotional response. Thus if employees held irrational expectations (musts or shoulds) that went beyond what could be realistically expected from their supervisor or manager, they would almost certainly feel angry.

Employee satisfaction was measured using a 5-point Likert-type scale ranging from (1) Very Dissatisfied to (5) Very Satisfied. If for any reason employees were unable to judge the performance of their supervisor or manager, they had the option to check (?) to indicate that they did not have sufficient information. To assure anonymity, the completed surveys were sent directly to an off-site scoring center where computer-generated reports were prepared.

Supervisory Effectiveness

In the Supervisory Effectiveness Questionnaire (SEQ), the following nine questions were used to assess supervisory performance:

1. Is your supervisor keeping you informed?
2. Is your supervisor telling you what is expected?
3. Is your supervisor asking for your ideas about work?
4. Is your supervisor letting you know when you have done a good job?
5. Is your supervisor counseling you about your career goals?
6. Is your supervisor understanding the technical aspects of your job?
7. Is your supervisor helping you to do a better job?
8. Is your supervisor anticipating problems and effectively planning for them?
9. Is your supervisor assigning work fairly, according to work-load demands?

Managerial Effectiveness

In the Managerial Effectiveness Questionnaire (MEQ), the following nine questions were used to assess managerial performance:

1. Does your manager place emphasis on improving work methods?
2. Does your manager support opportunities for career development?
3. Does your manager effectively administer policies and procedures?
4. Does your manager provide adequate resources to get the job done?
5. Does your manager recognize and reward good performance?
6. Does your manager encourage recommendations and suggestions?
7. Does your manager select the best qualified for promotions?
8. Is your manager responsive to results from employee surveys?
9. Does your manager consider the impact of organizational changes on employees?

Building Awareness And Receptivity For Change

To develop an awareness of problems identified by the employees and to facilitate movement within the Precontemplative and Contemplative stages, reports of the survey results were prepared for the president and key executive staff. Separate reports were also prepared for each supervisor and manager in the company. The report provided information regarding the average employee rating for both the importance level and satisfaction value for each of the nine items on the MEQ and SEQ. The results of the MEQ indicated that Items (1) the manager's emphasis on improving work methods, (4) providing adequate resources, and (5) recognizing and rewarding good performance, were the most important areas. These areas also had the lowest level of employee satisfaction. The results of the SEQ indicated that Items (3) the supervisor asking for ideas, (4) letting employees know when they have done a good job, and (6) understanding the technical aspects of their employee's job, were the most important areas. These areas also had the lowest level of employee satisfaction. The results of the survey clearly indicated that the vast majority of employees were dissatisfied with both supervisory and managerial work-related areas they considered important. As expected, the executive staff was quite surprised by the survey results. Although there was a recognition for some kind of change, many of the staff members were ambivalent and not ready to commit themselves to a major change effort.

Facilitating an Action-Oriented Management Attitude

To facilitate a movement into the Determination stage, meetings were held with the executive staff and the president. The advantages of changing supervisory and managerial work practices to improve employee satisfaction were discussed. Much of the ambivalence expressed by the executive staff was related to their not knowing how to proceed and their concern for further exacerbating the existing situation. In the final analysis, the team decided that there was greater risk of increased cost due to lower employee productivity in continuing with the current situation. Although the executive staff was clearly in favor of initiating some kind of change effort, they were not quite ready to take action. They were still somewhat defensive about the way they were perceived by their subordinates and not quite ready to handle skillfully future discussions with their employees regarding possible change efforts. To help supervisors and managers to analyze their reports and to plan an effective action strategy for each of the items, training workshops were scheduled. All supervisors and managers received a two-day workshop that provided instruction on how to analyze the survey report and how to manage discussions and problem-solving sessions with their employees effectively. The supervisors and managers also received instruction on how to manage irrational beliefs and dysfunctional emotions related to their employees' assessment of their performance. Based on the practical examples in using RET presented by Ellis and Harper (1975) and Walen, DiGiuseppe, and Wessler (1980), training sessions and small group exercises were developed to provide instruction on how to change dysfunctional thought patterns involving awfulizing, demanding, self- and other rating, and low frustration tolerance. By disputing these dysfunctional thought patterns, supervisors and managers could avoid developing dysfunctional emotions that might adversely effect their problem-solving ability and work relations with their subordinates.

In the training session, each of the participants received actual survey reports for work areas in the company that had very low levels of employee satisfaction. The participants were then instructed to imagine that the sample report was their actual report and that they would have to present and discuss the report with their subordinates. After spending a few minutes reviewing the report, the participants were then told to write down their thoughts and feelings about receiving this kind of feedback from their subordinates. The dysfunctional thoughts often expressed at the training sessions were:

1. It would be awful if I received a bad report.
2. If I got a bad report, my career would be over.
3. If I got a bad report, I could never face my employees.
4. I must get a good survey report.

After recording all of the thoughts and feelings, the participants were given a lecture regarding how their thinking is related to their emotions and behavior. The emotional effect of certain kinds of irrational thinking was discussed, such as demanding that situations like the survey results or employee attitudes be different than the way they actually are. Information was also provided regarding the deleterious effect that emotional distress has on problem-solving performance (D'Zurilla, 1986).

After the lecture, the participants were put in small groups and instructed (a) to analyze their thinking for unrealistic, irrational, and self-defeating thoughts, and (b) to replace them with more realistic or rational thoughts using the ABCDE model presented by Walen, DiGiuseppe, and Wessler (1980). In the final phase of the training, the participants were provided instruction on various ways to facilitate discussion of the survey report with their employees and how to create an effective problem-solving atmosphere (Miller & DelBazo, 1989; Miller, 1992). At the conclusion of the workshop, the participants reported less emotional distress and a readiness to move into an action phase that included meeting, discussing, and problem solving with employees regarding ways that work relations and work procedures could be improved. As part of the action phase, each supervisor and manager met with their subordinate employees and discussed the results of the survey and ways to improve areas of concern. Quality circles were established, and employees were challenged to think about ways to improve work-related problems.

Maintenance and Relapse Prevention

To support the supervisors and managers in the Maintenance stage of the change effort, time was provided for the managers and supervisors to meet weekly in small groups to discuss their progress openly. At these meetings, the supervisors and managers shared both successes and failures and provided suggestions and support for each other. Scheduled skill training sessions in group facilitation, problem solving, stress management, and cognitive restructuring using RET techniques maintained continued improvement and helped when relapse occurred. One-on-one or individual training was provided in modeling, stress inoculation (Meichenbaum, 1985), and problem solving (D'Zurilla & Nezu, 1982) for those managers and supervisors having the greatest difficulty.

Conclusion

Although the effect the survey process had on improving supervisory and managerial effectiveness was not measured directly, the response rate for all three administrations of the survey was more than 96%. Plans to administer a follow-up survey to measure the change in employee perceptions are made. Anecdotal feedback indicated that the survey process also provided an effective means by which employees could contribute their ideas for improving many of their work relations with their supervisors and managers. Productivity measures increased 32% approximately 60 days following the meetings the managers and supervisors had with their employees. Other measures, such as sick leave and employee turnover, are being carefully monitored for future evaluation of the program. The RET training helped supervisors and managers to modify their style of management and to improve their overall performance. Many of the supervisors and managers reported that they felt less threatened by feedback that was critical of their performance and believed they were more effective in bringing about changes in day-to-day work relationships. Similar success has been achieved by adapting the Prochaska and DiClemente (1982, 1986) change model to an RET format in implementing change programs directed at corporate wellness (Yeager & Miller, 1991).

The world is changing at an ever increasing rate. Today's global markets will continue to foster a competitive challenge for superior goods and services. If we understand the principles of change, we can manage its course of action more effectively. The value of knowing these principles is eloquently stated in the Ancient Chinese *Book of Changes* (Wilhelm & Baynes, 1950, p. 243): "If we know the laws of change, we can precalculate in regard to it, and freedom of action thereupon becomes possible." Managers and supervisors who have the knowledge and skill to increase the opportunity for change will have the greatest opportunity for success.

References

Argyris, C., & Schön, D. (1978). *Organizational learning*. Reading, MA: Addison-Wesley.

DiGiuseppe, R. A., & Miller, A. R. (in press). RET perspectives on organizational change. In M. E. Bernard & R. A. DiGiuseppe (Eds.), *Rational emotive consultation in applied settings*. Hillsdale, NJ: Lawrence Erlbaum.

DelBalzo, J. M., & Miller, A. R. (1989). A new organizational flight pattern. *Training Development Journal, 43*(3), 40-44.

D'Zurilla, T. J. (1986). *Problem-solving therapy: A social competence approach to clinical intervention*. New York: Springer.

D'Zurilla, T. J., & Nezu, A. (1982). Social problem solving in adults. In D. Kendall (Ed.), *Advances in cognitive-behavioral research and therapy* (Vol. 1). New York: Academic Press.

Ellis, A. (1977). *Anger: How to live with and without it*. Secaucus, NJ: Citadel.

Ellis, A. (1978). *Executive leadership: A rational approach*. New York: Institute for Rational Living.

Ellis, A., & Harper, R. A. (1961). *A guide to rational living*. Englewood Cliffs, NJ: Prentice-Hall.

Ellis, A., & Harper, R. A. (1975). *A new guide for rational living*. North Hollywood, CA: Wilshire.

Kanter, R. M. (1983). *The change masters*. New York: Simon & Schuster.

Lawler, E. E. (1986). *High involvement management*. San Francisco: Jossey-Bass.

Mackay, H. (1988). *Swim with the sharks without being eaten alive: Outsell, outmanage, outmotivate and outnegotiate your competition*. New York: Morrow.

Mahoney, M. J. (1991). *Human change process: The scientific foundations of psychotherapy*. New York: Basic Books.

Meichenbaum, D. (1985). *Stress inoculation training*. Elmsford, NY: Pergamon.

Miller, A. R. (1988). *Managerial and supervisory effectiveness questionnaire*. Commack, NY: Career Management Resources.

Miller, A. R. (1992). The application of RET to improve supervisory and managerial response to subordinate survey feedback. *The Journal of Cognitive Psychotherapy, 6*(4).

Miller, A. R., & DelBalzo, J. M. (1989, September). *Enhancing supervisory and managerial response to survey feedback.* Paper presented at the Annual Conference on Creativity and Innovation in Public Service by the American Society of Public Administration, Atlantic City, NJ.

Naisbitt, J. (1982). *Megatrends: Ten new directions transforming our lives.* New York: Warner Books.

Ouchi, W. G. (1981). *Theory z.* New York: Avon Books.

Peters, T. (1987). *Thriving on chaos: Handbook for a management revolution.* New York: Knopf.

Peters, T., & Austin, N. K. (1985). *A passion for excellence: The leadership difference.* New York: Warner Books.

Popper, K. R. (1969). *Conjectures and refutations: The growth of scientific knowledge* (3rd ed., rev.). London: Routledge & Kegan Paul.

Prochaska, J. O., & DiClemente, C. C. (1982). Transtheoretical therapy: Toward a more integrative model of change. *Psychotherapy: Theory, Research, and Practice, 19,* 276-288.

Prochaska, J. O., & DiClemente, C. C. (1986). Toward a comprehensive model of change. In W. R. Miller & N. Heather (Eds.), *Treating addictive behaviors: Processes of change* (pp. 3-27). New York: Plenum.

Taylor, S. E., & Fiske, S. T. (1981). Getting inside the head: Methodologies for process analysis in attribution and social cognition. In J. H. Harvey, W. Ickes, & R. F. Kidd (Eds.), *New directions in attribution research* (Vol. 3). Hillsdale, NJ: Lawrence Erlbaum.

Walen, S. R., DiGiuseppe, R. A., & Wessler, R. L. (1980). *A practitioner's guide to rational-emotive therapy.* New York: Oxford University Press.

Webster's new collegiate dictionary. (1983). Springfield, MA: G. & C. Merriam.

Wilhelm, R., & Baynes, C. F. (Trans.). (1950). *The I Ching or book of changes.* Princeton, NJ: Princeton University Press.

Yeager, R. J., & Miller, A. R. (1991, September). *Developing and implementing corporate wellness programs.* Workshop presented at the University of Bridgeport Institute for Addiction Studies' Seventh Annual Issues in Addiction Conference, Beyond Tradition: Contemporary Approaches to De-Addiction.

Index

About the Editors

Windy Dryden is Professor of Counselling in the Department of Psychology at Goldsmiths' College, University of London. He has written or edited more than 50 books on counseling and psychotherapy, and he edits the *Counselling in Action, Counselling in Practice* with E. Thomas Dowd, and *Key Figures in Counselling and Psychotherapy* series published by Sage Publications. Professor Dryden is also editorial consultant in chief of *Counselling News* and is on the editorial board of numerous professional journals in the field of counseling and psychotherapy.

Larry K. Hill, Ed.D., is currently in private practice in Rock Springs, WY. He is a Licensed Professional Counselor; a Certified Clinical Mental Health Counselor; a Certified Sex Therapist with the American Association of Sex Educators, Counselors, and Therapists; a Clinical Supervisor with the American Board of Sexology; and a Founding Fellow of the American Academy of Clinical Sexologists. He is an Associate Fellow of—and on the Board of Advisors for—the Institute for Rational-Emotive Therapy. Dr. Hill was awarded the Clifford Houston Award by the Colorado Association for Counseling and Development, and is the author of more than 140 publications, papers, and presentations in the areas of psychology, sex therapy, rehabilitation, and counseling.

About the Contributors

Robert Dain earned a Ph.D. in School Psychology from The University of Texas at Austin and is a Diplomate in Clinical Psychology of the American Board of Professional Psychology. He is Director of the Dallas Institute for Rational-Emotive Therapy and Director, RR-Texas. He is a Clinical Associate Professor in the Department of Psychiatry, Division of Psychology, of The University of Texas Southwestern Medical Center at Dallas, where he was full-time faculty for many years and served as Assistant Dean in the Graduate School of Biomedical Sciences from 1973 through 1977.

Albert Ellis is President of the Institute for Rational-Emotive Therapy in New York City. He is the founder of rational-emotive therapy (RET) and the grandfather of cognitive-behavior therapy (CBT). He has published more than 50 books and over 600 articles on psychotherapy, sex, love, and marital relationships. He sees about 70 individual clients and conducts five group therapy sessions each week at the psychological clinic of the Institute, supervises many RET practitioners, and gives numerous talks and workshops in the United States and abroad.

Nancy Haberstroh, Ph.D., is Director of the Department of Psychology at The Monson Developmental Center within the Massachusetts

Department of Mental Retardation Services. She received her bachelor's degree in English from Virginia Polytech, her M.B.A. from the University of Massachusetts, and her Ph.D. in counseling psychology from the University of Virginia.

Robert F. Heller, Ed.D., is a teacher, trainer, and psychologist. He received his doctorate from Boston University in 1974 and was awarded a prestigious Postdoctoral Fellowship at the Institute for Rational-Emotive Therapy in 1981. In 1990, he was awarded the Diplomate from the American Board of Behavioral Psychology, which attests to the highest level of professional competence. He is on the faculty of the Boston Center of Adult Education and the Continuing Education faculty of the Massachusetts School of Professional Psychology. He has conducted workshops on such topics as Confident Public Speaking, Dealing With Difficult People, Developing Self-Confidence and Self-Esteem, Overcoming Fears, Assertiveness Training, Overcoming Shyness and Learning to Relax and Manage Stress. His clients have included The Harvard Business School, Jordon Marsh, The American Bankers Association, Midas Muffler, Bay State Executive Association, and the St. Louis Department of Health. He has created a series of self-help tapes and has appeared on radio, on television, and in print.

Charles H. Huber, Ph.D., is an Associate Professor in the Department of Counseling and Educational Psychology, New Mexico State University, and a psychologist in private practice with Associates for Marriage and Family Therapy in Las Cruces, New Mexico. A Fellow and Approved Supervisor of the Institute for Rational-Emotive Therapy, he holds a Diplomate in Family Psychology with the American Board of Professional Psychology, as well as being a Clinical Member and Approved Supervisor of the American Association for Marriage and Family Therapy. He is the author and co-author of numerous professional writings, including *Rational-Emotive Family Therapy: A Systems Perspective.*

William J. Knaus, Ed.D., is a business consultant and psychotherapist in private practice. He has served as Director of Training, Insitute for Rational-Emotive Psychotherapy and taught at Queens College, City University of New York. He has written the seminal books on procrastination and authored other self-help books and articles on a broad range of topics. He originated and developed Rational-Emotive Education and first published his program in *Rational-Emotive Education: A Manual for Elementary School Teachers.* His present interest is in the psychology of change.

Valerie C. Lorenz, Ph.D., has worked in the field of compulsive gambling since 1972. Her master's thesis was the first systematic study of the effects of this illness on the family, and her doctoral dissertation focused on environmental influences contributing to this addiction, and identified the "soft signs" of compulsive gambling. In addition to serving on the Editorial Board of the *Journal of Gambling Studies,* she is one of the most prolific researchers and authors in her field and a major contributor to professional journals and conferences. She co-chaired the two-year Task Force on Gambling Addiction, convened by the Maryland Department of Health and Mental Hygiene. She has frequently testified before various state legislatures and Congress, and as an expert witness in state, federal, and military courts, leading to precedent-setting court rulings. She is in high demand, nationally and internationally, for training of mental health professionals and law enforcement officers, and has appeared at national and international media events in England, Germany, Canada, Holland, and Japan.

Alfred R. Miller, Ph.D., is a licensed psychologist and organizational consultant in private practice. He is a Fellow, Institute for Rational-Emotive Therapy, and Co-Director, Institute for Cognitive Development, Commack, New York.

Robert H. Moore is an Associate Fellow and Training Supervisor for the Institute for Rational-Emotive Therapy and was Director of the Institute for Rational Living in Florida from 1973 to 1990. He is a Fellow/Diplomate of the American Board of Medical Psychotherapists, a Diplomate in Professional Counseling of the International Academy of Behavioral Medicine, Counseling and Psychotherapy, and a past presenter for the International Society for General Semantics and the International Society for Traumatic Stress Studies with specialties in post-traumatic stress reduction and cognitive (marriage and family) therapy. He has co-edited and/or contributed to five books by Albert Ellis and authored chapters on "Inference Chaining" and "E-Prime" in books edited, respectively, by Dryden and by Wolfe. He has hosted his own nationally syndicated, daily talk radio program (in the United States) and produced a series of psychological vignettes for national radio and the Cable Health (TV) Network (Lifetime). He currently divides his time between clinical supervision, professional training, public education, and writing for the broadcast and print media.

Mitchell W. Robin, Ph.D., is an Associate Professor of Psychology at New York City Technical College, CUNY; a Staff Psychotherapist and Fellow at the Institute for Rational-Emotive Therapy in New York; an Associate Member of the Dramatists Guild; and an active member of Sea View Playwrights Theater on Staten Island. In the latter capacity he has directed more than 30 productions, acted in many more, and managed their children's theater. At the IRET he has initiated the Performance Anxiety workshops and conducts their ongoing Performance Anxiety Group for actors, artists, and "civilian" performers. He has also appeared on more than 200 radio and television shows, including the *Today Show* and *Entertainment Tonight.* He still experiences eustress whenever he performs.

Bertram H. Rothschild, Ph.D., ABMP, is Assistant Chief Psychologist and Training Director of the Psychology Service, DVAH, Denver, Colorado, where he is the past director of the Pain Clinic. Currently he is Director of SAFE program, an inpatient substance-abuse program, and leader of the Domestic Violence team. He is also a Fellow and Faculty of the Institute for Rational Therapy, and Co-Director of the Rocky Mountain Center for RET. He has several professional publications and writes book reviews for ARBA and the Colorado ACLU newsletter.

Richard S. Schneiman, Ph.D., is a licensed psychologist in private practice in Salt Lake City, Utah. He is an Associate Fellow, Certified Supervisor/Trainer of the Institute for Rational-Emotive Therapy, New York City, and he is Co-Director of the Intermountain Center for Rational Living, Salt Lake City. Dr. Schneiman is an Associate Adjunct Professor in the Clinical Psychology Department of the University of Utah, a member of the Board of Trustees of the Utah SIDS Foundation, a member of the SIDS Advisory Board of the

Utah Department of Health, and has served as a volunteer mental health adviser for the Utah SIDS Chapter for the past 14 years.

Jennifer-Ann Shillingford received her Ph.D. in psychology from Hofstra University, New York, in 1991. She is currently a postdoctoral fellow at the Clinical Research and Treatment Institute of the Addiction Research Foundation in Toronto, working with Dr. Linda C. Sobell. She is an Associate Fellow in the Institute for Rational-Emotive Therapy, where her clinical internship was completed. Her current research interests include motivational interventions in treatment of low dependence alcohol and drug abusers and assessment of cognitive changes in treatment for addictive behaviors.

Jack Trimpey, founder and Executive Director of Rational Recovery Systems, has had more than 20 years of clinical experience since receiving the M.S.W. degree in 1969 from Wayne State University. He has received extensive postgraduate training in rational-emotive methods with emphasis on the treatment of impulse disorders and chemical dependency. More recently, he has developed Rational Recovery Systems, a nonspiritual recovery program for alcoholics and substance abusers. He is editor of *The Journal of Rational Recovery,* and has recently done extensive lecturing concerning RR and its emergence in the mainstream of American addiction care. His articles have appeared in *Newsweek, The New York Times, The Washington Post, Counselor Magazine, Behavior Today, Glamour, Sober Times, The Los Angeles Times, The St. Petersburg Sentinel, The Detroit Free Press, New York Magazine, The Boston Globe, The Seattle Post-Intelligencer, Prevention Magazine, Today's Health,* and numerous local publications around the United States. In addition, he has appeared on all of the major networks, including CBS's *This Morning,* NBC's *Today Show,* two CNN special programs on Rational Recovery, the Fox Network's *The Ron Reagan Show,* and numerous talk radio programs nationwide. In conjunction with the Institute for Rational-Emotive Therapy, he is completing the design of a training program that will make Rational Recovery seminars and workshops available to the professional community on a regional basis during 1992, leading to professional certification.

Emmett Velten holds a bachelor's degree from the University of Chicago and a Ph.D. in psychology from the University of Southern California. His dissertation produced the Velten Mood Induction Procedure. He is Clinical Services Director of Bay Area Addiction Research & Treatment, a board member of Rational Recovery Systems, instructor in the Department of Psychiatry at California Pacific Medical Center, Assistant Clinical Professor at the University of California, San Francisco, and a past president of the Association for Behavioral and Cognitive Therapy. With Dr. Albert Ellis, he is coauthor of *When AA Doesn't Work for You* (1992).

Carolyn M. Yeager, Ph.D., is a clinical psychologist in private practice and is on faculty at the Seminary of the Immaculate Conception and at the SUNY College at Old Westbury.

Raymond J. Yeager, Ph.D., is an Assistant Professor in the Department of Counseling and Human Resources, and is Director of the Institute for Addiction Studies at the University of Bridgeport. He is a clinical psychologist in private practice and is co-director of the Institute for Cognitive Development. He has co-authored several texts including *Rational-Emotive Therapy With Alcoholics and Substance Abusers, Rational-Emotive Couples' Therapy,* and *Why Some Therapies Don't Work: The Dangers of Transpersonal Psychology.*